100 STEPS

to Financial Independence

The Definitive Roadmap to Achieving Your Financial Dreams

INGE NATALIE HOL

100 STEPS TO FINANCIAL INDEPENDENCE
The Definitive Roadmap to Achieving Your Financial Dreams
Copyright © 2018 Inge Natalie Hol

100 Steps Publishing
inge@100StepstoFI.com
www.IngeNatalieHol.com

Cover and interior design by Domini Dragoone - dominidragoone.com
Editorial services provided by Susannah Noel and Heidi Dorr of Noel Editorial - noeleditorial.com

ISBN (print): 978-84-09-05149-6
ISBN (ebook): 978-84-09-06205-8

Disclaimer

100 Steps to Financial Independence is intended to help others on their way to better money management. The information presented is for informational purposes only and is solely the expression of the author's opinion. The author is not offering any legal, investing, or tax advice and is not liable for any actions prompted or caused by the information in this book. While every attempt has been made to verify any information presented in this book, the author is not responsible for any errors, inaccuracies, or omissions. Consult a professional if you have any concerns or doubts regarding your actions to gain financial independence. No liability is assumed for losses or damages due to the information provided.

Contents

SHORTCUTS: *For a lighter version of the book, use the suggested shortcuts to design your own fast track.*

> ⬇ SHORTCUT: If you're keen to see some immediate results or if your main concern is paying off your debt, you can skip ahead to Part 4.

➚ SHORTCUT: If your current income covers your expenses, allows you to pay off debt as well as save enough money on a regular basis, you can skip ahead to Part 7.

⬖ **SHORTCUT:** If you don't want to invest or if you don't feel ready to start investing just yet, you can skip ahead to Part 9.

> ⬊ SHORTCUT: If you've completed the most important steps but would like to get the bigger picture first before going back to different parts of this book, you can skip ahead to Step 100.

Introduction

When it is obvious that the goals cannot be reached, don't adjust the goals, adjust the action steps.
—CONFUCIUS

Why this book?

Personal finance is a hugely important topic that applies to us all. Yet we don't generally learn about it in school, nor do most parents feel comfortable talking about money with their children. Many of us learn about debts, retirement accounts, and taxes "on the go" as we live life, making critical financial decisions without understanding the bigger picture. We buy a house without calculating how much the mortgage will really cost us. We take out a consumer loan without understanding how disastrous a low monthly payback can be. "Look at retirement accounts" is a long-term item many of us have on a to-do list that gets transferred to next year's list every January first (and we often don't even know what to look at anyway). Investing is scary and taxes complicated, so why waste effort trying to understand it all?

A few years after the global financial crisis of 2008, I, too, became aware I didn't know much about personal finance. Most shocking was that when that realization hit me, I had already made some major financial decisions in my life. Having grown up in the Netherlands, I decided to go to Spain for six months to finish my university degree. My mother wasn't too keen on my going to Spain, and she made me promise not to fall in love with a Spaniard and stay there. Unfortunately for her, I did fall in love with my (now) husband, who is from the UK but had been living in Spain for a few years by

then. Since he wasn't a Spaniard, I felt I didn't technically break my promise when I ended up moving to Spain definitively two years later, thereby moving my entire financial life to my new country. We have since bought a house, gotten married, and set up our own language school, all of which involve serious financial commitment and responsibility.

You'd think I knew a fair bit about finances by the time I made some of those decisions. But the truth is I didn't. By the time I started to take an interest in personal finance, a few years after the financial crisis, I had no clue as to why I had life insurance, what my retirement account provision would look like, and what assets or bonds were. I had never heard of the seven income streams and knew nothing about how much I was paying in taxes. Paying off debt or our mortgage as fast as possible seemed an impossibly illogical decision. As far as inflation, I had heard of it many times, but how it was even remotely connected to interest rates, I had no idea.

The moment I realized I was too old (i.e., a "real" adult) not to understand these things, I knew it was time to secure a good understanding of personal finance. I began to search for a book that covered all the major topics. But I didn't want to just read about finances. I needed a book that had a clear action-focused design that would help me implement directly what I'd learned and tackle my finances one step at a time.

I bought and studied many finance books and began reading financial blogs and listening to hundreds of podcasts. It soon became obvious that although there is a wealth of information available, there was no book that was a clear blueprint of where to start, what action to take, and what route to follow to get me started on that journey to financial literacy. Thousands of books have been written about money and finances, yet I couldn't find a single one that explained all the basic concepts and turned it into a practical course, a step-by-step guide that would take me by the hand and walk me through my own finances. The finance books I read were either very theoretical, leaving me to figure out the practical side of how to apply what I learned to my finances myself, or were mainly focused on just one topic—debts, budgeting, or investing, for example. They did not explain how it was all connected and how to make sure I was on top of *all* areas of my financial life in a practical way.

Since that roadmap I was looking for didn't exist, I decided to distill those steps from all the information available and put them together myself, to form my own guide to understanding personal finance. That project slowly morphed into *100 Steps to Financial Independence*.

After implementing each step myself and making tweaks where needed, what started as a personal project became something bigger. The more I spoke to people about this topic, the more I realized there was a real demand for a handbook to achieving financial independence, and I decided to turn what I learned into a book available to a wider audience.

Where this project initially started as a way to achieve financial independence (FI) to be able to handle my own finances independently without needing to ask others for help or advice, I slowly discovered another meaning of FI: having enough financial resources to do without a nine-to-five job to generate an income. I was soon taken in by the latter concept and decided that this book should not only cover the first meaning of FI, but also the

> ### ⚙ STAT BOX
>
> A 2016 study by the Transamerica Center for Retirement Studies found that women have a median of $34,000 in retirement savings against $115,000 for men.[1]

second, which you will learn about as you progress through the material.

Who this book is for

If you don't know much about personal finance and would like to improve your financial management, have more money left over at the end of the month, up your savings, get rid of debt, start investing, learn about retirement accounts, and become financially independent in either of its meanings, this book is for you. It is an introduction to, and step-by-step guide of many personal finance topics. If you, on the other hand, already know quite a bit about how to manage your finances, or don't aspire to any of the above, this book will probably not be very useful to you.

Men and women deal with finances in different ways; in fact, in many families it is still more the man than the woman looking after money and making financial decisions. This book is not an attempt to change that, nor is it solely written for women, but you might find it at times adresses women more than men in terms of some of the topics covered and examples given. The *100 Steps to Financial Independence* will give anybody reading it—both men and women—the tools and knowledge to start managing their money independently. I hope to inspire all to take action and become involved in their personal finance and that in doing so it will help close the gender gap in financial skills and knowledge that (still) exists.

There are moments in this book where I use female stereotypes to explain a specific topic or give an example, such as spending money on manicures or flowers. That is not to say that all women should identify with these representations of how women want to spend their money. (In fact, I've only had a manicure once in my life and only because my friends insisted I have one just before my wedding. Nor do I tend to buy flowers—I'd like to, but I don't.) My point here is that we all use money for different things and those things don't define us as men or women. Feel free to replace the examples I use throughout the book with ones *you* can relate to, to make the topics more applicable to your own life.

Personal finance or family finance?

This book will help you come to grips with the most important parts of your personal finances and allow you to put together a plan to master your money like a pro. A money plan is not of much value if it doesn't also tie in with your personal circumstances and priorities, however, nor is there much point in aiming to achieve financial independence if you aren't also content and happy with the other areas in your life.

One main challenge is making sure that your personal life and your financial life go hand in hand and that your personal finance plan is compatible with your family's or partner's plan and aspirations. Whether you are single, dating, in a long-term relationship, married, separated, divorced, widowed, remarried, have a partner who (sometimes) lives away from your home, have children, don't have children, are coparenting, a stepparent . . . your journey to financial independence will need to adjust to your personal situation.

Make sure your partner or family is part of your journey and in full support of your decisions and that you have joint goals and aspirations. But don't underestimate the importance of also staying true to your own financial goals, even if your partner's opinion is not exactly the same as yours. Find a middle ground that works for everybody and that allows you both to feel comfortable with the agreement, giving you both space to fill in certain parts of your financial lives, instead of one of you having to conform completely to the other person's wishes. Your partner and family will play a vital part in your journey to FI, so don't block them out or set out on your own. It'll be much more fun and easy if you share your dreams and have the support of your family, even if you don't fully share the exact same ideas.

In Step 23 you'll find a more detailed description of how to handle finances together with your partner, although this is not meant as a one-off step you complete in a day. It is an ongoing process and you'll want to involve your partner or family from the beginning. Feel free to turn to that step at an earlier stage if you'd like some ideas on how to find the right balance between both your goals at the beginning of your journey.

What if . . .

Now that we have covered some basic points regarding personal finance, you might have some specific doubts about the journey to financial independence. Let's cover some of the most common questions.

What if you are too old or too young to aim for financial independence?

There really isn't such a thing as being too old or too young for this journey. You can start this book at any time in your life, whether you're in your early twenties, you've been out of school or university for a few decades, or you're just a few years away from your retirement age. However, the earlier you start working toward achieving financial independence, the better, as a small step can lead to big results over many years. But even if you start well beyond your twenties or thirties, you can make huge financial progress that can be of great importance later on in life. The most important thing you can do is to start today and not tomorrow, regardless of how old you are.

What if you don't have much time?

It's impossible to predict how long you will need to implement and finish all steps of this book.

Depending on what your current financial life looks like, you might be progressing through certain parts a lot faster than through other parts. This is not a book that you will read and finish in a week and then never need to pick up anymore. Many parts of this book require weeks, if not months, to get on top of, such as building up your savings or paying off your debts. There might be moments when you feel things have stagnated because you are stuck on a step or in a section of the book. The most important thing you can do is to keep up momentum and continue going. Sometimes this might indeed mean that you can't move on to the next part as you haven't yet completed the bit before, but that's fine. Remember, you are still making progress.

I recommend setting aside time every week to evaluate your progress and see how you are doing and whether you are ready to proceed to the next part. Sometimes you might be able to move on even if you have not yet completely finished the previous step, whereas sometimes it is better to wait. Find out what works for you. Maybe you want to finish every part completely before moving on. Or you might want to continue seeing progress and start incorporating other parts even if you're still working on something from before. Either approach is absolutely fine.

Financial independence is not something you achieve in a few months. It requires years of planning and working the plan to get there. But remember that with every little step you make, you also get one step closer.

What if you don't live in the US?

I have tried as much as possible to keep an international perspective for the many different topics addressed in this book. While there might be many topics in the book that are fairly similar across countries, there are also parts for which the differences are more pronounced. One example of this is health care, which is often vastly more expensive in the US than in other parts of the world. Pension or retirement funds as well as costs for higher education are other areas that pose unique challenges for those in the US and some other countries. Of course, many other financial considerations, including taxes and disability insurance, differ from one country to the next.

It is unfortunately impossible to go into too much detail about the many differences that do exist among countries. To avoid getting too abstract, I have, where I felt this was needed or useful, decided to use the United States as a reference point for examples. I invite the reader to investigate the differences that exist regarding these points in their own country and/or to get the help of an expert to clarify how specific concepts might be relevant to them.

What if you're not very organized?

Becoming financially independent requires some level of organization, whether that is to do with regularly reviewing your progress and looking ahead at the next few steps to come, keeping your paperwork neatly filed to easily be able to refer back to your financial life, or even just implementing these steps one at the time—you will need to put in some time and effort to follow this journey with some level of organization. If you're not a very organized person, however, that doesn't mean you can't get through this book and make the most of it. You will just need to adapt your approach to some of the suggestions and find a way that works best for you. For example, if you are not the type of person who likes to plan ahead to schedule in their weekly money moment for the next few weeks (as described in Step 24), then that's fine, but make sure you still do this once a week, even if that isn't always at the same time or on the same day or in the same place.

Many of the steps in this book rely on developing new habits: from keeping track of what you're spending to making regular contributions to your savings and retirement accounts or involving your children in some of your financial life. People differ in how they develop and keep habits. Some need an external factor to hold them accountable (a friend or coach checking up on their progress), whereas other people find it easier to live up to internal expectations. Some need to schedule in an exact time and place to execute a particular activity, but others feel restrained if activities are too rigidly planned ahead of time. Find out what works best for you. If some of the suggestions in this book don't feel right to you, adapt them to fit with the way you'd best create a new habit.

An excellent book on habits is Gretchen Rubin's book *Better Than Before*. It provides some excellent insight into how different people best form new habits based on their tendencies and it might be a great book to consult when creating the new habits suggested throughout the 100 steps.

What if you don't make enough money?

To become financially independent, we all have to start somewhere. It doesn't really matter whether you make $20,000, $60,000, or $150,000 a year. Without taking the right steps, you will always be living paycheck to paycheck, not knowing how to plan your financial life to get ahead. Of course, it's beneficial if you make more money, but unless you're burdened in debt and not able to make ends meet in any possible way, this book will help you reduce your expenses, pay off debt, increase your income, start saving for retirement, and so much more, regardless of your current annual wage. Depending on your current situation, you might only be able to save $20 a month instead of $200 or $1,000 or even more, but if that's all you can save, that is still better than nothing. Starting small might be the only thing you can do, but that's better than standing still.

While you don't need to be making a minimum (or maximum) amount of money, nor be debt-free or have a minimum amount in debt, savings, investments, and so on, this book is most valuable if you are at least making enough money to pay for your basic needs such as housing, food, clothing, and other key expenses. If you are struggling to make it to the end of the month when it comes to your essential needs, this book will probably not help you. I recommend you first find ways to minimally be able to provide for you and your family when it comes to the essential expenses before starting this journey. Dave Ramsey's book *Total Money Makeover* might be a great place to start to see some quick results. *Zero Debt* by Lynnette Khalfani-Cox is particularly useful if you are buried in debt and feel you are stuck in a vicious circle of accumulating debt and not being able to pay it off at the end of the month. Alternatively, you might also want to consider getting help from a credit counseling agency before starting your journey to financial independence.

How this book is set up

This book describes the 100 most important steps to becoming financially independent. These 100 steps are divided into ten different sections that form the building blocks of successful money management. Starting with the most basic aspects of your financial life such as your expenses and debts, we slowly move to savings, then taking control of your income and retirement accounts, followed by investing, financial protection, taxes, and how to excel at financial independence.

Each of these ten parts starts with a short introduction to that topic before proceeding with the different steps in that section. Each part is concluded by a checklist that you can use to ensure you have completed all the steps and achieved their objectives.

All of the 100 steps first describe the main information about a particular subject before presenting the action plan, which is a bullet-pointed list of the actions to take to implement the information.

Every step also includes three key features:

- **Difficulty level:** a rough indication of how easy or difficult the step is for the average reader. This goes from *easy* (relatively easy or general information presented) to *medium* (some new financial concepts or information is presented and/or some more in-depth analysis is needed) to *difficult* (more complex concepts are discussed and/or long-term planning or projections are required).

- **Objective:** the objective of the step and how this will help you on your way to financial independence.
- **Review times:** how often I recommend you review the step. This can range from a quick review once a year to a weekly analysis of your progress and planning or even a daily implementation of a new habit.

Of course, all of the above are guidelines; what one person finds easy might be more difficult for somebody else. I have tried to gauge what the average reader might find.

In between each section, there are personal stories from people regarding each specific part. I hope these inspire you to take action and little by little improve your finances!

How to use this book

You are of course free to use this book however you want, but here are three recommended strategies I have found work best in order to get the most out of it:

1. Read a step, then implement its action plan before moving on to the next step.
2. Read a full section, then implement the action plans of all the steps in that part before moving on to the next area.
3. Pick and choose the steps to read and implement, depending on what you feel is most urgent or important to you.

If you decide on a fourth option and read the entire book first before implementing each step because you are just too curious and want to read everything, bear in mind you will likely feel overwhelmed by the amount of information and sheer volume of things to do. This book is meant to be

---

⇶ A NOTE ON CURRENCIES

In the examples throughout all of this book I have decided to use dollars ($) as a generic currency, in order to use a standard currency most readers are likely familiar with, although instead of dollars it could of course read euros, sterling pounds, yen, or any other currency you most use.

I've used -/- to indicate a negative value in order to avoid confusion with - signs.

---

very practical with many action-to-be-taken lists, not something you read cover to cover in a week. Considering the amount of information and tasks that will be discussed, I also strongly believe in the importance of creating small wins early on in your journey to financial independence. The sooner you start implementing each step, the sooner you can begin to experience these small victories and start experiencing your achievements.

There are some steps, however, that might be beneficial to look at earlier than later. I've tried to keep a logical order and divide the various steps into parts, but you might find it useful in your case to skip around. For example, I've put "Digitize Your Documents" in the ninth part of the book, but you might find you want to tackle this right from the beginning when you organize your paperwork in Part 1—or not at all if you prefer to keep a physical filing system. Similarly, as mentioned before there is a step in Part 3 on communicating with your partner about finances, but you might decide to go through this step a lot earlier and set off on this journey together from the beginning.

I've also included some recommended shortcuts in the table of contents for a lighter version of the book. Use this fast track to work on the personal finance topics that are most urgent first. You can always go back afterwards to complete the parts that you skipped.

What you need

Apart from this book, you don't need much to start your journey, although I recommend you keep the following on hand whenever you are working through the steps:

- A notebook to keep notes for some of the steps. If you prefer to work digitally, decide on a program or app that allows you to take notes and track some key numbers or targets. This can be a simple note taking app, or something like Excel or Evernote to allow for more flexibility.

- For some of the steps you might need to use an online calculator that allows you to calculate the effects of such things as inflation or interest over time. There are many available on the Web. Just find one you like through Google or another search engine. Other times the standard calculator on your phone might do just fine.

And with that, I think we are ready to start the 100 steps journey to financial independence!

PART 1

Before You Begin

Throughout this book, you will find out more about what financial independence can be and identify what it might mean to *you* in particular. Part of becoming financially independent is to start thinking outside the box and dreaming big. This book encourages you to discover those dreams and make them tangible goals to start working toward.

With each part of the book you will begin to link your big dreams to concrete objectives, which will form the basis of your journey to financial independence. Each step will in turn provide the necessary building blocks that will give you the practical tools you need to achieve those dreams.

In the first part of this book, you'll find out more about some essential skills and practices that will come in handy as you work through the action items. These are particularly strategic steps focussed on your objectives and the reasons for starting this journey. I strongly recommend you start your journey here and review these steps regularly. If you are anxious to get going and jump straight in, however, simply skip to Part 2 and read and implement the steps in Part 1 when you have time.

Commit to Your Journey

A journey of a thousand miles must begin with a single step.

—LAO TZU

DIFFICULTY LEVEL: Easy

OBJECTIVE: Find ways to commit to your journey to financial independence and hold yourself accountable

REVIEW TIMES: Daily

I know, I cheated—we're actually starting *before* Step 1. But this step really is the foundation of all others.

Applying the 100 steps

This book will walk you through 100 action plans that will help you achieve your goal of reaching financial independence, taking just one step at a time. With every step, you will feel more in control of your finances, as you consistently organize and improve part of your current, past, or future money affairs. During this journey, you will learn how to become financially organized, make more money, save and invest wisely, get rid of debt, build a more secure financial future, and ultimately achieve your financial dreams. Each step will dive into a financial topic and will arm you with all the information you need to use to your advantage.

That being said, the real magic of this book is not *learning* about money, as the key to success is not about *knowledge*; you can, after all, be highly educated about a subject but it will not get you anywhere unless you *do* something with it. The

true value of this book lies in the way it shows you step by step how to *apply, execute,* and *implement* everything you learn here, so that by the time you get to the end of your journey you can rightly call yourself a finance ninja well on your way to financial independence.

Expect some ups and downs

It is probably safe to say that this journey will at times be a bit of a wild ride, one in which you might get overwhelmed by information or feel you are not making any progress. Throughout your journey, please remember that all of this is totally normal. If it were an easy route, you would have already had your finances in high gear and you likely wouldn't need to read this book! Don't give up when things get difficult; it is (unfortunately) just part of the journey. If you have ever learned to ride a bike, you will remember that part of the process is having to fall off a good few times before you become a confident bike rider.

If you—like me and about a billion others—have ever set New Year's resolutions, you probably have firsthand experience of how we can all start a new project with a lot of enthusiasm and motivation, but after just a few weeks and maybe some tough moments, we unfortunately tend to give up. Think about how many times you have gone back to smoking or stopped hitting the gym as often as you'd like.

I want to make sure this will not happen to you on your journey to financial independence, even if you feel your motivation dipping at times. There-fore, the very first and also most important step on your journey is to make a true commitment to your mission.

You might feel you have already committed by picking up this book or because you have been thinking about getting a handle on your finances for such a long time that you sense your mind is completely ready for the challenge. But at some point, you will almost certainly lose the desire to continue after some initial hurdles. So do yourself a favor and commit to the 100 steps to financial independence right here today, now that your ambition is at its highest. (Remember those people with New Year's resolutions. They too were once just as motivated as you are now.)

Let's start with our very first action plan.

- -

There are many different ways to commit to your financial goals. Find one (or more) that works best for you. If you truly want to kick-start your financial life, there's no going back from here. So pick one or more of the ideas in the action plan, or add your own, and put it in place TODAY!

☑ STEP 0 ACTION PLAN

☐ Write down your goal on a card or Post-it, such as: "My journey to financial independence," "Getting my finances sorted once and for all," "On a mission to financial excellence," or something that works for you. Stick the card somewhere where you will see it daily: in your wallet, in your diary, on the inside of the bathroom cabinet, in the car. Find a place where you will be reminded a few times a day of your new intention and your commitment to reaching the end of the 100 steps.

☐ Alternatively or in addition to the above, write your commitment down on your mobile phone and set a daily reminder or alarm that reminds you to look at it. Or change the screensaver or desktop image on your computer to the statement of your commitment so that you will see it every time you use your computer.

☐ Write an affirmation that you read every morning and/or evening. An affirmation would be slightly longer than the commitment, and could read: "I am committing to getting my finances in order and indeed grow my wealth, so that I know I am using my money in the best way possible for both the present as well as the future. Despite the fact that I have not put my financial health front and center to this point, I know I am capable of getting on track and improving my financial status and organization to become financially independent." Make it part of your morning or evening routine to read the affirmation, and you will find that with time you will start to believe in it more and more, and it will help keep your motivation up.

☐ Find an accountability buddy, be that your romantic partner, a friend, a colleague, or anybody else you trust and feel comfortable sharing your struggles and goals with. Tell them you are starting this journey and ask them to check in with you regularly to see how you are doing and to hold you accountable for your actions and results.

☐ Take the idea of an accountability buddy one step further and find a friend who is willing to start this with you. You can check in daily and make sure you do not let each other down. You might even find several people willing to join and you can create your own social media group for daily accountability checks and to help each other with the various challenges.

☐ Write a short summary in your journal or find a new notebook and reflect on your progress daily.

☐ Put a status update on your social media platforms, post a photo on Instagram of you and this book, or start a blog on every step or every day you have worked toward completing a step. Add the hashtag #100stepstoFI to your social media posts as another way to feel accountable for your success on this journey. Doing this means other people can find you, see how you are doing, and encourage you.

☐ Follow the 100stepstoFI Facebook page or follow #100stepstoFI on other social media such as Twitter and Instagram to get frequent inspiration and to find other people on the same journey.

Discover Your "Why": Define Your Financial Independence Vision

> *Wealth is the ability to fully experience life.*
> —HENRY DAVID THOREAU.

DIFFICULTY LEVEL: Easy

OBJECTIVE: Define your vision for financial independence

REVIEW TIMES: Read daily, update yearly

It's exciting times as you're about to embark on your 100 steps to financial independence! Or better yet: now that you've picked up this book and have begun to read it, I think it's safe to conclude you have indeed already set off on your journey and will soon find yourself progressing nicely along your very first step. I hope you are as eager to complete these 100 steps and set yourself up for efficient money management and achieving financial success as I was when I first set off on this adventure!

All along these 100 steps, we will be talking about financial independence. But what exactly is financial independence to you? And most important, why specifically are you pursuing it? Now that you have started the journey to financial excellence, you want to dedicate some time to determine your long-term goal and discover the reason(s) you embarked

on this path. This will allow you to connect the dots between the hard work you need to put in and your ultimate goals.

Five common reasons to aspire to financial independence

Below are five common reasons to pursue financial independence. They are presented in a progressive order; whereas goals one, two, and—to a certain extent—three should be easy to achieve if you follow this journey all the way, goals four and five require some serious hard work and dedication. It is up to you how far you want to go with these steps.

1. A HEALTH CHECK OF YOUR FINANCES

You might be pursuing a level of financial management that will allow you to know your finances thoroughly and stay apprised of how you are doing on a daily, monthly, and yearly basis. Perhaps you want to feel confident that you are not wasting money at the expense of building a secure future, your bills are always paid on time, your financial paperwork is up to date and easily accessible, and you are making wise investments for your current as well as your future self. You're looking for peace of mind and would like to know enough about finances to trust that yours are at a healthy stage.

2. STOP MONEY WORRIES OR PROBLEMS

Your money situation might be worrying you, whether that is with regard to your current circumstances or your future ones. Are you concerned about an ever growing debt? Do you not have the means to provide for yourself and your family at the moment? Would you not be able to pay for any emergency expenses that you might be faced with such as a car or home repair? Do you fear not having enough funds when you retire, or are you worried you have not taken all the necessary precautions to protect yourself or your family financially if you are hit by a major event such as illness, death, or other emergency? If that is the case, you probably want to achieve more than just a check of your finances. You likely have some areas that need a fair bit of attention and work, and if you remain at the status quo, you will likely end up with even more worries.

3. STOP NOT HAVING ENOUGH MONEY AND MISSING OUT

If this is your goal, financial independence means having some extra money that you can spend on your hobbies, your family, a vacation, or to give to others in need. By being financially organized and aware of what is happening with your money, you hope to save some cash here and there, use opportunities to reduce expenses, and look for ways for more money to come in. You are aiming for some extra financial breathing room that will allow you to spend more on fun or build a more secure financial future. That way, when you retire, you don't have to skimp and save every penny and can instead focus on enjoying life.

4. HAVE MORE TIME

You might want to work less to spend more time on other things you care about, such as your family and friends, or following a dream or passion project like doing volunteer work, writing a book, or working

on a new income stream. Financial independence to you means that you have enough money coming in to reduce your work hours in your current job and focus on something else. A next logical step might be to stop working altogether and spend all of your time doing what you love without needing to worry about money. Your goal is to not need to work to have money coming in, and you are looking to replace your regular income with one you generate yourself, be that from savings, investments, or your own business.

5. FINANCIAL FREEDOM

Financial freedom is a stage at which you can live out your dreams that are far beyond your current lifestyle. It means you can do whatever you want to do (financially), and that money is no concern to you. Your reason for beginning this journey might be to be able to buy various cars, live half the year in your second house in the Caribbean, and gift everybody in your family the latest gadget. Or you might want to take it another way and give away substantial parts of your wealth to charity or set up your own charity, become a philanthropist, or help rescue our planet. Extreme as this reason to pursue financial independence might sound, there are many people who achieve this goal, so who knows whether you might also, with time?

Find your own vision

Whichever vision you have for your financial independence depends on what you feel comfortable with and whether you are willing to push yourself beyond your current beliefs, habits, and limitations. You need to discover your own "why" for becoming financially independent. Maybe you love your current job or work in general as it gives you a sense of purpose and a structure in your life and you may have no desire to reduce your work hours or to retire early. Or alternatively, you might want to set up your own company and need to find the time and motivation to finally do so. Maybe all you need right now is some extra money left over at the end of each month to do something fun with your family, support your parents, or invite your friends for a meal out. Or is your real purpose in life making more money in order to give back to others in need?

Whatever your goal is, make sure it reflects your real intentions. If you want to have more money in order to go on vacation more often, that is absolutely fine—don't feel you need to give a socially accepted answer. This is your journey and the why of your mission should reflect you.

Determine your vision so you have a clear end point in mind. Keep that vision with you and remember to work toward it every single day.

☑ STEP 1 ACTION PLAN

☐ Get out a notebook, document, or app and brainstorm why you started this project. Start writing what comes to mind, whether it be single words, sentences, or your life story. The format doesn't matter; just write down what inspired you to start following these 100 steps.

☐ Is there anything in particular you want to achieve from this journey? Below are some questions to help you get started:

- Is your paperwork a mess and do you have no idea what you are spending every month? Are you looking to get organized so that you have a clear picture of what happens to your money?
- Do you spend too much and are you looking to cut your spending?
- Do you want to save (more) money?
- Do you have debts that are smothering you?
- Are you worried about your financial future and do you want to plan ahead for your retirement?

☐ Identify any worries or concerns you have about your finances and your financial future and determine how big of an impact they have on your life. Use a rating system between 1 and 10 or use pluses and minuses to quickly see the biggest challenges you might be facing.

☐ Describe the role of work in your life at the moment and in your goals: Do you want to get a promotion, move to another company, get a new job, work less, work more, set up your own company, or stop working altogether?

☐ If you are looking to reduce your work hours or quit working completely, what would you spend your time on? Your family? A hobby? Travels? A creative endeavor? Volunteering?

☐ If you had to identify your ideal financial future in the next five, ten, and twenty years, what would it look like? What would you have, do, possess, give back to the world? Write down what you would like your money situation to look like in the short and long term.

☐ Refer to the reading list in Appendix D for some specific books on goal setting to help you get started and implement this step further.

Discover Your "What": The Eight Stages of Financial Independence

At least 80% of millionaires are self-made. That is, they started with nothing but ambition and energy, the same way most of us start.

—BRIAN TRACY

DIFFICULTY LEVEL: Easy

OBJECTIVE: Determine what financial independence looks like to you

REVIEW TIMES: Every three months

As with many things in life, if you start looking closer at a concept that at first might seem simple, there is more than just a black-and-white division, a yes or no, a fail or succeed. Even with financial independence, the reality is there is no easy distinction between being financially independent or not. Instead, there are many different financial phases that one can reach along the way.

You have determined your vision and set your "why" of wanting to reach financial independence in Step 1, but here at Step 2, we'll have a closer look at the "what" you want to achieve on your journey—in other words, your end goal. As Stephen Covey famously wrote about in his highly recommended book *The 7 Habits of Highly Effective People*, beginning with the end in mind makes you more likely to achieve your goals.

The eight stages of financial independence

Below are the eight most commonly defined stages of financial independence, starting with financial dependence and going all the way up to financial abundance.

1. FINANCIAL DEPENDENCE

Your journey starts with dependency: when you are born, you completely rely on others for financial resources. The support of your family or caregivers is essential when you don't yet have the means to provide for yourself. Little by little you move away from this stage, once you start earning your own money and become responsible for your own finances.

2. FINANCIAL SOLVENCY

When you get to the solvency stage, you are able to look after your own bills and financial commitments. You no longer need the help of others to pay your expenses. Although you might have a debt in the form of a mortgage, a student loan, or an outstanding balance on your credit card, you are taking care of your finances yourself, even if that involves accumulating debt along the way.

3. FINANCIAL STABILITY

You get to the stability stage once you have been able to build up some savings and emergency money that will help you if and when you face unexpected adverse financial situations. Having some emergency money will stop you from falling back down the ladder to stages 1 or 2 in case you need to deal with an urgent situation. It provides you with a buffer that gives you the chance to bounce back, even if you are dealt an unexpected card.

4. DEBT FREEDOM

Reaching stage 4 might take a while, especially if you have substantial amounts of debt that you need to pay off, but once you get to this stage you no longer need to worry about monthly loan repayments, compounding interest building up, and losing money on money you once borrowed. At this stage, you do not owe anybody money anymore, and you no longer have any obligations to any creditors. You are now in full control of any money you earn. You reach this stage the moment you pay off the last of all your loans, including your student debt, car loan, credit card debt, and mortgage.

5. FINANCIAL SECURITY

To get to the financial security stage, you need to have some of your essential expenses covered by income that is not coming from your job but from a passive income source. This can be rental income, investments (dividends, capital gains, or interest), or any other type of income stream you have created that generates enough money to cover at least some of your utilities, food, insurance, and transportation costs. The more of these expenses you can cover with your other income streams, the higher your financial security. This means your job only needs to fund your less essential overheads, i.e., the fun stuff you do in life! Reaching this stage signifies that if you were to lose or quit your job, you have the security of being able to pay for at least your basic expenses from other income sources.

6. FINANCIAL INDEPENDENCE

You achieve financial independence once you have enough income from sources other than your job to cover *all* your current financial needs. This includes any of your discretionary (or fun) expenses, or at least the ones you expect to have if you decided to retire from work. It means you can maintain your current lifestyle from just your investments or other income streams, without being dependent on a job. This of course doesn't mean you have to stop working, but the option to quit is now there, and it can give peace of mind in case you're worried you might at some point lose your job.

7. FINANCIAL FREEDOM

You are financially free when your various income streams cover not only your current lifestyle needs but also a few luxury goals. This could be going on several long vacations and trips every year, buying another car, or maybe even buying a small condo for vacationing.

8. FINANCIAL ABUNDANCE

When you reach the financial abundance stage, your passive income can pretty much cover whatever you want. You are well past the stage of covering your current lifestyle or even those two or three things you splurge on each year. At the financial abundance stage, you can do pretty much anything you want to do, whenever you want to (financially speaking).

- -

Knowing about the eight stages of financial independence and identifying where you currently are and where you want to get to will make your journey a little more real. Use them to keep you motivated during your mission to financial independence! (Or to financial stability, or financial freedom, or whichever stage you have decided is your goal. . . .)

☑ STEP 2 ACTION PLAN

☐ Get out your notebook or open your digital file and determine at which of the eight stages you currently are. Most people will be somewhere around stage 2 or 3, although you might already be on your way to stage 4.

☐ Decide on your goal. Which stage do you want to get to? Just because others around you might be aiming for stage 4 does not mean you cannot aspire to get to the next one. Similarly, not everybody wants to reach the last two stages described above, so there is no point pushing to reach those levels if they don't resonate with you.

☐ Describe what reaching your target stage looks like to you. Make it as detailed as possible and write down exactly what you would be able to do as well as what you would not need to worry about anymore when you reach your target stage.

☐ For each of the stages in between your current stage and your target stage, identify what exactly will indicate you have made it. For example, imagine you're currently in stage 3 and want to get to the next stage. Indicators of reaching stage 4 could be:

- Having paid off the $200,000 remaining principal of your mortgage.
- Having paid off $40,000 in credit card debt and student loans.
- Never having to pay monthly bills on outstanding debt.
- Never having to worry about debt again.

☐ During your journey to financial independence, come back to this step regularly to track your progression. Each time you do, identify if and how your goals might have changed. Maybe you started off hoping to become debt free but have since started to realize that deep down you want to quit your job and therefore need to generate a passive income stream. Or maybe you'll decide in a few months that you are going to dream big and pursue reaching financial freedom. Plans can change, so don't be afraid to also change your goal identified here.

Visualize Your Dreams

It always seems impossible until it is done.

—UNKNOWN

DIFFICULTY LEVEL: Easy

OBJECTIVE: Identify your (financial) dreams and regularly remind yourself of your goals

REVIEW TIMES: Daily

The journey to financial independence is designed to make you achieve your (financial) dreams. Now that in Step 1 and 2 you've thought about what financial independence means to you and why you want to achieve this in this step you're going to create a vision board of your dreams. By doing so, you are taking the ultimate step to all of the following:

- keeping up your motivation during this journey and beyond,
- making goals more real and reminding yourself of these goals,
- not forgetting to live in the now by identifying what is important to you.

While the first two points are easy to understand, the third one can sometimes be overlooked. I would like to highlight the importance of that third point before we move on.

Live in the moment

Imagine a couple who feels really inspired to become financially independent. They make a budget, cut expenses, start a side hustle to earn some extra money to invest, and they see their efforts paying off as the number in their bank account slowly increases. So they hustle a little more, cut another few expenses, and find other ways to speed up the process.

But with time, they become so absorbed by this life project that they cut other things, too. Even though they have a fair amount of money in the bank, family vacations are "too expensive," clothes are recycled well past their "best before" date, and any real family togetherness disappears quickly as the side hustle takes up all their valuable time.

After many years of dedication and hard work, they finally reach that milestone of a $1,000,000 net worth they set for themselves. The couple gets ready to celebrate this moment and to loosen the reins a little, only to find that their children have gone off to college and friends from the past have ceased to be friends as they have hardly seen each other in recent years. They no longer belong to any sports clubs and realize they don't know that many people in their area anymore. They see no albums on the shelves with photos of happy family vacations, there are no memories of fun days down at the beach or up in the mountains, and they cannot recall having taken their children on any visits to the theater, a museum, or even the movies.

And what was it all for? What is the point of having $1,000,000 in your bank account if you can't enjoy it? What is the value of money if not to be used and help you enjoy the little things in life, such as spending time with the people we love and giving others opportunities to live a better life? More than the million dollars, is it not important to have time to do what truly makes you happy or to make a difference in the world?

The pursuit of happiness

Of course you have embarked on this journey for your own reasons, but I hope that becoming financially independent is only a means to another goal and not a goal in itself. There is of course nothing wrong with wanting to have that money in the bank, but never lose sight of your why. If you know why you want that money (to become a stay-at-home-parent to spend more time with your family, to travel, to live a more fulfilling life by volunteering or being able to set up your own company, and so on), whatever it is, you need to keep just that in mind, as that is what will bring you happiness. The money in itself will not; it will only allow you to achieve your goals faster.

Creating a dream or vision board

A vision board is a lot simpler but also a lot more powerful than a list of goals. It is a visual representation of your goals: a big poster or collage, usually made up of photos, pictures, or drawings along with quotes or short statements that represent the key objectives you are working toward.

When you place a vision board in a strategic place (like on the fridge or bathroom mirror or inside of your wardrobe door), you are constantly reminded of your goals, your why's, and the reason for planning your financial life meticulously.

STAT BOX

The 2016 Transamerica Retirement Survey found that the most commonly cited retirement dreams for workers are traveling (66% women, 60% men), spending more time with family and friends (60% women, 54% men), and pursuing hobbies (46% women, 52% men). Interestingly, 22% of women and 33% of men said their dream is to continue to do some type of work.[2]

As we discussed above, ideally your goals will not all be financial. Therefore, a vision board should not just include future savings or investment targets, but also your values and current joys. That way, you never forget to enjoy life as it is now, to appreciate what you already have, and to use that to become even more motivated to keep up the hard work.

Once you start using your vision board regularly, you will discover how much more focused your efforts at becoming financially independent will become. When you are reminded of your dreams and goals daily, you will progress even faster. It also turns the process into something more enjoyable.

☑ STEP 3 ACTION PLAN

☐ When you make your vision board, decide on your top six, eight, or ten aspirations for your (financial) life. You are looking for the ultimate targets that reaching financial independence will help you achieve, such as early retirement, setting up your own company, having time to learn a new skill, buying a vacation house somewhere else, traveling the world for a year, buying a boat, paying for your children's education, or donating $20,000 to a charity that you strongly identify with.

☐ Include a mix of short-term goals (i.e., goals you have set for the next two or so years) and long-term goals. (Use some of the ideas your brainstormed in Steps 1 and 2.) In this way, your vision board is not all about the distant future, but will remind you to enjoy the milestones you reach along the way.

☐ Your goals should not just be materialistic goals. Remember the example from above about the family who never stopped to enjoy life? Your goals can be retiring early to go hiking every weekend, reducing work hours to spend more time with your (grand)children, or adopting a pet from the local shelter and giving it a second chance in life.

☐ Going through your own photos and using the Internet or magazines, find one or two photos per goal that most represent your target. Be creative, and make sure you identify with the pictures and have a strong positive feeling toward each of them.

☐ Add what is important to you in life: your family, friends, pets, hobbies, or (volunteer) work. Make sure to add pictures of these areas so that you do not forget to appreciate and enjoy life now.

☐ Find or buy a big piece of paper and write "financial independence" or some other sentence, word, or quote in the middle or at the top.

☐ Stick your pictures up on the paper.

☐ Find a few powerful quotes, habits, or mottos to complete your vision board, or start writing them down in the next few weeks whenever you come across one.

☐ Take a moment to look at your goals and imagine achieving them one by one. Visualize how you would feel each time and how you would enjoy the effects.

☐ Stick your vision board somewhere where you will be able to look at it every day.

☐ Make it a daily habit to start your day looking at your vision board, reminding yourself of what is important in life and visualizing yourself reaching each of your dreams.

Set Your Financial Objectives

The imagination is literally the workshop wherein are fashioned all plans created by man.
—NAPOLEON HILL

DIFFICULTY LEVEL: Easy

OBJECTIVE: Set your financial goals

REVIEW TIMES: Read daily, update every three months

One of the most important steps you can take on your way to becoming financially independent is making your goals clear. There is nothing more powerful than having a specific end point in mind that you are working toward. Without stating your intentions, it is easy to give up after only a few initial attempts as you get distracted by day-to-day life and slowly forget why you started this journey in the first place. Without clear objectives, furthermore, you have no way of measuring whether you are any closer to your targets and whether your efforts are paying off.

This step bridges the gap between your dreams about the financial life you want to live and the practicalities of how you can get there. By setting specific, clear objectives, you can start working toward them on a daily basis.

Setting objectives

Once you have set objectives, they become your guiding financial principles, the cornerstones of all future money decisions and your encouragement to not give up when the going gets rough and the temptation to abandon your goals increases. Numerous studies have shown that the likelihood of achieving your goals increases significantly if you have clearly defined objectives that you remind yourself of continually.

When stating your objectives, they should be challenging, specific, and with a clear time frame. For example, "I want to save more money" is not a very powerful target as it is neither specific nor time bound. A more effective objective could be, "I want to have saved $10,000 in two years' time." Bear in mind that you want your goals to be challenging enough to require some effort. If you are already saving about $500 a month, you will easily get to those $10,000 in even less than two years, in which case you might need to think of a more challenging goal.

Once you have your goals written down, you have completed a very important part of the journey: clarifying what some of your aspirations and (temporary) destinations are. That will allow you to get started with some practical steps.

☑ STEP 4 ACTION PLAN

☐ You probably have several financial goals in mind already that were likely major reasons for starting this journey. Write down as many as you can think of for now. They might take you a week, a few months, several years, or even decades to achieve. As long as you feel strongly about them, that is absolutely fine. Later we will look at areas such as your expenses, debts, savings, income, investments, and retirement accounts, and although you will be setting specific targets in each of the corresponding sections of this book, writing down those you have at the start ensures you will remember your initial goals. A few examples could be:

- I want to put $250 a month into a savings account.
- I want to pay off my credit card debts or student loans in three years.
- I want to have paid off my entire mortgage by 2025.
- I want to start investing.
- I want to be a millionaire by the time I am fifty.

☐ As you can see, some targets might be farther in the future than others, some can be slightly more ambitious, some might not be applicable to you (maybe you do not have any consumer debt), and some you might not even aspire to at all (maybe you do not want to be a millionaire). Set what is right for you and what you feel is going to motivate you to put in the time and energy to ultimately get to your goal.

☐ Pick just a few objectives to start working toward. That might be just one or two, or you might feel comfortable having four or five goals at a time. Pick the right number of goals you feel you can handle and leave the other ones for now. We will come back to them. Make sure the ones you select are all doable at the same time. For example, "I want to pay off my $50,000 student loan in two years" and "I want to save $40,000 for a deposit on a house in one year" might not be achievable at the same time. Maybe you first want to pay off your loan and then start thinking about buying a house?

☐ Every time you achieve a goal, simply replace it with a new one. So even if you identified fifteen goals above and only selected three or four to start with, you will eventually get through all of them.

☐ Write your objectives on a card that you can take with you, add them to your cell phone reminders, share them with your social media group, write them in your journal, or use any of the other ideas listed in Step 0 to remind you about your goals daily and feel accountable for them.

☐ With time, some of these goals might need to be tweaked to keep up with changes in your lifestyle, interests, and ideas, making them more relevant to your current situation. You will also be setting new or additional goals throughout this book as we go through the various financial topics. For now, there is no need to worry about those goals you have yet to identify. Little by little during this journey, you will start incorporating them into your list of goals to focus on.

Create Progress Trackers

You cannot change what you don't manage; you cannot manage what you don't track.

—VALENTINO CRAWFORD

DIFFICULTY LEVEL: Easy

OBJECTIVE: Start tracking your progress on some of your key financial goals

REVIEW TIMES: Daily / weekly / monthly

One of the most enjoyable aspects of setting goals to reach financial independence is seeing yourself getting closer to them with each step you take. Throughout this book there will be many times when you will set (new) goals. Before doing so, the current step encourages you to set up or gather ideas for some visual, fun, or creative ways to track your progress. In doing so, becoming financially independent is not just a great end goal in itself, it will also become a fun journey with many smaller milestones to work toward and keep track of along the way. Tracking your progress can furthermore increase your motivation and likelihood of success, so there are many reasons to keep on top of your goals!

Goal tracking put in practice

Compare the following two situations:

- **Situation 1:** You decide you want to save $10,000 for a specific goal. You start off the first few weeks feeling very motivated and eager to get the money together as you cut out some expenses so you can assign some extra money to

your goal. Yet little by little, as your regular day-to-day life happens, you start to forget about your goal and stop your efforts to find extra savings. Within a few weeks, you cease to put any money aside at all.

- **Situation 2:** You decide you want to save $10,000 for a specific goal. You get out a piece of paper and at the top write: $10,000 for [insert your goal]. You decide that for every $10 or $25 you save, you will write that amount in a big circle on the paper. You stick the paper in your notebook, on the inside of your bathroom cabinet door, or on the fridge. Every time you see the paper, you're reminded of your goal and of how much you have saved already, which stimulates you to take another small step so you can contribute just a little more and add another amount to your paper. The more you save, the more motivated you become as you see the amount increasing.

As you can see, even a small daily reminder of your objective can have a big effect on your progress and motivation and help you stick to your new target.

How to track your progress

Below are some ideas to track your progress. Depending on your creativity and how much time you want to spend on this step, feel free to adapt these ideas to what would work for you personally. Remember these can be applied to any type of goal, be that saving, becoming debt-free, investing, or increasing your income or revenue, so you will likely end up with various trackers as you progress through this book.

- On a piece of paper, write down the amount of your goal, for example, $10,000 if you are looking to save $10,000. Every time you put money toward your goal, write down how much you contributed, cross out the old amount, and update it with the new outstanding amount.
- Get some graph paper—the one with the little squares—and determine how much each square represents: $5, $10, $25 . . . . Draw a box around the number of squares that represents the amount of money of your objective. For example, if you are trying to pay down a $5,000 debt and you decide that each square represents $50, then you need 100 squares: 100 x $50 = $5,000 to represent your entire goal. Every time you pay off $50, color in one of the squares.
- Instead of going for a plain box of squares, get creative and draw a figure. Say you are saving up $3,000 to buy a secondhand car. Why not draw a car out of the 60 squares you need?
- If you know that you sometimes might be able to set aside $25 but other times only $10, draw a shape with different-sized parts, such as a big flower with various leaves. Bigger leaves represent bigger amounts and you can add in the exact amount every time you put money toward your goal, meaning you do not have to determine the

amount each leaf represents beforehand. Do a search on sites like Pinterest or Instagram for more ideas on fun drawings.
- Alternatively, make a mural on which you draw something small or apply a sticker for each specific amount you save. This can be anything: from smiley faces to stars in the night sky or fish in a big fish tank.
- If you are saving your money in a bank account or paying down debt directly to your creditor but like the idea of a piggy bank to see your progress (see also Step 46), you can find a jar and put in items (buttons or marbles work well) for every $25 saved. In this way you can see your contributions to your goal increase even if the money is safely tucked away in a bank account.

- -

Tracking your progress can be great fun, as you get to see how you're moving closer to your goal bit by bit, even if your goal is big and might take a long time. Having a visual way of recording your progress will keep you motivated and focused to not give up. Don't be surprised if, with time, you realize you enjoy seeing your progress so much that you end up spicing up your trackers a little more as you go. But if, for now, you don't have the time to make your tracker(s) as beautiful or inspiring as you'd like to, just use a plain piece of paper, write your target amount and simply get started.

☑ STEP 5 ACTION PLAN

☐ Decide what is the most important financial goal you have right now, one that you can and would like to track. This can be a savings goal, an income goal, or a debt payment goal.

☐ If you want to keep it simple, just grab a piece of paper, write the amount of your goal at the top of the paper, and anytime you make any progress toward it, write down how much you added and how much is still pending.

☐ If you feel particularly creative, have a look on the Internet for some fun ideas or start with the suggestions offered above.

☐ Put your tracker in a visible place so that you are reminded of your goal every day. Make sure to update it daily or weekly during your money moment (see Step 24) or whenever you make a contribution toward your goal.

☐ Whenever you complete one of the 100 steps during this journey in which you set yourself another goal or would like to track your progress, come back to this step and create another tracker, so you can monitor your work in various areas at the same time.

Celebrate Your Victories

People often say that motivation doesn't last. Well, neither does bathing—that's why we recommend it daily.

—ZIG ZIGLAR

DIFFICULTY LEVEL: Easy

OBJECTIVE: Break down goals into smaller achievements and celebrate your success

REVIEW TIMES: Monthly

Setting goals is one thing, but achieving them is a whole different matter. Goals are usually easy to set, but difficult to achieve. They require real commitment and dedication. This can be especially true for such radical goals as "quit smoking" or "exercise daily," which require an almost all or nothing attitude.

Yet these type of goals have one big advantage over many long-term financial goals: it is easy to see how successful you are. Every hour you do not light a cigarette is an immediate success: your goal is to stop smoking and your success is easily measured with a simple yes or no at the end of each hour: Did I smoke a cigarette or not? The same is true for a goal such as "exercise daily": at the end of each day you can simply ask yourself: Did I do this today? A yes will make you feel good, and a no will hopefully give you a kick up the backside to try again tomorrow.

Long-term goals do not have daily successes

Many financial goals do not have this luxury. If you do not see a lot of progress quickly, it can be difficult to keep your motivation up after the initial few weeks. Say your goal is to increase your net worth by $1,000 per month, which roughly corresponds to $33 a day. But at the end of each day, you cannot exactly ask yourself, Did I increase my net worth by $33 today? Or imagine you have decided that you need to get $20,000 together for a down payment for a house, something that will likely take you a fairly long time to achieve. Or what about saving for retirement? How long will it take you to get that money together?

With none of these goals can you actually say, I achieved this today! Instead, they require you to change small things in your life every day in order to reach your goal little by little, and the results are often not very visible until many weeks or months (if not years) down the road.

As you continue on your journey to financial independence, your goals might become bigger and more abstract, which in turn makes it even more difficult to see your daily efforts paying off. Yet without focusing on your goals today, you will not be any closer to reaching them tomorrow. It is a continuous process of small steps and changes. Focus on them now and you will likely achieve your future goals; forget about them and nothing will ever come of them.

How to find regular successes

Even if you can't evaluate the immediate achievement of your goals on a daily basis, they should become an essential part of your day-to-day life, and you should evaluate every day how well you did on your way to achieving them. You can make them more tangible by not focusing on the end goal but on smaller milestones along the way, breaking them down into smaller steps and making it easier to see progress. Then—and here is the most important part—you should celebrate your victories. Once you've got half, a quarter, or even just 10% of your $10,000 savings goal—celebrate. I'm not talking about spending lots of money on a meal out in a high-end restaurant (that might set you back on your way toward your goal anyway). A celebration can be as big or as small as you want it to be: open a bottle of wine, have a picnic in the park, or build in time to go for a walk along the beach. By celebrating your victories, you keep yourself (and your partner or family) motivated, which makes you appreciate what you have already achieved instead of focusing on what is still to be done. And you deserve it! You have made the effort to cut expenses or increase your income, so why not a small celebration and a pat on your own back?

When to celebrate your victories

Regardless of the size of your goals, in this step you are going to think of ways to break them down, as well as how to celebrate your achievements. Have a look at some of the following ideas on setting smaller milestones regarding some topics that will be coming up in this book:

- **Net worth:** Celebrate every time you increase your net worth by $5,000.
- **Emergency fund:** Celebrate when you get to $250, then to $500, and finally when you reach $1,000.
- **Three-months-expenses fund:** Celebrate every time you save another month's worth of expenses.
- **Debt:** Celebrate for every $2,500 you pay off.
- **Savings:** Celebrate every time you save $2,000 or your savings rate increases by 3%.
- **Investing:** Celebrate every time your portfolio grows by $5,000.

Depending on your particular situation, adjust the ideas and figures to make them your own. The point is, you don't have to wait to pay off your very last debt before you celebrate. You can determine the achievements along the way. Think of it as a child going on a walk with their parents and getting a treat after every twenty signposts they see. Every time you hit a milestone, it makes you feel proud of your achievement, but it also keeps you going in order to claim your next reward.

- -

Looking back and appreciating what you have achieved is a great practice to include in your daily life. By starting small, you gain momentum, and celebrating your victories will help you keep up that momentum and give you confidence in yourself, knowing that if you can save $100, then you can also save $1,000. And if you can do that, you can also pay off that $10,000 debt. And if you can pay off your debt, you can also pay off all your other debts . . . and so it continues. Have fun celebrating!

☑ STEP 6 ACTION PLAN

☐ Every time you set yourself a new objective, break it down into smaller accomplishments and clear celebration moments. Determine how often you would like to celebrate (more often for more difficult or challenging goals to achieve, maybe not as often for goals that you find easier).

☐ Write down every single milestone. For example, if your goal is to increase your net worth by $10,000 in two years, you might decide that the moments to celebrate are every $2,500. Write down all:

- Net worth up by $2,500
- Net worth up by $5,000
- Net worth up by $7,500
- Net worth up by $10,000

☐ For every single small goal, determine a celebration. They don't all have to be different. Following the example above, you might create an in-home spa with a hot bath and some scented candles for the first three triumphs, then throw a Sunday afternoon barbecue party when you get to the last one. It's not about how creative you can be; it's about celebrating and appreciating how far you've come each time.

☐ Set aside for now any goals you have not yet started working toward. You will get to those every time you complete another goal. It will be fun to come up with new celebrations every time you move on to a new goal (or just repeat your favorites).

Organize Your Paperwork

Getting paperwork under control makes me feel more in control of my life generally.
—GRETCHEN RUBIN

DIFFICULTY LEVEL: Easy

OBJECTIVE: Organize and tidy your paperwork so you can always retrieve any papers you need

REVIEW TIMES: Yearly

Now that you are about to get serious regarding your financial life, one of the worst things is to try to take full control over your journey to financial independence and then not being able to find important financial documents when you need them, such as insurance policies, warranties, bank statements, or income stubs for your tax return. Come to think of it, is it even possible to become financially organized without having your home filing system organized?

An organized system

Having a proper, up-to-date, and easy to understand filing system does not only guarantee less stress and less time lost when you are looking for things, it also ensures you do not, for example, waste money on a new product if your old one still has a manufacturer's guarantee. It allows you to quickly check you still have the right insurance and update your assets, debts, and cash flow overview, and it makes it easy to see if your credit card statements are correct. If you're like I used to be, there might

 MAKE IT FUN:

Because this step can be tedious, make it enjoyable by breaking it up and setting yourself challenges: put together a playlist with your favorite energizing songs of thirty minutes and see how much you can get done in that half hour. Take a photo of the amount of papers you collected when going through your house, or of the state of your home office before you start. Then take a photo at the end of each day you have worked on this step, either of your home office, your folders that are slowly becoming organized, or of the amount of paper you've been able to sift through or envelopes you're putting in the recycling. Or set yourself the target to organize 1 folder per day.

have been some—if not many—occasions when you could not find anything you needed in the labyrinth also known as your financial dumping ground and wished you had one of those immaculate home offices from the pictures.

Good news: this step will walk you through the actions needed to set up a home filing system that ensures you will never (again) end up in a situation where you cannot find your important financial statements.

Having an organized filing system makes dealing with any paperwork a breeze. But the below action plan might all sound incredibly old-fashioned, time-consuming, or space-hungry to you. If that's the case, Step 92 tells you exactly how to convert your paperwork to a digital format. You can either jump straight ahead to that step now, or complete the current step and hold off digitizing until you get to the end of this journey when you've gone through the majority of the book.

☑ STEP 7 ACTION PLAN

☐ Make sure you have several empty folders or a filing cabinet available.

☐ Grab a big box or basket and put in any papers you can find lying around your house that should be sorted and/or filed. Go around the various rooms and check any drawers, baskets, and other areas where you might have paperwork that should be processed. Don't forget to look in closets, under your bed, and behind decorative vases on your shelves.

☐ Take the box with all the documents you have gathered to your home office or paperwork area. If you don't have such an area (yet), use your kitchen or dining-room table.

☐ Divide the documents by topic into piles: car papers, electricity bills, bank statements, phone bills, mortgage overviews, etc.

☐ Examine any previous attempts at a filing system if you tried to set one up before and be prepared to slightly overhaul this if it is relatively outdated or overly complicated.

☐ Assign one folder to each specific category or use dividers to create more space within each folder. Depending on how many papers you have for each topic, some might need more or less space and some categories might require an entire folder for itself.

☐ You will probably have documents and papers for the following categories, which you can use to preassign some of your folders:

- Income/pay slips and annual statements
- Insurance policies
- Bank and credit card statements
- Savings and retirement account overviews
- Car documents
- Utilities contracts and bills (electricity, water, phone, etc.).
- Tax returns
- Warranties, manuals, and receipts
- House- and home-maintenance-related issues
- Official paperwork such as birth certificates, marriage license, and diplomas
- School documents
- Mortgage and property documents
- Medical documents
- Paperwork regarding your pets

☐ Put your documents per category in reverse chronological order—oldest ones at the bottom, newest ones on top—and start filing documents that are merely for information, such as statements and contracts.

☐ Any document that requires action (for example, a bill that needs to be paid or a subscription you need to cancel) should be kept aside to deal with later.

☐ If you find a document that replaces another one, throw out or recycle the oldest one if you no longer need it. Shred anything that contains personal information that can be used to identify you, such as account information, credit card details, your address, phone numbers, or an email address.

☐ Throw away or recycle any documents for any services you no longer use or regarding objects that have since been replaced or disposed of.

☐ Set up a command center, mail station, or organization station (ideally close to your mailbox or main entrance) where you have the following five baskets or boxes available for any paperwork:

- To pay: bills that need to be paid (although try to automate these where possible; see also Step 33).
- To do: items that require some sort of action, such as canceling or renewing a subscription.
- To read: anything you want to read before filing it away or recycling it.
- To file: any paperwork that's been processed that you need to keep and that can be filed.
- To recycle: any papers that can be recycled immediately.

☐ Make it a daily habit to go open any mail you receive and put it in the appropriate baskets. Do the same with any documents you bring home, such as warranties or receipts for purchases you made that day.

☐ Schedule in a monthly time to go through your baskets and process, pay, read, and/or file the contents. (One idea is to plan this for your monthly finance review; see Step 35.)

☐ With every paper that you receive, decide whether you really need to keep the document and/or whether you can do anything to make the paperwork unnecessary: Is it a bill or payment you can automate, or a paper bank statement you can opt out of?

☐ Once you have a filing system that's clear and easy to use (don't make it too complicated because that could cause you to stop using it), you can be sure all your paperwork is always where it should be: in the corresponding folders, or in the basket if you have not yet processed it. Therefore, you should always be able to find important documents and financial statements when you need them.

☐ Schedule in a quick review of your filing system once a year to update categories or throw out/ recycle paperwork you no longer need.

Plan Your Money Allocation Strategy

If plan A fails, remember that you have twenty-five letters left.

—CHRIS GUILLEBEAU

DIFFICULTY LEVEL: Difficult

OBJECTIVE: Start putting together your ultimate money plan

REVIEW TIMES: Yearly

A difficult question that many people on their journey to financial independence quickly encounter is how to make a solid financial plan with the aim to get the most out of their money by making it work for them. Throughout this book you will start to cut down on your expenses, or to up your income or earnings from a side hustle, and once you manage to do so, the question as to what to do with the extra money you will then have can be a difficult one. In this step, you will make a money allocation strategy that will guide you through some financial decisions you will need to make at different points on this journey.

How money can make you money

In these 100 steps you will learn about some of the following avenues to "make money with your money":

- **Paying off debt:** this strategy saves you money on interest and compounded interest paid over the years.

- **Saving:** putting money toward savings generates money due to interest received and the power of compounding interest. It also ensures a financial cushion, helping you avoid having to go into debt in the future.
- **Income:** investing money to start your own business or launch a product can generate another income source.
- **Investing:** generates money due to capital gains, interest, and dividends received.
- **Retirement accounts:** builds up the income that you will receive after your retirement age.
- **Personal capital:** increases your earning potential as a professional or entrepreneur.

These are the most common strategies to pursue in order to leverage what your money can do for you. But where to start? Say you saved an extra $100 this month and you are happy to invest this money into your future. Where do you actually put this money? Which of the above options do you choose? And how do you prioritize these strategies?

Money allocation

The question of where to allocate your money does not have to be an either/or proposition. You can start investing while still having a mortgage. You will want to save up for an emergency fund while also paying off credit card debt. And once you start investing in your personal capital, you will likely want to keep that up on a regular basis and the fact that you are investing in the market does not rule out this option.

That said, some people feel more comfortable paying off all their debt first or hitting a specific savings goal before starting to invest. It is important to do what you feel most comfortable with and what seems most logical for your personal situation. Below are tips and guidelines you can use to put your own money allocation strategy together. Some of these points might not be very clear at this stage, but don't worry, they will be once you've completed the corresponding section on that particular topic. For now this just serves as an overview that you will probably need to return to at various moments on your journey.

Debt payments

- Based on the annual interest rates of your various debts, prioritize any debts over a certain percentage. A good guideline is to pay down any debt as quickly as possible with an annual interest rate over 5%. The compounding effects of these debts make them very expensive, and especially credit card debt can have high interest rates of around 14% or more. Consider paying off these debts as an absolute priority if you have these.
- Apart from that, your own opinion about debt is very important to consider, too. If you feel uncomfortable about owing money to somebody else, prioritize paying off debt over any of the other strategies or assign the biggest chunk of money to this.

Savings

- Your savings strategy can greatly depend on your job stability as well as how variable your income is. If your job stability is relatively high and you have a sufficiently guaranteed monthly income, then you might not need to get together a three-months-expenses fund (see Step 45) as quickly as somebody whose job is less secure or whose income varies greatly from one month to the next.
- Your savings goals can further determine whether you should allocate more or less to your savings. Are they short-term or long-term goals? How important are these goals and when do you hope to have saved the money together? Do you feel comfortable with keeping a three-months-expenses fund in your savings account and investing everything else, or do you want (or need) more money in a savings account?
- You should also consider the interest rate on your savings to decide whether to adjust your savings strategy. At the time of writing, some banks in many parts of the world offer an interest rate of just a little more than 0%, and some even offer a negative rate, meaning customers pay to store their money with a bank! During times like this, it might be much more interesting to pay off debt or invest more, at least until interest rates go up again. Especially when the interest rate is far below the rate of inflation, money quickly loses its value in a savings account, making it not a great candidate as a way to make more money.

Investing

- Consider your returns on investments, i.e., how much you expect to get on your investments. Especially if a savings account is not giving you much return, you might want to give investing more priority for a while.
- The possible risks of losing a substantial amount of money that is invested might make paying off debt more interesting before you start investing, as your money might give you a lot more value. This is especially true at the height of a bull market when investments are expensive.
- With higher average returns, long-term investments can often generate a very nice portfolio, especially with the power of compounding interest. As a long-term strategy,

therefore, investing is usually the one with the most potential.

Retirement accounts

- If your employer matches your retirement account contributions, it is often worth maxing out your contribution, especially (but not only) if your retirement account is based on cheap index funds.
- If you have tax advantage accounts, putting extra money toward these might again be favorable, even more so if you expect your tax rates to go up in the future.
- Retirement accounts have the disadvantage of often having less flexibility when it comes to choosing investments (especially in the case of workplace retirement accounts) and deciding when to start withdrawing from them. If you start withdrawing before the official retirement age, you often will be charged a substantial fee. In contrast, investments you manage personally offer much more flexibility.

Personal capital

- Investing in your personal capital, be that books, podcasts, or training programs, might deserve priority when the expected outcomes or returns of the program are far bigger than any of the other strategies and if the course fits with what you are looking for. The world of online courses is growing rapidly and more are being launched every week. Whether you invest in an online course, a book, or a college degree, nowadays you can pretty much find a course for anything you could possibly need.
- The returns can be less predictable with this strategy than with others, but also more satisfying. Investing in personal capital might have not only direct financial advantages, but also psychological ones. Do not underestimate the positive effect that feeling motivated and inspired in your job can have on your long-term earning potential.

Plan your strategy

When it comes to planning your own money allocation strategy, you can make this as simple or complex as you want. A relatively simple, linear strategy in which you complete each step before moving on to the next one could look like this:

1. Save for a $1,000 emergency fund
2. Become debt-free
3. Invest an average of $25 per month in your personal capital
4. Save a three-months-expenses fund
5. Max out retirement account contributions
6. Pay off your mortgage
7. Start investing

If you want to go for a more complex and customized strategy, an example strategy could be:

1. Save for a $1,000 emergency fund
2. Aggressively pay off any debt over 5% annual interest rates
3. Put together your own plan of a proportional money allocation strategy, including: debt payments / saving / retirement account contributions / investing / personal capital growth
   a. If you want to get rid of any debt as soon as possible, your contributions might look like: 80% / 5% / 5% / 5% /5%
   b. If you might want to put money toward all of these areas but in different proportions,

you can make any allocation, such as 25% / 10% / 10% / 50% / 5% for an aggressive investment strategy, or 30% / 20% / 25% / 20% / 5% for a more balanced approach.

With time, adjust your strategy as you reach your various targets or whenever your situation changes. You don't have to stick with the same percentages—after all, once you pay off your debt, you free up money that can go elsewhere. Similarly, factors such as a higher or lower income, changes in your family situation, or market developments can affect where you can and want to put less or extra money.

Do not regard your list of money allocation percentages as being set in stone. As your situation changes, your pay increases or decreases, interest rates change, and the stock exchange experiences a bear or bull market, you will want to modify your plan. Accept that your plan will need adapting, but that having a flexible plan that you constantly mold to your needs is better than not having a plan at all. It will help you when setting your budget and building your secure financial future. Enjoy planning!

☑ STEP 8 ACTION PLAN

The below action plan is designed to be consulted every time you complete a new part of the book. The first time you do this when you haven't yet read the rest of the book, this might be more arbitrary, but every time you come back to this list at later moments, your plan will start to become more solid and comprehensive. It is helpful to put together a plan now and update it as you progress through this book, rather than only making a plan when you reach the end of your journey to FI. Not only is it easier to update an existing plan that started off basic than it is to put together a complex plan from scratch, but it will also provide valuable insight into how your financial priorities are changing over time.

☐ Start with determining your feelings about debt and your risk levels in terms of saving and investing. How bad is debt for you and how badly do you want to get rid of it? Do you feel comfortable to start investing even if you still have debt? How big are your savings goals? Are you happy to have a big chunk of money in the stock market or would you rather first have a substantial amount of savings built up?

☐ Make a list of all the various money allocation strategies you want to pursue and put them in a logical order as per the examples above. What is your number one goal that you will stick to before moving on to any of the other targets? What about number two? Which targets do you want to complete first before starting a divided money strategy in which you assign parts of the extra money to various targets?

☐ Go back to the vision and goals you set out during the various stages of this journey. Are they represented in this plan? Do you want to modify any of those goals? Do you need to adjust your plan to incorporate some goals you had forgotten about?

☐ Review your list and make sure you feel absolutely confident and happy about it. If you want you can assign target dates for the various goals to be achieved.

☐ Make any necessary changes to your budget to reflect your new strategy. If you have been budgeting too much or too little for some of these goals, adjust the amounts now and make any necessary changes in automatic transfers or standing orders to savings or investment accounts.

☐ Review your list annually and make any changes as needed.

Checklist Part 1

Use the following checklist to make sure you have done everything in Part 1 and are ready to continue with the next section.

☐ You have written an affirmation that identifies your commitment as well as your belief in your ability to succeed and accomplish this journey. You keep this affirmation close by and read it at least once a day.

☐ You have set reminders in your calendar and have visual reminders in your car, bathroom, wallet, or on your phone or computer about your commitment to this journey.

☐ You have defined your vision for financial independence—your reason to embark on this journey and pursue financial success.

☐ You have determined which of the eight stages of financial independence you want to pursue, what reaching that stage would look like to you, and which targets you need to set yourself to get from your current stage to your aspired stage.

☐ You have made a vision board to remind you of your goals daily, to keep up your motivation, and to not forget about what you are working toward and why.

☐ You have set at least a few financial goals.

☐ You have set up a progress tracker for one of your most important financial targets in order to keep up your motivation and quickly see how well you're doing on your key goal.

☐ You have decided on small rewards for yourself when completing different milestones for the various targets you have and will be setting on this journey.

☐ You have set up and organized your filing system and you can easily access all your important documents and statements if needed.

☐ You have put together an initial money allocation strategy that will guide you on how to spend your money long term. This plan will likely change with time, as you adjust it to the various goals you are still to set in the different areas of money management.

> ## 💬 PERSONAL STORY: LIZ
>
> After the birth of my first child, I made the decision to step away from my full-time position to dedicate more time to my family. It has been a financial adjustment by only working part-time, but the emotional payoffs have far outweighed the pay cut.
>
> My kids won't remember what toys I was or wasn't able to buy them or whether their clothes were hand-me-downs or from a designer shop. They will remember that I was there for them when they came home from school, I wasn't always rushing off to a meeting, and when I was home, I was home not only physically, but also mentally.
>
> I have the work-life balance that works for my family's needs at the moment. That being said, my future plans are to return back to work in a full-time teaching position, which is why I am currently studying for my master's degree. An investment in my education will hopefully prove to be fruitful in the future professionally as well as financially.
>
> —Liz Grabo, United States

Your Starting Point

After having gone through some key habits and good practices in the first part of this book, and getting a good understanding of what exactly you are hoping to get out of this journey and what you are working toward, Part 2 focuses on getting a good picture of your current financial situation.

Without knowing your starting point, it can be almost impossible to see any progress later on, or even find the direction in which to go. By first drawing up a clear representation of the current state of your finances, you can then start identifying action plans in order to improve your finances one step at a time.

In this part you will gain insight into where your money goes each month, find out more about your net worth and create an overview of the value of all your debts and assets.

Track Your Expenses

Always bear in mind that your own resolution to succeed is more important than any other.
—ABRAHAM LINCOLN

DIFFICULTY LEVEL: Easy

OBJECTIVE: Track your expenses and uncover your spending patterns

REVIEW TIMES: Register daily, review monthly

When defining your starting points, you first need to work out where all your money is currently going. Once you know your spending patterns, you can evaluate whether they align with your financial goals, and if not, how you can start working toward achieving those goals.

Understandably, your expenses are different from week to week and month to month. To map your spending patterns accurately, you are going to track your expenses daily for a prolonged period, at least three months but preferably more. By registering your spending, you not only get a good idea of how you spend your money, you are furthermore becoming more *conscious* of spending it, which is likely to result in a slight decrease in your expenditure in general.

Tracking options

There are various options available to track your expenses: You can carry around a notebook to register all your payments, you can create your own spreadsheet in a program such as Microsoft Excel, or you can get an online program or mobile app (both paid and free), such as YNAB (You Need a Budget), Mint, and EveryDollar, to name just a few.

The advantage of online programs and apps is that they allow you to record transactions on your phone in the moment and do away with the notebook. Some even allow you to directly import your bank statements, which can save some time long term. These programs also often provide detailed spending reports. Have a look around and decide what you prefer and what works best for you. Of course, you might want to keep it simple and go for the paper-and-pen option.

If you don't have time to investigate the options right now, just start registering your expenses on paper or in a digital file and transfer them into your definitive method of tracking once you have made a decision.

If you ever forget to register an expense, don't worry about it too much, and most importantly, do not give up on this entire step only because you missed one or two expenses. It will require a fair bit of time to get used to this new habit, so you'll likely forget now and again. Missing out on one or two expenses is not a big issue as long as you just pick up from where you left off as soon as you become aware of this.

☑ STEP 9 ACTION PLAN

☐ Starting today, keep a register of everything you spend, no matter how small or insignificant the expense might seem. Don't record just cash; remember to also include any debit or credit card payments, standing orders, checks, PayPal transactions, and any other form of payment.

☐ Record your expenses in one place. Don't worry about whether or not it is the perfect system or whether it's set up in the most logical way. The most important thing for now is to get started and then with time start making small tweaks.

☐ Keep receipts until you register the expense. If you don't get a receipt, make sure to note the payment elsewhere immediately.

☐ Check your bank, PayPal, and other online accounts regularly to register any transactions that were made from there.

☐ When you get a moment, investigate some programs available to track your expenses in digital format. If you want to use a digital expenses tracker on different devices, such as your computer, tablet, and phone, it will need to work on all of them and updates should be synced automatically and instantly.

☐ Settle for an option that you feel is easy to use and that fits with what you need. If you choose a system that looks snazzy but you're not motivated to use, you are unlikely to stick to it over time.

☐ Log your expenses for at least three months to get a good amount of data and to see how much your expenses fluctuate.

☐ Even better than three months, aim to implement this step as a permanent habit, as it will help you stay on top of your money month to month and see how your expense patterns change with time. If you don't follow this practice, yearly expenses and emergency or one-off payments might go unnoticed.

☐ If this is the first time you are registering your expenses, accept that they will be a long list of uncategorized outtakes for now. In Part 3 of this book, you will add structure and organization to this list, but that is not your objective at this stage.

☐ Add this step to a Post-it, your mobile phone, or your journal so you are reminded of your new daily task. You might also want to set an alarm twice a day to remind yourself to write down any expenses you forgot to register in the moment. If you leave it until the next day, you are likely to forget some of them.

List Your Debts

> *If you're walking down the right path and you're willing to keep walking, eventually you'll make progress.*
> —BARACK OBAMA

DIFFICULTY LEVEL: Easy

OBJECTIVE: Create a list of your outstanding debts

REVIEW TIMES: Update monthly

Now that you are tracking your expenses, and since you need a solid, reliable log with several weeks of data about your expenses before you can do much with it, let's continue with some other steps in the meantime. To start with, in this tenth step you will be pulling up an overview of your outstanding debts.

Being reminded of how much you owe others is usually not very pleasant, but since these debts are probably also one of your biggest worries or financial strains, this step is necessary to find out how bad (or not) your situation is to begin with.

A borrowing society

Borrowing money is a relatively common phenomenon in our current society. Although it seems like a great way to finance big purchases, the problem is that as long as you have debts, you are not only tied to paying back money all the time, you are furthermore consistently losing money, much more than you might think. Borrowing money comes at a high price, which is why debts are also known as liabilities: the interest you are charged can be substantial,

something we will look at more closely in Part 4 of this book. Yet we seem to constantly be borrowing money these days—first to get through college, then to buy a car, a house, that fancy vacation, until slowly it becomes more and more normal to get something first and pay for it later.

Any debt you have is a sign you are not financially free. To improve your situation, you need to first get a clear picture of exactly how much money you are paying off monthly, how much you are still due to pay, and how much longer you will be tied to paying back these loans. Once you clearly understand your liabilities, you can start taking control of your situation and make some positive changes to your finances.

I appreciate this can be a slightly discouraging step, but remember that all beginnings are tough. If you feel a little depressed by the total amount of debt you have, put your feet up, brew a cup of coffee or tea, grab your favorite book or run a bath, and celebrate the fact that you've made good progress already! You are soon going to attack these debts and stop them from controlling you and your finances once and for all. And—spoiler alert—the next step will be a more positive one in which you will look at a list of what you own. It should provide some balance to today's list of what you owe.

☑ STEP 10 ACTION PLAN

This step requires some investigation, so hopefully you completed step 7 and have your paperwork (semi) organized. If not, don't let that put you off. Just grab your phone and contact your bank or loan provider(s) and get the necessary information that way. Commit to getting this step done regardless of how organized your home office is.

☐ Make a list in a notebook, journal, or digital spreadsheet of any outstanding debts. Think about:

- Student loans
- Mortgage
- Car loan
- Credit cards
- Overdraft fees on your bank account
- Loans or financing plans with stores, travel agents, etc.
- Personal loans from friends/family

☐ Find statements, contact providers, or log into online accounts to find the current outstanding balance (the money you still owe) on each one of the different debts. Write this down in the second column next to each loan. For example, if you got a mortgage for $200,000 but have since paid off $50,000 of the principal, then write down the current outstanding amount of $150,000 next to "mortgage."

☐ Find out how much you are paying back monthly on each of these debts and write this payment next to each loan in a third column.

☐ A fourth column will be for the interest rate for each debt. Make sure to note down the yearly percentage, not the monthly rate! If you only know the monthly rate, such as for your credit card, simply multiply the rate by twelve to get your yearly rate.

☐ For the fifth and last column, find out how long you have left to pay the loan back, if applicable (this is commonly for a mortgage but can also apply to other debts).

⚏ STAT BOX

According to a 2017 publication by the Federal Reserve System, almost 44% of Americans carried credit card balances in 2016, just under 34% had a loan for their vehicle, and 22% of Americans had a student loan.[4]

List Your Assets

> *The biggest obstacle to wealth is fear. People are afraid to think big, but if you think small, you'll only achieve small things.*
>
> —T. HARV EKER

DIFFICULTY LEVEL: Easy

OBJECTIVE: Create a list of all your assets

REVIEW TIMES: Update monthly

Now that you know exactly what your debts (or liabilities) are, in this step you are going to look at what your possessions—also known as assets—are. Assets add a positive value to your financial balance sheet: they are the things you own and that can provide you with money if you chose to liquidate them—i.e., sell them.

Making an overview of all your assets will not only allow you to know exactly how much you own at present, but also provide insight into how you could increase the total value of those assets, such as through investing or saving more money, something we will look at in Parts 5 and 8.

What counts as an asset?

When it comes to making an assets list, there are different opinions about what to include. You can decide to focus on your big assets alone, or you can make the list as detailed as possible and include small assets such as your furniture, electronics, and cars.

I personally recommend you don't worry about the smaller possessions you have (how much would you really get for your furniture anyway?) unless you own a piece that is really valuable, such as an antique or some very expensive jewelry. With anything else, such as cars and computers, remember that their worth goes down with each day, so my advice would be not to include these, unless you feel particularly strongly about making a very detailed list. As long as you are consistent from one time to the next when you make your list, you can include as many or as few items as seems logical to you.

The value of some of your assets (such as your money in a checking account) might fluctuate more from month to month than others (such as your house). That is not something to get very concerned about. For now, you just want to have an approximate overview of your different assets in order to monitor changes over time.

☑ STEP 11 ACTION PLAN

☐ In the same place you noted your debts, be that a journal, spreadsheet, or online program, proceed with making a list of everything you own. Think about the following categories:

- Your house/apartment if you have bought it—even if you have not yet paid off the mortgage
- Any other property you own (a second house or apartment, any rental property)
- Savings money
- Any money in other (checking) accounts
- Your pension(s) and other retirement funds
- Investment portfolios such as stocks, bonds, gold, etc.
- Endowments
- Antiques or jewelry
- Permanent or whole life insurance

☐ Find out the value of the different assets and write these down next to each item. Make sure to put down the current value, regardless of what you once paid for it. For example, if you bought your house for $200,000 but the current value is $30,000 less, then list the value as the amount at the moment, or $170,000. Ignore the amount you still need to pay on your mortgage; in this step, we are just looking at the value of your assets, so even if you still have a $100,000 loan on your house, list the value as the full $170,000.

☐ You may not know the exact current value of your house, in which case you can do some investigating, online or with a real estate expert, to find out what similar houses in your area are going for.

☐ Contact retirement account or savings providers to get the latest statements.

☐ If you have a whole life insurance policy, you can work out the current value if you decided to cancel the insurance. Bear in mind that in nearly all cases this would involve a penalty or cancelation fee, and similarly, the amount of money you are due would most likely be taxed if it were paid out at once. If you have term insurance, none of this would be applicable as you would not be paid out anything if you canceled, meaning your term insurance is worth $0 (and that can be absolutely fine, as you will discover in Part 9).

☐ In terms of retirement accounts, you can decide whether to add them or not. The slight issue with these accounts is that they are not an asset, but a future income. Another problem with retirement accounts is that over time they are usually corrected for inflation while at the same time regularly overhauled to adjust to current changes in society, making the amount unpredictable, especially if you are still a long way from retiring. (See more on retirement accounts in Part 7.) One option is to include the current value of any private and workplace retirement plans, but leave out any state or federal retirement accounts that you might be eligible for, as these are more likely to change over time. Alternatively, you can decide to include an estimation of all of them or leave them all out.

Calculate Your Net Worth

Money is in some respects life's fire: it's a very excellent servant but a terrible master.

—P.T. BARNUM

DIFFICULTY LEVEL: Easy

OBJECTIVE: Calculate your current net worth

REVIEW TIMES: Update monthly

After having completed the previous two steps, you are now ready to work out your overall financial starting position by calculating your net worth. Surprisingly this step is a lot easier than it might sound, as you have already done the preparation work in the last two steps by digging up those financial statements and creating your assets and liabilities lists.

What is net worth?

Simply put, your net worth indicates what would happen if you decided to sell all of your possessions and pay off all of your debts today. Would you have any money left over or would you still be in debt? How much money would you walk away with or still owe? Your net worth is your total amount of assets minus the total amount of your liabilities and is an indicator of your financial health: the higher the number, the healthier your finances.

If your net worth is negative, your liabilities are bigger than your assets. Even if you sold everything you own, you still would not be able to pay off all your debt. If, on the other hand, your net worth is positive, this indicates that you own more than what you owe, which of course is a more financially attractive situation to work toward. It probably means that you have paid off (a lot of) your debts or that you have used your debts to invest cleverly in assets that have increased in value (more on that later).

The advantages of knowing your net worth

What makes calculating your net worth useful is threefold:

1. It gives you a realistic picture of your current situation and how positive or negative this starting point is.
2. It gives you an easy method to calculate your financial progress over time, as you can recalculate your net worth on a regular basis and monitor how it changes.
3. It allows you to set financial goals with a clear time frame attached; e.g., you can set yourself the goal of increasing your net worth by $10,000 in two years.

What should your net worth be?

There is no one indicator of what your net worth should be, and often people's net worth changes a lot over time. Most people in their twenties have a negative net worth when they come out of college and are starting off with their adult lives. It is usually not until they get to their thirties that their net worth slowly starts to increase, but average net worth per age varies hugely across different countries. If you would like to know the average net worth per age in your country, have a look online for the latest figures by searching for "net worth per age + [your country]."

Do not despair if your current net worth is negative. Many people are in the same situation, so turn this into a challenge to start working toward getting a positive figure. If, on the other hand, you currently have a positive balance—congratulations, as it means you are already a little ahead! Don't see that as a reason to relax, however, as I am sure you will want to increase your net worth even more and keep working toward financial freedom.

☑ STEP 12 ACTION PLAN

- [ ] Get out your journal, spreadsheet, digital app, or online document and write down today's date.

- [ ] Write down "total value assets," "total value liabilities," and "total net worth."

- [ ] Pull out your list of assets with their estimated values from Step 11. Add up the numbers to get the total value of your assets. Add this number to your document next to "total value assets."

- [ ] Look back at your list of debts that you put together in Step 10. Add up the outstanding amounts of each debt to find out your total amount of debt. Write this number next to "total value liabilities."

- [ ] Take your total value of assets and subtract the total value of your liabilities to find out your net worth.

  - For example, if your total value of assets is $40,000 and you have a total of $70,000 in liabilities, your net worth would be -/-$30,000 at the moment. Write this figure down next to "total net worth."

- [ ] Make it a habit to calculate your net worth monthly at either the start or end of each month. Take out your calendar or journal and mark the next time to do this. If you are using a digital calendar, set up a recurring reminder.

Set a Net Worth Goal

Something mystical happens when we commit something personal to writing. We somehow begin to live out our plans.
—DAVE RAMSEY

DIFFICULTY LEVEL: Medium

OBJECTIVE: Define a six-month goal for your net worth

REVIEW TIMES: Review monthly, reset biannually

Your next step of the 100 steps to financial independence is to set yourself a goal for what you would like your net worth to be in six months. This gives you a specific target to work toward during this journey. Six months is a good time frame to start with, as it is long enough to see a substantial change and the direct effects of goal setting, yet short enough not to forget about or lose track of.

With time you will decide how exactly you want to raise your net worth: by increasing your savings, paying off debt, boosting your investments, or any other means. Any way that increases the total value of your assets or decreases the total amount of liabilities will work. Later parts of this book will of course give you more details on each method. In this step, you will simply set yourself a target.

You can set yourself a net worth goal by either stating a specific amount or setting a percentage by which to increase your net worth. Let's look at these two different approaches.

A set amount for your net worth goal

Imagine your current net worth is $25,000 and you set yourself the goal to increase it by $5,000 in six months, to a total of $30,000. Your plan is to do this by paying off debts—your mortgage, for example—and by saving money. Now, say that after six months you have achieved your goal so your net worth is now $30,000. You decide to continue to set yourself a new goal with regard to your net worth every six months, in particular to increase it by another $5,000. Five years after starting off with a net worth of $25,000 and assuming you achieved your goal every time, your net worth would have increased to $75,000, as shown in Table 1.

It would be logical, however, that with that increased net worth (most likely due to having less debts and therefore less interest to pay or thanks to more savings or investments with interest generated) it becomes substantially easier to keep increasing it with $5,000 per half a year than when your net worth was "only" $25,000. Sticking to the target of $10,000 a year might therefore mean you are not achieving as much as you might be able to if you adjusted your target up every time your net worth increased.

Table 1: Net worth increases based on a set amount

	Net worth	Target increase
Start	$25,000	$5,000
6 months	$30,000	$5,000
1 year	$35,000	$5,000
1.5 years	$40,000	$5,000
2 years	$45,000	$5,000
2.5 years	$50,000	$5,000
3 years	$55,000	$5,000
3.5 years	$60,000	$5,000
4 years	$65,000	$5,000
4.5 years	$70,000	$5,000
5 years	$75,000	

Table 2: Net worth increases based on a relative increase (20%)

	Net worth	Target increase
Start	$25,000	$5,000
6 months	$30,000	$6,000
1 year	$36,000	$7,200
1.5 years	$43,200	$8,640
2 years	$51,840	$10,368
2.5 years	$62,208	$12,442
3 years	$74,650	$14,930
3.5 years	$89,580	$17,916
4 years	$107,496	$21,499
4.5 years	$128,995	$25,799
5 years	$154,794	

Note: Amounts rounded to closest dollar.

A relative amount for your net worth goal

If, on the other hand, you set yourself the goal of increasing your net worth by a certain percentage, you increase your goal as your net worth increases. Say that your net worth is again $25,000 at the moment you start, and you set yourself the goal of increasing it by 20% in six months. You will see that for the first six months, your increase would be exactly the same as before: 20% of $25,000 is $5,000, so after the first half a year, your new net worth would also be $30,000. But after those first six months and with a net worth of $30,000, 20% is no longer $5,000 but $6,000, and after that, your next target is to increase by $7,200. As you can see in Table 2, this increases the value continuously, and after five years—providing you successfully achieve your goals—it would not be $75,000 but over $154,000.

You can see how a simple shift in expectations adds up to a lot more money over time—in this case, more than $79,000 in just five years. Whichever approach you choose for this step, you can of course always adjust your targets up or down or switch from one to the other.

- -

If you feel your goal is a little bit of a wild guess, that is fairly normal; with time, this will become more accurate, especially once you have had a better look at your expenses and income patterns (in Parts 3 and 6). For now the main thing is that you have started thinking about the evolution of your net worth and that you have set yourself a goal. Perfecting it can be your focus at a later stage.

☑ STEP 13 ACTION PLAN

☐ Make a rough calculation of how much of your debt you already pay off each month. You have to be careful here, as even if you pay $200 monthly, that does not mean your outstanding balance goes down by $200, since part of what you pay is interest (more on that later!). So contact your loan provider or compare the last two statements of any of your debts to find out how much of the core debt (or "principal") you are paying off per month—which should be indicated on your statements—and write this down.

☐ If you are increasing any assets on a monthly basis (investments, savings, retirement contributions), estimate how much you roughly add per month.

☐ Total how much you decrease your debts and how much you increase your assets on a monthly basis and multiply the total by six. This is how much you can expect to roughly increase your net worth in six months (not looking at capital gains, market fluctuations, and compounding effects, all of which we will discuss later), provided you continue doing what you are currently doing, do not add any other debt, and do not sell off any of your assets.

- Let's say your current net worth is -/-$30,000. You pay $200 toward your student loan provider on a monthly basis, of which only $170 goes to the loan, and the remaining $30 is interest. You also put away $50 into a savings account. That means that in six months, you expect to have paid $1,020 ($170 per month) toward your loan (the $30/month interest you pay does not count), and you should have added $300 to your savings account. That means that your net worth would have increased to -/-$28,680 without doing anything different from what you are already doing.

☐ Set a realistic target for how much to increase your net worth, bearing in mind that with all else staying the same, you should already achieve the net worth that you calculated above. Make it challenging but at the same time not too difficult to achieve. In the next parts of the book, you will be encouraged to spend less and save more, so the idea is that as we progress through the steps, you should contribute more to your net worth than you are currently on a monthly basis.

- Looking at the earlier example from above where you started with a -/-$30,000 net worth, getting to $0 in six months is probably not very realistic. Similarly setting yourself the target to get to -/-$29,000 might not be challenging enough.
- You might in the above example set yourself the challenge to get to -/-$27,500, which is $1,180 above what to expect if you made no other changes, corresponding to roughly $200 extra per month.

☐ Next month when you recalculate your net worth, check how you are doing with your target. If you are not on track to reach your net worth goal, see if you can make any adjustments to your spending patterns to get back on track. Alternatively, if you are well ahead of your target, see if you want to set yourself an even higher goal.

Checklist Part 2

Use the following checklist to make sure you have done everything in Part 2 and are ready to continue with the next section.

☐ You have decided how or where to track your expenses and are updating your expenses log daily.

☐ You have compiled a list of all your outstanding debts along with their details.

☐ You have compiled a list of all your assets with their current values.

☐ You have calculated and registered your current net worth.

☐ You have set a target for your net worth in six months.

☐ You have set a reminder or appointment with yourself to update your debts, assets, and net worth at the start or end of each new month.

💬 PERSONAL STORY: ILSE

I started my own veterinary acupuncture practice for dogs and cats after I had worked for about eleven years for a boss. It was a relief. Why? Well, I have a couple of reasons, but the most important ones are that it gave me a lot of freedom and energy.

I am totally not a morning person; I perform much better in the afternoon and in the evening. I get very tired and receive too much stimuli when I have to get up early in the morning and get myself stuck in traffic like the rest of the working people. I have a toddler at home whom I'm taking care of without the help of a child day care. I want to be there for him as much as possible the first years of his life before he goes to school. During the day I take care of him. When he does his nap I relax, too, and when he goes to bed and my husband is at home, I visit patients. Once a week my mother helps me out, and I can treat patients during the afternoon. Sometimes I even treat some patients on the weekend.

But freedom and energy are much broader. I can practice my profession the way I want. I don't have to justify anything to anyone, except to myself, my family, and my clients. There is no boss who tells me when and how I have to do the things in which time span. I want to do the things my way, the way which fits me most. I have high standards for the health care I want to deliver and it's more time-consuming than a boss can offer me. I hated the feeling of someone breathing down my neck and a waiting room getting full with patients waiting for me. Now I don't need to make concessions in the quality I deliver.

Despite the fact that I now earn less compared to when I was employed, I am so much happier and it has been worth it. My husband is also a freelancer, so we both have a lot of flexibility to live the life we want: taking as much care of our son as we truly want and believe is good for him, touring with our camper van more frequently and for longer periods of time, working when we have a lot of energy, and relaxing when we are tired or haven't got much inspiration. I know, sometimes you have to work while you don't feel like it or you have a very sick patient or a strict deadline, but at least you have the feeling that you're doing it for your own business, and that's a whole other feeling than doing it for someone else's. Furthermore, to work in my own way and to treat the animals of clients who feel comfortable with my methods cost me less energy; in this way there is more space in my head for other fun things!

Live your own life, not someone else's!

—Ilse van Driel, Netherlands
http://www.felicanipunctuur.nl

PART 3

Your Expenses

Now that you have defined your starting points and have set yourself up for this journey in Part 2, we will be looking at each area of your finances in turn and start making changes and applying the knowledge you learn along the way.

Part 3 is completely focused on your expenses and you'll gain invaluable knowledge about the way you spend your money. After you first analyze your current expenses in more detail, you will proceed to develop a plan of action that ensures you are building up a more secure financial future. You will be making some very firm decisions regarding the way you are spending your money and identify ways to reduce expenses that don't fit in with your long-term goals.

At the end of this part you should have a much more streamlined expense pattern that is aligned with they way you plan to spend money from here on.

Categorize Your Expenses

Too many people spend money they haven't earned to buy things they don't want to impress people that they don't like.

—WILL ROGERS

DIFFICULTY LEVEL: Medium

OBJECTIVE: Classify your monthly expenses into categories

REVIEW TIMES: Update monthly

By now you have (hopefully!) been tracking your expenses for a while and you should be starting to see some patterns emerge. Ideally you have at least a month of data to look at for this step, but if you are too eager to start and do not have a full month of expenses yet, complete this step anyway and try to fill in gaps in your data as best you can. Then make sure to come back here again once you have more data to complete the missing information.

Categorizing expenses

In this and the next few steps, you will be looking at your expenses in detail to get a better idea of where your money is going, how much you spend on various categories, and most important, whether this spending pattern is aligned with the way you *want* your money to be spent. The best way to start is by categorizing various expenses into groups. This will allow you to analyze in which of these areas there is a potential to save more (or less) money in later steps.

When categorizing your expenses, you are looking to create categories that consist of various

STAT BOX

According to the 2016 Transamerica Retirement Survey, men said "saving for retirement" was their main financial priority, whereas women more frequently cited "just getting by—covering basic living expenses," as their greatest financial priority right now.[5]

expenses grouped together that are more or less related. An example of this can be housing costs, which includes costs such as mortgage or rent, utilities, TV or cable subscription, and your Internet connection.

There is no one set way of doing this; everybody should classify their expenses in their own way depending on their personal situation. For example, you might travel a lot for work and rent cars regularly, in which case you might want a "travel" category with "car rental" as a subcategory. If you do not travel a lot nor rent a car very often, you probably won't need this category. Various expenses depend entirely on your personal situation: whether you have a job, work from home, have children or pets, your hobbies, and so on. Because we all have different expenses as well as preferences, there is no one right way to classify your system.

Adapting your system

Using your expenses log, you can set up a classification system in a way that works for you. Play around with it until you are happy with the categorization, but know that you can always change it again later on, so don't wait until you have the perfect categorization mapped out in your head. With time, the way you classify your expenses might need to be modified anyway: some overheads might disappear, new categories could emerge, and

you may move a specific expense into a different category. These changes are normal, so see this as a logical consequence of your increased understanding of your finances as well as your life evolving, which shifts your expense categories as well.

Once you have a total for each expense category, you are done for now. In the next few steps we will look at the various expenses in detail, although be sure to come back to this step regularly at the end of each month to update your expenses list.

☑ **STEP 14 ACTION PLAN**

☐ Pull out your list of expenses of the last month(s)

☐ Look at all of your costs and identify different expense categories by grouping them together in a way that is logical for you. Below is an example, but feel free to adapt this to your own needs and expenses.

- House (Household goods and furniture, Home maintenance, Rent/mortgage)
- Utilities (Electricity bill, Water bill, Gas, Cable and TV)
- Telephone, Internet
- Groceries
- Restaurants and bars
- Hobbies, sports, books
- Medical expenses
- Clothes
- Other general expenses/spending money
- Pets
- Car (Gas, Maintenance, Insurance, Toll payments)
- Travel and vacations
- Toiletries and makeup
- Monthly or yearly bills (Taxes, Insurance (life, health, home)
- Savings and investments (Loans and debt payments, Savings contributions, Investment payments, Retirement account payments)

- Charity
- Presents
- Other

☐ Again, make the above list work for you by adding in and taking out (sub)categories or moving some of the subcategories elsewhere.

☐ Looking at your list and working with a full month's data, start listing the various expenses into each (sub)category so you get a total amount spent per category for the last month. For example, under groceries, find all your groceries expenses from the last month (or however long you have been tracking) and total them. If you are using software to track your expenses, you may not need to do this yourself as the program most likely can do this for you once you have set up your categories and assigned each expense to the corresponding category.

☐ You might find that you do not have all your expenses fully categorized or you are missing expenses that were never registered. That's okay! With time you will become better at tracking your money, as well as fine-tuning your categories, so that the method really works for you. For now just work with what you have and adjust as needed.

☐ If you have more than one month of expenses tracked already, complete this step for each month separately: first total all the grocery expenses for month one, then month two, and so on, and register them next to each other. This will allow you to compare and find a more average pattern.

☐ If you do not yet have a full month of expenses, add a note in your calendar or notebook at the end of the full month to repeat this procedure for the remaining days and list your full expenses for each category.

☐ Make sure to keep up your habit of registering any expenses. Not only will it come in handy in later steps, but also the farther down the 100 steps journey you get and the more financially literate and independent you become, the more insight you will want to gain in your money affairs, including your spending patterns.

Identify Your Fixed Expenses

Financial peace isn't the acquisition of stuff. It's learning to live on less than you make, so you can give money back and have money to invest. You can't win until you do this.

—DAVE RAMSEY

DIFFICULTY LEVEL: Easy

OBJECTIVE: Identify and calculate your monthly fixed expenses

REVIEW TIMES: Update monthly

From the previous step, you should have your basic expense categories identified. In the next few steps, you are going to dissect these expenses and classify them into four different *types* of expenses, each requiring their own planning and budgeting approach.

We start with having a closer look at the first expense type: your fixed expenses.

Fixed expenses

Typically a fixed expense:

- is a set amount that you have little to no control over,
- has a regular time interval (e.g., monthly or yearly),
- cannot be cut down without making a big change or posing a substantial financial risk,[6]
- is needed for day-to-day living.

The first two criteria are easy to understand: for an expense to be considered a fixed expense, you need to be able to predict when the bill will be due

and how much it will be. For the third criterion, you need to decide whether cutting the expense will have a big impact on your current day-to-day life or lead to an increased financial risk. Where things get more difficult is deciding what classifies as "necessary for day-to-day living" and what does not; that is, you need to determine whether you can reasonably live without it. Below are two examples to clarify these criteria further and help you establish what a fixed expense is.

Rent or mortgage

When we check rent or mortgage payments against the four characteristics of a fixed expense, the following pattern appears:

- **A set amount that you have no control over.** Yes: you will be charged the same amount every month regardless of how much you have been at home that month.
- **It has a regular time interval.** Yes: usually these bills come at a set day of the month.
- **You cannot cut down the expense without making a big life change.** Yes: you might be able to reduce the expense by moving to a different house or apartment, but that is indeed a big change with a substantial impact on your life.
- **It is needed for day-to-day living.** Yes: you need shelter and a place to live.

Applying the four criteria, it is clear that your mortgage or rent payment is indeed a fixed expense.

Cable TV

To illustrate fixed expenses further, let's check how cable TV holds up against our four criteria:

- **A set amount that you have no control over.** Yes: regardless of how much TV you watched that month, you generally pay a set monthly fee.
- **It has a regular time interval.** Yes: usually monthly or every three months.
- **You cannot cut down the expense without making a big life change or running a substantial financial risk.** No: cutting out cable is not a big life change. Contracting a service via a cheaper alternative or an online company such as Netflix is not a major life change. There is no financial risk involved in canceling your cable, either.

- **It is needed for day-to-day living.** No: you don't actually need cable to survive.

As you can see, cable TV is not a fixed expense and canceling your subscription will not result in any big life changes. But this is not to say you have to give up cable TV. I am not advocating that you should cut all nonfixed expenses, nor am I saying you should give up pleasures in life. If having cable TV is important to you, by all means keep that contract going. Our only conclusion here is that the expense should not be classified as a fixed expense.

Having it clear what your fixed expenses are will give you a good idea of some of your base recurring monthly costs.

☑ **STEP 15 ACTION PLAN**

☐ Go through your expenses log to identify your fixed expenses. There might be some you haven't yet registered, especially yearly bills that have not yet come due, so don't forget to look through your papers for payment statements or policies for bills that you pay infrequently. Also, carefully analyze each category as you might be able to come up with some expenses yet to be paid by thinking about what other expenses might fall into each category.

☐ Below are some possible payments to include, depending on your personal situation:

- Mortgage or rent payments
- Insurance: car, life, medical, etc.
- Taxes: income, property, etc.
- Bank fees

☐ Once you have identified your fixed expenses, note down in your notebook or digital file the current average monthly expense for each. If any of them are a yearly bill, make sure to divide the total yearly amount by twelve to get the monthly cost.

☐ Come back to this list and update your total monthly fixed expenses at the end of each month to make sure you have them all registered and to check that none of the fees or rates has changed.

Identify Your Variable Expenses

Just because you can afford it doesn't mean you should buy it.

—SUZE ORMAN

DIFFICULTY LEVEL: Easy

OBJECTIVE: Identify and calculate your monthly variable expenses

REVIEW TIMES: Update monthly

After identifying your fixed monthly expenses, this step continues with the second type of overhead you have: your variable expenses.

Variable expenses

A variable expense generally:

- is an expense of a variable amount that you have some control over,
- has a semiregular time interval,
- is needed for day-to-day living,
- can be cut down by making small lifestyle or behavioral changes.

An example of variable expenses are groceries: you need them for day-to-day living, they have a semiregular time interval since you probably go to the supermarket a few times a week or month, but contrary to your fixed expenses, you have some control over the total amount on your grocery bill, as you can buy more or less groceries or select either cheaper or more expensive products.

Another type of variable expenses are your utilities bills. Although you need water and electricity for the daily running of your household, you can usually influence the amount on the bill by turning off appliances when not in use, regulating the temperature of your house, or reducing the time you spend in the shower, to name just a few.

Identifying a variable expense

Even more than with fixed expenses, it can be difficult to decide whether a cost is variable. Opinions differ on this issue. Is your Internet connection a necessity for daily living? One can argue it is these days and that you cannot do without it. At the same time, I think most people would agree that groceries are slightly more necessary than an Internet connection, although if you work from home and need Internet access to generate an income, it might be much more important than if you just used it to browse your social media accounts.

As you can see, determining whether something is a variable expense is partially up to your own opinion and situation. There is no good or bad answer. You simply need to take some time to determine what makes most sense to you and your individual situation.

Although your variable expenses will always be different from one month to the next, having an overview of the average cost will help you predict your monthly payments later on.

☑ STEP 16 ACTION PLAN

☐ Go through your expenses log and identify all your variable expenses. As before, depending on how long you have been tracking your expenses and with how much detail, you likely won't have all possible expenses included yet, so be sure to think outside of your current log.

☐ A few examples of variable expenses can include:

- Groceries
- Utilities (gas, water, electricity)
- Car expenses such as gas, repairs, or maintenance
- Phone/Internet
- Medical checkups and health care
- Clothes
- House maintenance

☐ Once you have identified your variable expenses, register the average monthly costs for each one individually. The more months' data you have, the more accurate your average becomes. If your bills vary a lot (such as utility bills that change with the season), you will need to look further back and find the bills of a full year in order to get a reliable amount. For example, if your electricity bill is $60 in summer and $100 in winter, put down the average of $80 per month.

☐ Come back to this list and update your total monthly variable expenses at the end of each month.

Identify Your Discretionary Expenses

I'd like to live as a poor man with lots of money.
—PABLO PICASSO

DIFFICULTY LEVEL: Easy

OBJECTIVE: Identify and calculate your monthly discretionary expenses

REVIEW TIMES: Update monthly

Next up are your discretionary expenses, which belong to things you don't absolutely need to survive or run your household. They are often optional expenses that mainly enhance your daily life and allow you to have some fun, such as restaurant dinners, vacations, or going to the movies.

Discretionary expenses

A discretionary expense:

- is an expense of a variable amount that you have more or less complete control over,
- might or might not have a regular time interval,
- is not needed for day-to-day living,
- can be reduced or cut out altogether relatively easily.

Discretionary expenses are usually the type of expense that people cut back on first during tough financial times and the first ones that increase again

MAKE IT FUN!

Although you don't want to eliminate discretionary expenses from your budget altogether, use this step to think of other, sometimes more fun alternatives to some of them. Instead of buying presents, could you make a present or offer an experience or companionship that might be even more fun to prepare, give, and receive? Or can you organize a get-together with your friends and give each other a manicure instead of paying for it in your regular salon?

when economic situations improve. That coffee you get every day at Starbucks on your way to work? That is a discretionary expense: you have complete control over it, you do not need it for day-to-day living, and you can cut it out easily by making your own coffee when you get to work or bringing one from home in a travel mug.

Identifying discretionary expenses

Despite these straightforward criteria, there is unfortunately no 100% clear distinction between a discretionary expense and the other expenses. Is a gym membership an essential expense or not? What about your mobile phone plan? Any distinction will always be slightly arbitrary or at least a personal decision. With time, you might move an expense from the variable to the discretionary category or the other way around. Do what feels right to you. If a gym membership is essential to you for healthy living because you will not otherwise go for a run or do any other form of exercise, mark it as a fixed expense. If a mobile phone plan is something you see as an essential part of life or if you could not do your job without it, then put it in your fixed or variable expenses (depending on whether the amount fluctuates according to usage). There is no perfect answer to how an expense "should" be classified, so again use what seems right to you.

Some expenses might even fit into two categories—for example, clothes, which to a certain extent are a basic need and therefore a variable expense. At the same time, sometimes you might just want to buy a new item of clothing even if you don't strictly need it, which is why this category is also included in the list of discretionary expenses below.

- -

Your discretionary expenses are likely the ones that vary most from one month to the next. The longer you track these, the more accurate the average will be to make educated decisions regarding these costs.

☑ STEP 17 ACTION PLAN

☐ As with the last two steps, start by putting together a list of any discretionary expenses you can think of. You might have to rack your brain a little more as many of these will not be regular expenses and therefore will not appear in your expenses log (yet). Think of the following areas:

- Clothes
- Dining out: bars, restaurants
- Entertainment: theater, movies, concerts
- Vacations and days out: theme parks, city trips, hotels, transportation
- Presents
- Personal care: haircut, manicure
- Hobbies
- Books and magazines
- TV and music subscriptions
- Courses or lessons
- Home decoration

☐ When you can no longer think of other examples, go through your bills, online bank statements, or receipts and check whether you have forgotten anything.

☐ Calculate how much you have spent in total in the last month on each of these categories.

☐ Now for the hard part: as these expenses can vary quite a bit, you will probably need to allocate more time predicting how much you spend on each category on average to better budget for these later on, as last month's total might be different from your typical discretionary expense pattern. You likely will not be able to make this completely accurate, but do try to get a rough figure.

☐ Depending on your situation, you might need to research more months back. For example, do you buy clothes every month? Or do you only tend to buy new clothes every three to four months, or even just once or twice a year? And when you do, do you spend about the same amount each time or does this vary? If what you spend changes a lot, you will need to go further back to find out what you spent on average or try to estimate it as best you can.

☐ Write down your predicted average monthly expense per category until you have a fairly accurate figure for each expense. Remember to account for occasional spending; for example, if you go shopping just once every six months for clothes and spend $300, your monthly average for clothes is $50.

☐ Come back to this list and update your total monthly discretionary expenses at the end of each month.

Identify Your Savings Expenses

If saving money is wrong I don't want to be right.

—WILLIAM SHATNER

DIFFICULTY LEVEL: Easy

OBJECTIVE: Identify and calculate your monthly savings expenses

REVIEW TIMES: Update monthly

There is one last type of expenses that needs to be identified: your savings expenses. Savings expenses are any expenses that are related to improving your financial situation now or in the future. They are payments you make toward your financial goals, and they typically increase your net worth.

Distinguishing savings expenses

When you were going through your expenses in the previous three steps, you might have been wondering how to classify your savings expenses. You may have even included them in your list of fixed expenses, as they can easily mask as such. The reason to distinguish your savings expenses from other types, however, is that they are generally very different in nature from fixed, variable, or discretionary expenses. Savings expenses help you achieve a financial goal, improving your financial prospects and moving you toward financial independence. The other types of expenses revolve more around daily living.

Even though it might sound counterintuitive, payments toward an outstanding debt are therefore also savings expenses, as they reduce your liabilities and therefore increase your net worth, reduce interest payments, and improve your general financial situation.

In all likelihood, not many people will have a goal along the likes of, "This year I want to spend at least $1,500 on eating out in restaurants." It is more common to hear, "This year I want to add at least $1,500 to my savings account," or "This year I want to pay off my $1,500 credit card debt." As you can see, the first example of spending a certain amount in restaurants will not improve your financial situation, whereas the other two goals would improve that situation significantly and are therefore savings expenses.

Your savings expenses are the ones most closely linked to your long-term financial goals and will with time likely increase, as you start to align your expenses more with the various targets you'll be working toward.

☑ STEP 18 ACTION PLAN

☐ This will probably be familiar to you by now, but start by making a list of any savings expenses you currently have. Examples include:

- Debt reduction payments
- Savings account payments
- Investments
- Payments toward emergency funds
- Retirement account contributions

☐ Once your list is ready, write down your monthly payments for each individual expense. If this varies and depends on the month, try to get to an average for each by looking at the last few months and calculating the average.

☐ If you have any debts you are not paying off at all at the moment (i.e., not even the minimum amount), do not include them. Or if you do because you want to have a full list, add them to your list and write $0 in the column next to it, so you know that debt is still there but is not actually reducing.

☐ Come back to this list and update your total monthly savings expenses at the end of each month.

Calculate Your Cash Flow

Annual income twenty pounds, annual expenditure nineteen six, result happiness. Annual income twenty pounds, annual expenditure twenty pound ought and six, result misery.

—CHARLES DICKENS

DIFFICULTY LEVEL: Easy

OBJECTIVE: Calculate and register the difference between your monthly income and spending

REVIEW TIMES: Update monthly

Now that you have a good starting point regarding your various expenses, we are moving on to another very helpful indicator of your financial management: cash flow. Simply put, your cash flow indicates how much money you have coming in on a monthly basis, how much is going out, and whether there is a positive or negative difference between these two numbers.

Positive cash flow

As you might expect, having a positive cash flow, where you earn more money than you spend, is what you likely want to aim for (although see "Neutral cash flow" below). It means that even after deducting all of your expenses from your income, you still have money left over at the end of the month, which signifies that you are living within or below your means and working toward building a secure financial future.

Negative cash flow

If the reverse is true and you have more money going out than you have coming in, you have what is called a negative cash flow. One of two things is generally happening to sustain this:

- you are building up debt
- you are eating away your savings

Avoiding a negative monthly cash flow is therefore essential, although this might sound easier than it is: there may be some months when you have more money coming in than going out, but other months when the opposite might be the case. Especially if your income fluctuates, maintaining a consistent cash flow might be more challenging to control.

Neutral cash flow

There is an argument that a neutral cash flow of $0 might be the ultimate goal to work toward, as that indicates you are using all of your money for a purpose. This of course is especially true if your savings expenses are well represented within your overall expenses. So even if you have $50 left over at the end of the month, if you pursue a neutral cash flow, you might decide to put that toward an extra debt reduction payment or building up savings instead of having extra money building up that is just sitting around.

Whether you want to pursue a positive or neutral cash flow also depends on some of the objectives you are working toward. If your goal is to pay off your debt as soon as possible, using any extra money left over to reduce debt might be the right thing to do. If, on the other hand, your goal is to build up a $500 cushion in your bank account, then keeping those $50 safely in that account is likely your best bet, in which case you will want to pursue a positive cash flow for a while.

Calculating your cash flow

To calculate your cash flow, you need to add all your monthly expenses together, including your savings expenses. Even though the latter are generally "positive" payments because they improve your financial situation and help you to work toward your goals, this is still money leaving your account, regardless of whether you use it to pay down debt or put it in a jar for safekeeping. In Step 48, you will calculate your savings expenses separately from your cash flow to find your savings rate, but for now, to calculate your cash flow you should include payments toward savings.

- -

Once you get used to calculating your cash flow on a monthly basis, you'll find it will greatly help you make more informed decisions about your spending.

☑ STEP 19 ACTION PLAN

☐ You will want to update your cash flow overview regularly, so you need to give yourself enough space in your log. Start with a new page in your notebook, a new tab in Excel, a new note in Evernote, or a fresh page in whatever program you are using for your 100 steps.

☐ To calculate your current net cash flow, start with last month's income. Depending on how you have calculated your expenses, either put in:

- your net pay, i.e., what you take home after paying taxes (if you have not included your income taxes in your expenses lists);
- your gross pay, i.e., before taxes (if you have included your income tax as an expense).

☐ If your income varies a lot—for example, if you are self-employed or you work on commissions or with bonuses—either put down your average or your absolute minimum monthly income.

☐ Total all of last month's expenses (fixed, variable, discretionary, and savings).

☐ Subtract your expenses from your income to get your monthly cash flow.

☐ If you have several months' data of income and expenses, repeat the above step for those months to get a better picture of your average and how much this fluctuates.

☐ If the difference is positive, you are in a great position as it means you have more money coming in than going out. The only challenge you will have is that you want this money to "do" something for you. Whether it is $20 or $600 you have left over, you don't want your money to sit idly in your account doing nothing if it could be making you money elsewhere, unless of course you have a specific goal for that money.

☐ If the balance is $0, you either always put all your money to work for you, or you often run out of money toward the end of your paycheck and need to cut back in order to make it to the end of the month. Getting a $0 cash flow is not bad if all of your money is doing exactly what you want. But if it you can barely make it to the end of the month, you have some work to do in the next few steps.

☐ If the result is negative, you have a bigger problem as it means you are spending more money than you are bringing in, which is not sustainable, especially over the long term. It means you are either losing money from your savings, or building up debt.

☐ Set yourself the goal to work toward increasing your cash flow, either by getting out of having a negative cash flow or by improving your current positive cash flow. Set a specific amount by which you would like to improve your monthly amount over the next three months.

☐ Set a reminder in your calendar to calculate your cash flow every month and update your log monthly to get a better idea of what it looks like over a prolonged period and see the effectiveness of any changes you have made. Check how close you are to reaching your new monthly cash flow goal and adjust your goals or ways to achieve it if needed.

Create Your Money Map

Make a decision to be successful right now. Most people never decide to be wealthy and that is why they retire poor.

—BRIAN TRACY

- -

DIFFICULTY LEVEL: Easy

OBJECTIVE: Create a visual representation of your accounts to streamline your money flow

REVIEW TIMES: Update every three months

- -

Now that you have identified and classified your expenses, it is time to link them all together. When it comes to knowing where your money goes each month, things can get complicated quickly when you consider all the various accounts, credit cards, and bills involved. Knowing how all your finances are connected can provide valuable insight into your money flow and will make it easier to see the bigger picture and identify money leaks or inefficiencies. A money map gives you exactly this bigger picture as it presents a visual representation of your monthly expenses, which will create not only an overview, but also a basis for further planning and money management.

A closer look at a money map

A money map is a visual representation of the following:

- Your bank and investment accounts
- The credit cards associated with those accounts
- Your expenses and bills that are paid from each account
- The connection between each account, i.e., how money flows from one account to the next
- The percentage each stage and account takes up of your total monthly income

The more accounts, cards, and bills you have, the more complex your money map will be.

An example money map

Below in Figure 1 is an example money map of various accounts, credit cards, and bills of somebody with both a private as well as a joint account she shares with her partner for communal expenses. Note that this chart is based on net income only. If you make any pretax savings or retirement account contributions, you might want to start with your gross income and then indicate any pretax deductions as well as taxes that are taken out before you add your other expense patterns. (We'll look at retirement accounts and taxes further in Parts 7 and 9, respectively.)

Figure 1: An example money map

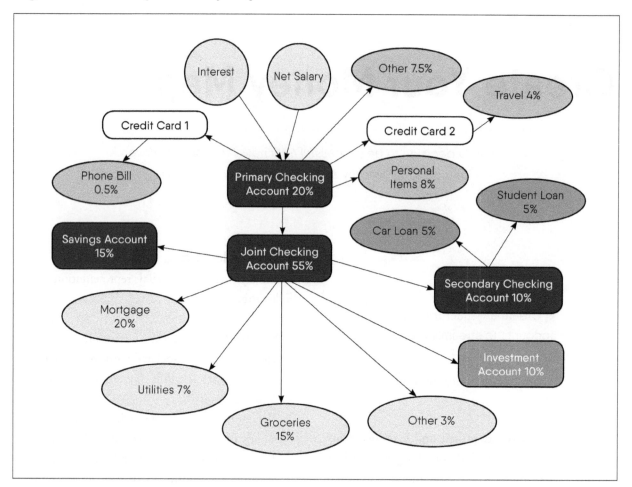

Note: The percentages in each of the four accounts (primary checking, joint checking, secondary checking, and savings account) indicate how much of the original total income was sent to each. The percentages for the various payment categories (utilities, groceries, etc.) indicate how much of the original total income was spent on those expenses.

As you can see, a money map is a useful tool to keep an overview of your expenses. It also shows you where your money goes, how it gets there, and how big or small each account or bill is in relation to your income.

Keep your money map with you when you review your expenses and see how you can further streamline your cashflow, especially when your income or expense patterns develop over time.

☑ STEP 20 ACTION PLAN

☐ You can either draw your money map by hand on a piece of paper or in your notebook, or render it digitally in a computer program or online app. Of course, you can also start with a manual version and when you have the final draft you can put it in digital format. This saves messing around with boxes, arrows, and information until you more or less know what your map looks like.

☐ Start by identifying your sources of income. This can be your salary from your job as well as any interest or income from a side hustle.

☐ If you work with your gross wage, include any deductions, taxes, and pretax savings contributions that are taken out.

☐ Add any bank accounts into which your net income is sent. You might have different accounts for different income sources, or maybe you have one holding account from which your money gets sent on to other accounts.

☐ From these first bank accounts, where does your money travel to? Think of savings accounts, retirement accounts, investment accounts, other checking accounts, and credit cards.

☐ Add categories or specific bills to each account and think of your fixed, variable, discretionary, and savings expense categories. Assign them under each account so you can visualize where each bill is charged from.

☐ For clarity, add colors to the different categories in your map: give one color to all of your bank accounts, a different one to all of your savings expenses, another color to all costs coming out of your checking account, and so on.

☐ Add in the rough income percentage each account or credit card gets each month. This provides a very quick and easy way to see how much of your income gets spent on various expense categories.

☐ Check whether you are wasting any money or opportunities in any part of your money map, such as extra transfer fees, and pay special attention to each part of your system and whether your money flow can be streamlined more. For example, can you link accounts or take certain bills from one account and put them elsewhere? This is especially useful to keep any accounts or credit cards active or to have the same type of expense coming out of the same account.

☐ Make any necessary changes to your bills and accounts if that's what you decide, and then update your money map.

☐ Review your map regularly to make sure it's still up to date. Make sure to check whether your percentages have changed.

Beware Lifestyle Inflation

A wise person should have money in their head, but not in their heart.

—JONATHAN SWIFT

DIFFICULTY LEVEL: Easy

OBJECTIVE: Identify the reasons you are not investing more in a better financial future

REVIEW TIMES: Review yearly

In the next steps, you will start planning for your monthly expenses by setting up a budget and becoming more purposeful with your money. But before you start with that, our current step aims to make you aware of what might be holding you back when it comes to progressing financially so you can use this information to your advantage when starting your budget.

No matter what stage you are at in your life, there is a good chance you feel you do not have enough money. Especially now that you have started setting goals and becoming more conscious of your money, you might have come to realize you need a lot more to achieve your goals. When planning to put money aside to save, invest, or pay off a debt, it is tempting to justify holding off on cutting costs until that one thing you have been waiting for finally happens. . . .

Excuses to put off investing in your future

Until you get a promotion? Until you have finished your postgrad course? Until you have bought a house? Until your children go to preschool? Until

you find a new job? You can come up with dozens of reasons, many of which are probably valid in their own way, so let's look at some of the most common excuses for waiting to improve your financial future. The truth is, with every change in your life, your spending patterns will most likely also change, thereby always giving you an excuse not to progress.

There are two main reasons why the thinking pattern of "I will start investing in my future when . . ." never really works:

1. CHANGED DEMANDS

With every change in life, new financial demands need to be met. This can range from buying a house to having children to getting older and needing medical care. To make it even worse, each new stage tends to be more expensive than the previous one.

2. LIFESTYLE INFLATION

Most people, when they earn more, start spending more. We want more and more from life every time our income goes up, and what was once acceptable as part of our lifestyle changes as soon as we can afford more. This is known as lifestyle inflation. Where we were once happy to earn $1,200 a month and managed to only spend just that amount, as soon as we start earning $1,500, we quickly adjust our expenses, and soon we cannot imagine spending any less than $1,500. When we double our income, we tend to also double our expenses. Without prioritizing and getting ahead on our long-term financial goals by also increasing our savings expenses, we are never able to catch up on our debt or savings goals.

Lifestyle inflation and changed demands through the ages

Below is a closer look at how these factors affect your spending and savings at different stages of life.

YOUR TWENTIES

When you're in your twenties and have just finished your education, will you likely have spare money to set aside and invest in your future? Probably not: you're still at the base of the career ladder and so is your income, and you can probably not imagine taking money out of your income to save or pay down debt. Additionally, you probably feel you have loads of time for that ahead of you. Now that you are no longer in college, lifestyle inflation also kicks in: where it was once acceptable to share an apartment with friends, this suddenly seems no longer desirable, so you find your own place. Low-budget vacations seem like something from the past; now that you're working full-time, you surely deserve more luxury and are happy to pay a little more for it. Changed demands (your professional job) require you to buy a car, so you take out a loan to finance that car.

YOUR THIRTIES

Maybe when you're in your thirties and earn some more you can start saving? But what if you were planning on having children at some point? Babies are expensive! You also started paying off your student loan a few years ago and will be doing so for quite a while, so there's not so much money left at the end of the month. That promotion you got means you have to look much more professional, so the increased income goes to high-fashion suits or a more expensive car. You have furthermore bought a house with your partner. Apart from paying for the mortgage, you have added expenses for any repairs and maintenance work and for property taxes, and you also like to buy new furniture every now and again to redecorate.

YOUR FORTIES

In your forties, things will have calmed down. You will be earning even more due to promotions, so this will for sure be a good time to start saving aggressively. . . . Although now that your children are a little older, they also cost more: toys, clothes, extracurricular activities, not to mention vacations for four or five instead of two. You might even need to buy a bigger house for more space to live, play, and study, possibly also a second car, and your partner has a tendency to always buy the latest gadgets to keep up with the lifestyle that the people around you have.

YOUR FIFTIES

Okay, so what about your fifties? By that time, your parents might need extra help. Your children will likely now be in college and potentially living farther away; apart from perhaps paying at least part of their college fees, you also now need to make more time to see your family. And to be honest, you could do with more time for hobbies and friends. So you consider working fewer hours. Apart from earning less, this also adds extra costs to travel to see those family and friends. But instead of scaling down your expenses, you also see other people around you in their fifties and sixties taking early retirement and traveling as often as they can, splurging on hobbies such as golf or other expensive activities, and you feel you, too, deserve this, so you keep spending more and more instead of less.

YOUR SIXTIES AND BEYOND

At any stage in your life, there are many reasons why you cannot save (more) money. But the problem is, this will always be the case. What happens in your sixties and seventies if you let your life be controlled by lifestyle inflation is that instead of having a financial cushion, you are drawing up more and more debt. When you get older, you will likely need more medical care, your income will go down if you decide to cut back your hours or disappear altogether when you stop working, and although you might have a retirement account, this is likely a lot less than what you are used to, regardless of whether you were used to getting $1,000 or $10,000 a month. You might end up working until you are a lot older than you had hoped and older than other people around you (at least those who started saving early!). It's possible you will have little money, let alone time to visit your children and your grandchildren.

As you can see, whether you're in your twenties, fifties, or seventies, there are always other things to spend your money on. You could have children or not, a huge mortgage or high debt, an expensive hobby, or you like splurging on traveling, cigarettes, new clothes, gadgets, you name it . . . there are many reasons why you cannot save and build up a secure financial future if you let yourself use these excuses.

- -

Many of the decisions you make now can make a tremendous difference later on. Although it will always be difficult to make the "right" decisions, being aware of how lifestyle inflation and changed demands work will help you find the balance between increasing your lifestyle and investing in your financial future at the same time.

☑ **STEP 21 ACTION PLAN**

☐ Grab a pen and paper or your digital file and write down different time periods in your life. They do not have to correspond to the decades as above. Start with when you finished school all the way up to today. For example:

- 18–21: college
- 24–28: first entry-level jobs
- 28–35: promotion and birth of children
- And so on

☐ Now for each of these periods, identify excuses you (could) have used or are using to not invest in your future.

☐ Continue the mental exercise and identify why you are not investing in your future just yet at this very moment—or, if you are, why you are not making higher contributions. Work up to when you are seventy or eighty. Think of possible excuses you could use in your future depending on the lifestyle you envision.

Start a Budget

> *A budget is telling your money where to go instead of wondering where it went.*
>
> —DAVE RAMSEY

DIFFICULTY LEVEL: Medium

OBJECTIVE: Create a spending budget and stop overspending

REVIEW TIMES: Review weekly, update monthly

Although budgeting might sound negative, boring, or limiting to some people, it also offers huge advantages on the way to financial independence. If you have any negative associations with budgeting, I encourage you to dispel them now. By learning how to budget and using your plan in the right way, you will develop an absolutely vital skill in making sure you achieve your short-term as well as your long-term financial goals and prevent lifestyle inflation from taking over your money management.

What is a budget?

When you make a budget, you assign your money a specific role for what it will get spent on. You state explicitly where every single dollar will go, from the very first to the very last day of the month. Across your fixed, variable, discretionary, and savings expenses, you assign a specific amount to all of your expense categories (such as groceries, utilities, and eating out) at the start of each month, before you have even spent anything.

Will you know exactly how you will be spending all your money at the start of the month? Of course this is highly unlikely: your grocery bill might be higher or lower than expected, you might have an extra lunch out, and that present you were going to buy might end up being a lot cheaper than you expected. So a budget is never rigid. It will invariably need to be adjusted and modified depending on a variety of factors.

So if it's not going to be completely accurate, why do you need to budget?

The advantages of a budget

Although it might indeed be impossible to know precisely how much money you need for every single category down to the last penny, there are some specific advantages of having a budget:

- A budget ensures you do not live beyond your means. You know what you have available to spend, and by budgeting, you *plan* how to spend that money instead of waiting to see how it all turns out, a strategy that can often lead to spending more than you have available or not making it to the end of the month. A budget keeps you from racking up more debt or eating into your savings.
- If an expense turns out higher than expected, you can easily review your budget to see where to take the money from to adjust for the rest of the month. In this way, you can quickly

nobody ever accidentally saved $10,000. To achieve your savings goals, you need to work out how to get that money together and spend and save accordingly.

Budgeting is a continuous learning process, a skill you will have to develop, adjust, and simply get on with in order to learn. It will take practice to master and perfect this new habit, and with time you will figure out how accurate you are at predicting your expenses, how flexible your various expense categories are, and how to plan ahead for bigger irregular expenses, including big ones like a car replacement.

So let's get started and put a budget together for next month!

decide how to prevent that higher expense from affecting you in a big way.

- If an expense is lower than planned, you can assign the money left over to a goal you are working toward, using the opportunity to make the most of this extra money.

- A budget will control your spending and help you work toward achieving your goals by planning ahead. Instead of realizing at the end of the month that you have spent $200 on meals out, you can set yourself a limit ahead of time and make decisions based on your plans and financial goals. By reducing your eating out money to $150, you can assign $50 a month to a savings goal, for example. Remember that

Making a budget is a new habit that you need to develop over time. As with all new habits, there will be disappointment or frustration when you find it difficult to follow through. But remember that your determination and persistence are what will get you there in the end, not whether you're perfect at it from the start. If you're struggling to stick to your plan, reread your commitment (Step 0) and your financial goals (Step 4) and remember that it will become easier with time.

☑ STEP 22 ACTION PLAN

- [ ] Pull up your log with your monthly expenses.

- [ ] On a separate sheet or in a new window in your digital file, write down your expected income for next month. This can include any source of money you have: from your job, social security benefits, annuities, retirement income, etc.

- [ ] Your goal is to not spend any more than what comes in next month by preassigning your money. First, assign an amount for your fixed expenses. Check your list of these expenses and write down how much you will need to spend on these next month. If any of these are not paid monthly but less frequently, then budget for the expense proportionally. For example, for a payment that occurs every three months, set aside one-third of the total amount.

☐ Next, assign your variable expenses. As you know, these are more difficult to predict because they can fluctuate, but check the average per category that you calculated or estimated in Step 16. Based on this, make an estimation of what you will need for next month.

☐ Assign your savings expenses—any debts you are repaying or any savings or investments you are making. Make sure to check your savings expenses register for the details.

☐ Check how much you have left and assign whatever you have left to your discretionary expenses. Think ahead: Do you have a birthday, wedding, or trip coming up? If so, make sure to set aside enough money to pay for it.

☐ Be realistic. There will be some expenses you know you cannot cut out, but at the same time be strict with yourself where possible. If you do not have money to buy a new outfit for that party, then don't buy it. Commit to reusing an old one and see if you can buy a new dress next time you need one. This might be the most difficult part of budgeting as it requires you to control your impulses and be sensible with your money. (But isn't that why you signed up for this journey in the first place?)

☐ Keep your budget with you and remember to track any expenses in the right category throughout the month, per Step 9.

☐ Stick to your budget. Whatever happens, whatever bargain you encounter or however tempted you are to buy something, *stick to your plan* . . .

☐ . . . Unless you can move money from one category to the other and it makes complete sense to modify your budget halfway through. Imagine you see that beautiful pair of trousers at a 30% discount, but have no money set aside for clothes this month, although you still have $50 to spend on a haircut. If you feel you can leave that haircut till next month, by all means go for it, buy that amazing pair of trousers. Then update your budget, moving the $50 that had been set aside for a haircut to your clothes budget and making sure you set aside money next month for your haircut.

☐ Once a week, check your budget and see how you're doing: Are you still on track? Have you got enough left over for each category for the rest of the month? Do you need to make adjustments? Have your plans for the rest of the month changed? Modify your budget if needed. Better to face it now than realize at the end of the month your budget was way off and you overspent.

☐ At the end of the month, review how well you did. How accurate were you in predicting your expenses and how successful were you in controlling them? Create a new budget for the following month based on your experience from the first month and repeat the process.

☐ There are lots of communities about budgeting on social media; I recommend finding one that appeals to you. It's a great way to lift yourself up when things are difficult and you find your budget is not yet completely working. These communities are also a great way to pick up budgeting tricks and tips.

Discuss Finances with Your Partner

Opposites may attract but I wouldn't put my money on a relationship of financial opposites.

—SUZE ORMAN

DIFFICULTY LEVEL: Medium

OBJECTIVE: Ensure you and your partner are compatible on key financial topics

REVIEW TIMES: Monthly

Now that you're making some progress toward taking full control of your finances, it's a good moment to discuss and share your financial planning with your partner, if you haven't done so already. Discussing money matters and making sure you have the same short-term and long-term goals is essential to not only achieving your financial objectives but also keeping your relationship healthy and happy. At the end of the day, if you're trying to save, invest, or grow your capital while your partner has more of a "let's spend it all now" attitude, you will likely both wind up frustrated with each other, meaning both your financial goals and your relationship will take a hit.

Joint financial planning

It's sad but true: finances and a lack of shared financial goals or financial compatibility are not uncommon reasons for couples to have arguments, get frustrated, and even end a relationship.

STAT BOX

Couples who reported disagreeing over finances once a week or more are 30% more likely to get divorced than those who disagree less often, according to a 2008 study by Jeffrey Dew at Utah University. Money arguments were more predictive of divorce than conflicts over chores, in-laws, free time spent together, and sex.[8]

Discussing individual and joint financial beliefs and goals on a regular basis is a worthwhile practice. You might not have exactly the same ideas about how to spend or save your money and you maybe never get to a point where you agree completely, but discussing it will at least create more understanding and hopefully pave the way to an agreement and long-term plan that satisfies both and leaves some room for either to do their own thing.

Of course your partner might not be into finances at all and might be happy for you to take control of the (majority) of the money decisions and responsibilities. If that's the case, it may sound easier in the short term to simply assume that role and to not inform or consult your partner, but long term, this might not be in the interest of either your relationship or your finances.

If your partner does not know much about finances at all, consider sharing these 100 steps so they, too, can familiarize themselves with common and important money themes and become more financially literate. It will only help both of you when it comes to discussing your money matters and achieving your mission.

Important considerations

Before starting a meeting, bear in mind that talking about money matters with your partner can be difficult, even when things start off with the best intentions. Fights about money are common, so when you discuss finances with your partner, always remember to give each other time to talk without being interrupted or judged. When your partner responds, try to just listen and to reflect first on what was being said before talking. Remember that even if you have read this book and your partner hasn't, that doesn't mean you are automatically "correct" and her or his opinion is "incorrect." Lastly, if you're experiencing difficulties with any of this, absolutely consider getting the help of a financial advisor or counselor to help you through these conversations.

Especially during the first meeting, you want to take it easy on your partner and remember that even though you might be totally psyched to reach financial independence, your partner might feel overwhelmed, intimidated, or scared of anything to do with money. Remember that only together will you be able to work toward the same goals and enjoy the journey along the way.

☑ STEP 23 ACTION PLAN

Below is a guideline on how to make this a successful and worthwhile finance chat with your partner. In addition, Appendix B has a detailed list of suggested points to talk about with your partner. Please note though that there are some topics in that list that have not yet been covered and will be discussed in later steps. You can omit them for now until you have familiarized yourself with them later on, after which you can slowly add them to your "meeting points" with your partner.

- [ ] Start by proposing a day and time for a conversation or meeting. If you feel this might be met with resistance by your partner, consider making it into a nice event by doing it over dinner. Offer to cook a nice meal, but be honest and tell your partner what you would like to discuss so he or she does not end up feeling disappointed if this does not turn into a romantic dinner by candlelight (although you can still light up some candles, of course!).

- [ ] Prepare the topics you would like to bring up. Refer to Appendix B for a full list of possible topics and questions to talk about. You might be really inspired to discuss everything you believe to be important, but maybe you don't need to comment on everything in great detail yet. There might be no need to discuss the concept of your investments if you feel the biggest area that needs your attention is your debt spiraling out of control. Or maybe all you would like to comment on is this journey in general and your dream about financial independence without going into any of the specifics.

- [ ] During the remaining part of this book, you will be looking into more areas of your financial life, so the topics you'll discuss with your partner will likely evolve. Every time you finish a part of the book, make sure to add a new topic so your partner will be involved in your joint financial decisions.

- [ ] Together, set plans for any targets for the next month, such as saving goals or cutting costs on a specific expense. You can either have the same target or a different one for both of you to focus on.

- [ ] Once you have had a first financial meeting with your partner, make it into a regular event, minimally monthly if weekly seems like too much right now. Agree on a set day and time when you will do this again.

Start a Weekly Money Moment

Don't tell me where your priorities are. Show me where you spend your money and I'll tell you what they are.

—JAMES FRICK

DIFFICULTY LEVEL: Easy

OBJECTIVE: Check your progress and update financial targets

REVIEW TIMES: Weekly

Step 24 is about starting another new and very powerful habit, one that will allow you to quickly check your progress, realign your spending and savings patterns to your goals, and thereby propel you forward on your journey to financial independence.

This new habit is to start a weekly money moment during which you go through your goals and expenses at a set moment each week. As you continue working your way through the remaining steps in this book, little by little you will add a quick update or review of those steps to this weekly check-in. In this way, you consistently hold yourself accountable for your success as you review whether you are on track (or not) for the rest of the month and what adjustments need to be made to ensure you will achieve your goals for the week, the month, the year, and longer term.

Schedule your review

Every week at a time that suits you best (Saturday morning, Sunday afternoon, a set evening during the week; you decide what works for you), make an

appointment with yourself to review your finances. Although I call it a moment, it will likely take you about thirty minutes to complete, so make sure you have enough time available when you schedule it. At the start of each weekly money moment, the very first thing you do is schedule your next appointment with yourself to keep up this habit and ensure you make time for it. If for whatever reason you cannot have it on your regular day or time next week, you should immediately decide when you can do it that week instead and reschedule it in your calendar. This review moment will simply become too important to risk forgetting about if you do not schedule it straight away.

From now on, that weekly money moment is *sacred*. It is your time to plan for what you have set out to achieve. Do not budge and do not move this appointment, unless you decide it is absolutely necessary. If your mom and dad are visiting you for a few days from the other side of the country, you of course can move the appointment ahead of time and schedule it to just before or after your parents' stay. But if you're playing a new computer game that you are really into and you just want to keep on playing . . . that is probably *not* a necessary reason to move your appointment. Give yourself a (metaphorical) slap in the face, turn off your game console, and just get on with it.

YOU determine your level of success

Your level of success on this journey depends on one thing, and one thing only: YOU. Only you can make it work or fail. It is this appointment with yourself during which you hold yourself accountable, review your successes, and set new ways to achieve your goals that will determine your success or failure on the 100 steps. Give up on this money moment and you will slowly be giving up on your goals, your mission, and your financial success.

(After the thirty minutes' review, you can go back to playing that computer game, by the way.)

Whatever you are hoping to achieve, you need to just get on with it and make continuous steps toward that goal, even if each action seems insignificant. Only by keeping your end goal in mind and continuously reviewing your progress and adjusting will you achieve what you set out to achieve. Your weekly money moment will help you greatly to stay on track.

☑ STEP 24 ACTION PLAN

☐ Take your agenda or calendar and find thirty minutes in your schedule this week to have your first money moment. Try to find a time and day that you feel might be your long-term moment to do this. If you don't know what the best time might be, just schedule it in for now and experiment with different days and times.

☐ During your review, go through the following tasks:

- Schedule your very next money moment. Do this first, not last, so you don't forget.
- Read your financial vision and objectives. Ideally you do this often (i.e., every day) anyway, but you definitely want to do this at the start of this money moment.
- Update your expenses log. In an ideal world your log is always up to date, but we all know that things slip through at times or you might not have updated your automatic payments yet, so this is a good moment to double-check all your expenses.
- Empty your wallet or purse and go through any receipts. Register anything that was not yet registered, then throw them out if you no longer need them or file them if needed for tax or warranty purposes.
- Check your budget and see whether you're on track for all of your expenses. Make adjustments as needed in your budget or in your spending plans for the rest of the month.

☐ If there's anything else you want to review weekly, add it to an ongoing list of notes to review or update.

☐ As you complete the remaining steps in this book, more points will be added to your money moment to update and evaluate, in particular for any monthly goals you will be setting yourself, so little by little this review will start to encompass more of your financial situation. Appendix A provides a full overview of tasks and steps to include.

Translate Expenses into Time Costs

Time is more valuable than money. You can get more money but you cannot get more time.

—JIM ROHN

DIFFICULTY LEVEL: Easy

OBJECTIVE: Know your hourly income and use this to determine the true cost of your expenses

REVIEW TIMES: Calculate yearly, apply monthly

Here is a useful piece of financial wisdom to remember: every time you spend money, you're spending time. It's not the good old "time = money" adage you should be concerned about, but the exact opposite: "money = time." Although at first blush the two might seem the same, it's much more pertinent and important to become aware that money = time.

Money = time

If you're like most people, the bulk of the money you have available to spend each month probably comes from your job in the form of income. Each month you start afresh with a new paycheck coming in on the one hand and also fresh bills to pay on the other. (If you're not receiving an income from a job at the moment but have other sources of income, this step is probably not as applicable to you.)

Regardless of your profession, your job is designed to trade time for money. You put your skills and expertise to use and in exchange your company or your clients give you compensation. Change from a full-time job to a part-time one and you will likely earn less (less time = less money) and vice versa.

Of course, some jobs pay better than others, some give you more or less vacation time, and some might offer bonus options, but the essence is nearly always the same: you trade your time to do a job and in exchange you get money you are then free to spend.

Jobs are the heart of our society

The key part of any job is generally that they contribute to society and keep the world going. They supply for a demand that exists. Thanks to people working their jobs, our children are educated by teachers all around the world, doctors are saving people's lives, new technology is developed by the hour, houses are built, restaurants enable people to relax together with friends and family over a meal out, and flights are operated to let people travel to other parts of the world. The list is endless and our society could not exist without people dedicating time to their profession in order to make a living, thereby enabling other people to use the services or products that jobs create. We would not be able do a lot of our day-to-day activities if it were not for people working in a job.

All of this being said, let's not forget that your time is your time and you can never make more time. Your money is also your money, but you can always make some more. But time spent on something is time that can never be recuperated. Be wary of working around the clock for forty years without enjoying life. Yes, you need to work in order to pay those bills, but with every increase in expenses, you also need a way to generate more income.

Be critical of what you really need. Is a new car really essential or can you do with a used one to avoid taking out a huge car loan? Do you really need the latest smartphone or is your older version still doing fine?

Know the time cost of your expenses

One way to counter the vicious circle described above is by becoming aware of the time cost of every expense. From now on, start thinking about money in terms of time. Figure out for each expense how long you had to work in order to get the money together to pay for the expense. You will suddenly become a lot more critical of certain purchases and start to question whether you really want to eat out in a restaurant for a third time this month, or whether you absolutely need another pair of jeans if you still have three pairs that are totally acceptable.

To illustrate this, let's say you make $15 net per hour and you're planning to buy a new flat-screen TV for $599. This means it would take you $599 divided by $15 = almost forty work hours to earn that money, which is one whole week if you work full-time. Use this to decide whether the money is worth the time you spent to earn it.

- -

Knowing the time cost of your expenses suddenly makes it much easier to understand that money = time, and that for every dollar you have in your wallet, you have given time to your employer or your clients. It will help you make better decisions on which expenses are worth the time you gave up for the money you made and which are not.

☑ STEP 25 ACTION PLAN

☐ Start with calculating your net (after-tax) income per hour. Since some months are longer or shorter and some have more workdays than others, you need to calculate your hourly wage based on your yearly income.

- Take your yearly net income.
- Figure out how many weeks you work: There are fifty-two weeks in a year, so subtract the number of unpaid vacation weeks you have. For example, if you take three weeks of vacation a year without receiving a salary, you work forty-nine weeks per year. If you have paid vacations, then count the full fifty-two weeks.
- Multiply the number of weeks you work by the number of hours you work per week to find out how many hours a year you work.
- Now divide your yearly net income by the total number of hours you work per year to find your net hourly income. For example, if your yearly net pay is $40,000 and you work fifty weeks a year, which at forty hours a week equals 2,000 hours per year, you make $40,000 / 2,000 = $20 an hour.

☐ From now on remember that for every $20 (or $15, or $30, or whatever your hourly wage is) you spend, you had to work one hour. Divide any expense by your hourly wage to work out how many hours of work the purchase represents.

☐ At the end of each month, look at your budget and monthly expense register and calculate how many hours you work to cover each of these monthly costs per category.

Limit One Expense

> *Wealth consists not in having great possessions but in having few wants.*
>
> —EPICTETUS

DIFFICULTY LEVEL: Medium

OBJECTIVE: Cut down one expense and start saving

REVIEW TIMES: Weekly

By now, you should have a good overview of your expenses and how much you spend on the various expense categories. But to create momentum and to experience some immediate positive results, now is the perfect time to begin making a change. Starting today, you are going to limit one expense consistently for a whole month.

Limit or cut out?

To limit an expense, you can either cut it down or cut it out altogether; which option you choose is up to you. It might be that, now that you're looking at your expenses, you have become aware of how much you spend on your smoking habit. Maybe you decide now is the moment to quit, in which case you would probably eliminate the expense altogether. Or maybe you are surprised at how much you spend at the bar on weekends with friends. If (understandably) you are not prepared to give up those nights of fun altogether, maybe you can make a commitment to staying in once a month, or going home an hour earlier and thereby reducing the expense without having to cancel the nights completely.

✔ MAKE IT FUN!

As extra motivation, find a glass jar and put a nice label on it. At the end of each day or week, put in the money you've saved. Say, for example, that you're giving up on your Starbucks coffee on your way to work. Make sure to drop $2 or $3 (or however much your coffee is) in your container at the end of each day you managed to not buy a coffee. There's something very enjoyable in seeing that money build up.

Focus on just one expense

For a whole month, you are going to cut down on one expense and one expense only. You are not looking to take it to the extreme and reduce all your expenses or focus on too many categories. Remember in Step 0 when we talked about New Year's resolutions and how so many people give up on them after only a few weeks? That is partially due to having to break an old habit and replace it with a new one, a process that requires time and effort. By aiming to do too much at one time, in this case focusing on too many expenses, you will likely spread your effort and energy too thin and end up giving up completely.

Chances are you will cut back on a discretionary expense for this step. Remember these are the ones that add fun to your life. Imagine what happens if you try to reduce too many of these expenses: life might just become a little boring, in which case you are also unlikely to see things through to the end.

In short, focusing on one expense requires more than enough effort, so just stick to one for now. After you make that one area work, you can always move on to another one.

This step marks the first real applied action step on your way to financial independence. Keep up your commitment, but do not fret or give up altogether if you lapse one day. Remind yourself we are all human, and these things happen. So you "accidentally" bought a Starbucks coffee and missed out on saving those $3 today. . . . Oh, well. Try again tomorrow. Nobody is perfect or indeed becomes perfect overnight, so don't be too harsh with yourself. Tomorrow is a new opportunity to continue where you left off.

☑ STEP 26 ACTION PLAN

☐ Take out your budget and have a close look at all your expenses and how much you've set aside for each category.

☐ You might want to pick a discretionary expense to limit, as these are easiest to control and influence, although there is nothing stopping you from picking a variable expense that you know you can easily work on if you make an extra effort. Here are some suggestions:

- Car expenses. Can you leave the car at home more often and walk/bike/take public transportation?
- Meals out. Can you set a limit on the number of meals out or money spent in restaurants?
- Utilities. Can you turn off lights and heaters more often?
- Groceries. Can you pay more attention to offers or cheaper versions of your usual products?

☐ These are just some ideas; brainstorm a list with more. Use the information from the previous step on time costs to help you decide what you feel is worth the money and time invested to pay for it and what is not.

☐ Pick *one* expense to limit that seems best for you and that you feel 100% committed to achieving.

☐ Now look at your average monthly cost for this particular expense and try to predict how much money you should be able to save in one month. Write this number down on your phone, on a new page of your notebook, as a social media update, on a Post-it, or wherever works for you to hold yourself accountable for this goal.

☐ The purpose of this step is to save on your expenses and end up with some money at the end of the month (you will find out exactly what to do with this money in Step 28). Any cash you save by cutting down, KEEP! Don't give up smoking and then spend that money on beer or dining out, as you will be using that money for something specific in just a few steps.

☐ Update your budget by decreasing the amount you set aside for the expense you've chosen to cut. Then add in a new category called "extra savings" and write how much you expect to save, even if this is just $10.

☐ Find a clean sheet of paper to stick in your notebook or on your fridge and note down every day how much money you managed to save each day or week.

☐ During your weekly money moment, check how you're doing with the challenge. How much have you saved already? Do you need to adjust the amount you think you will have saved by the end of the month up or down? Can you try a little harder to achieve your goal if you have fallen behind?

☐ At the end of the full month (mark the date in your calendar), review how much you've saved and how close you were to the goal you set. For now, set aside the money you saved.

☐ For the next month, continue the challenge and once again pick one expense to save on. It can be the same as the previous one or you can try out a new one. Remember to work on just one expense at a time until you feel reducing that particular expense has become a habit and you're ready to add a new one.

Set Up Your Bank Accounts

Beware of little expenses; a small leak will sink a great ship.

—BENJAMIN FRANKLIN

DIFFICULTY LEVEL: Easy

OBJECTIVE: Compare banks and open a new savings account

REVIEW TIMES: Yearly

Your bank accounts form the backbone of your financial organization as this is where you are constantly managing your finances, growing your savings, and paying your bills. You want to be sure that your accounts are set up in the best way possible, but also in a way that works for you.

In this step, you're going to analyze your current accounts and check that they offer what you need. If you find they don't, you'll evaluate what else is available and set up new ones that meet your requirements.

Accounts you need

You likely already have at least one bank account, but it's worth spending some time investigating the various offers of accounts available these days and comparing them to what you already have. If you discover you're not getting the best conditions, consider switching banks or accounts, or at least renegotiating your conditions. Added to that, for Step 28 you are going to need a new savings account, even if you already have one. Because it can be helpful to have different accounts allocated to different savings

goals, it never hurts to have more than one account, as long as none of them involves any costs.

Most people need at least the following:

- A checking account for paying bills and taking out cash.
- At least one savings account to use for savings goals. Consider getting a new account for each new savings goal.

So what should you look for when comparing accounts? Below are the main points to consider when analyzing and comparing banks' different conditions.

Costs

Some banks might charge you setup costs to open an account, apply yearly maintenance costs to "maintain" your account, or charge for the debit or credit cards associated with your account. Make sure to check these details and see how often you're charged. A monthly fee of $5 is obviously a lot more than $30 a year, so make the effort to find out exactly what the costs of each account are.

A note on credit and debit cards: I strongly recommend you *not* take out cards on a savings account if this is at all possible. Having no associated card makes it so much easier to resist the temptation to pay for something with your savings money. In that way, you likely only have access to your money at a desk in one of the bank's offices or online by transferring it into another account, which might in some cases take a few days if the accounts are at different banks, reducing the temptation to spend your savings money even more.

Another important area to consider when comparing costs is that of transfer costs. If you think you'll make several transfers from this account to other bank accounts, make sure you know the rates. Some banks offer this for free, whereas others can charge hefty fees, sometimes depending on the total amount transferred or the bank where it's transferred to or from.

Interest rate

An obvious one to look out for, especially for savings accounts: How much interest will you get on your money? Bear in mind that rates vary widely—not just between banks, but also over time. When financial times are rough, banks might lower the interest rate every few months, so a bank offering the highest interest rate at the moment will not necessarily still be the highest in six months. Added to that, when the economy is growing, banks generally offer higher interest rates again. Also, rates or special offers might be different for new customers as banks try to attract new clients, so you might sometimes get a better deal with a new bank.

Periodic payment of interest

Some banks pay interest out at the end of the year, whereas others pay out at the end of each quarter or each month. A 5% annual interest rate with a monthly payout is far more attractive than a 5% yearly payout as it means you are compounding interest during the year and not just after a year. If you get 5% once a year, you are paid $50 on every $1,000 at the end of the year. But if you get 5% a year and are paid monthly, you get 5% divided by 12 = 0.4167% a month, which, due to compounding interest where you receive interest on interest (see Step 36), ends up being 5.116% a year, or $51.16, providing you leave your money compounding during the year. This might seem like a small difference, but compounding interest can have a huge effect over time (we will look at this further in Step 36).

Other

Other details to look at when comparing accounts include how easily you can get access to your money (or not), whether you are required to make set monthly contributions, whether you need to tie your money up for a certain number of months or years, and if you need a minimum down payment to open the account. There might be other features that interest you as well, such as the user-friendliness of the bank's online website or app, their customer service, or the closeness of the nearest branch. This all depends on your personal preferences and situation, so I recommend you write down the main features you're looking for to start with. Lastly, I suggest you check that the banks you're looking into have financial protection in case the bank has financial problems or, in the worst case, collapses, to avoid significant financial loss. Unfortunately, recent years have shown that these scenarios can happen. Making sure your bank is backed up is no longer a luxury but an essential requirement.

- -

Once you have a designated place for your money, you can start working toward your first main savings goal, which we will get to in the next step.

☑ STEP 27 ACTION PLAN

☐ Make a simple spreadsheet with the main details you'd like to compare among the various banks and accounts. You might consider keeping it simple and just sticking to two or three key features, or doing a more advanced analysis and adding in more important main points as well as subpoints, which might be slightly less important but still important enough for you to consider them.

☐ Start with your own bank and check out or request to receive information regarding their checking and savings account options. Make sure you get the details you have identified as important and start filling them in on the spreadsheet.

☐ Ask friends or family which bank they use and how satisfied they are with the services. Request information from these banks and add to your comparison chart.

☐ Shop around on some online banks. They often offer better conditions for savings accounts since they have lower costs than traditional banks with offices.

☐ Once you have details on several banks and accounts (I recommend at least four or five), use your chart to compare the various offers and conditions. If none of the banks offer what you're looking for, keep looking until you find a bank that meets your key criteria, such as free accounts (i.e., no maintenance fees and other costs) and a user-friendly online interface.

☐ Remember that regardless of whether you already have a savings account that passes the test or not, you will need a new one for the next step's specific savings goal anyway. Once you've found an account that satisfies you, request the necessary paperwork to open a new cost-free savings account, and make sure to do so before the end of the week. If it helps, schedule time in your calendar to submit the paperwork or go to the bank in person.

Start an Emergency Fund

That some achieve great success, is proof to all that others can achieve it as well.

—ABRAHAM LINCOLN

DIFFICULTY LEVEL: Medium

OBJECTIVE: Build an emergency fund to cover unexpected expenses and avoid going into debt

REVIEW TIMES: Yearly

No matter how carefully you plan and budget for the next month, there will always be surprises that hit you financially at unexpected and often inconvenient moments: a car repair you hadn't planned for, a plumbing issue that needs immediate attention, a sudden vet bill for one of your beloved pets, or your washing machine that breaks down. I'm sure you can think of several examples that have happened in the past few years that threw you off track financially for weeks.

If you don't plan for the possibility of sudden expenses, you probably won't have the money to take care of them when they do happen. Then you're forced to borrow money or dig into your savings when they do arise.

This step focuses on building a fund for key emergencies that are usually one-off expenses. This is different from Step 45, "Build a Three-Months-Expenses Fund," where we will talk more about a long-term cushion to cover expenses in daily life if you're without an income for a while.

An emergency fund

Imagine what a relief it would be if you had an emergency fund with some money set aside that you can draw from in case of unforeseen emergency expenses. You wouldn't need to worry about scraping the money together, or getting into (more) debt—you could just pay the bill and get on with your life. Over the next few months, you'd simply rebuild your fund until it was back up to its original amount for when the next unexpected emergency expense came up.

That emergency fund is exactly what you will start to build in this step using your new savings account from the previous step. A good target number to aim for is generally $1,000. This would allow you to deal with most emergencies you might face.

⚏ STAT BOX

A 2017 Federal Reserve Board report found that 41% of Americans could not cover a $400 unexpected emergency expense in cash from savings.[9] In addition, a 2018 Survey by Bankrate survey showed that 23% of American households have $0 emergency savings.[10]

Of course, whenever you take money out of this fund, you will want to get it back up to the $1,000 as soon as possible.

Before we look at how to build an emergency fund, there is one thing worth pointing out: as the name says, this is an *emergency* fund. You should not touch it unless there is an emergency. That great outing that your friend invites you on but that you don't have any money for? That is *not* an emergency. Wanting to buy a new outfit for the upcoming wedding? You guessed it: not an emergency. Instead of using your emergency fund for these types of expenses, you should save up for them separately (see also Part 5 of this book). It might be tempting at first to use that money for other things, but when a real emergency comes up, you will be incredibly grateful you didn't.

How to build an emergency fund

You can build an emergency fund in many different ways; in the action plan for this step, there's a more detailed list of ideas on how to get this money together. But the main point to start from comes from Step 26 in which you set yourself the goal of limiting one expense for a whole month and keeping track of how much you saved. All that money you saved or will be saving will go directly into this emergency fund. Whether it's $100, $50, or just $10 each time—it doesn't matter. The key is to start putting money together so that unexpected bills no longer throw you off-balance.

You might only need a few weeks to get to your target of $1,000, but it might equally take you a

---

✔ **MAKE IT FUN!**

Join a no-spend challenge. Many financial bloggers run these every so often on their blogs or on social media. This might run for several days and your aim is not to spend any money (except certain specific payments for your basic need such as rent, groceries and utilities). This can be a great way to speed up this step.

---

few months or more than a year to get there. That is okay. You'll find that once you start saving up for your fund, it gets easier to keep adding money to it, and even if you start with $10 now, you might be able to increase this with time or in certain months.

Setting up your emergency fund adds a tremendous amount of peace to your life, as you know that for those unexpected bills, you now have the flexibility to deal with them without upsetting your entire finances. This is a key step to achieving financial security and stability.

☑ STEP 28 ACTION PLAN

☐ Use your new savings account you set up in the previous step as your emergency fund account. It should be separate from any other accounts you have. Make sure it's a fee-free account for which you do not pay for your cards, transactions, and maintenance costs.

☐ At the end of each month, add the money you saved by limiting one expense from Step 26 directly to this account.

☐ Have another look at your income and expenses and decide if and how much you can regularly pay into this account monthly, apart from the money you're saving by limiting one specific expense. Can you commit to another $10 or $20 by adjusting your budget a little?

☐ Are you currently setting aside some money to save for purchases in the short-term, such as for a vacation or a new laptop? If so, consider first funding this account before continuing to build up other savings. (If you are also saving money for long-term goals such as your retirement or child's college fund, you probably don't want to change your contributions to save up for an emergency fund. Those are big and important goals that need a consistent amount of funding on a regular basis.)

☐ How about your cash flow? If that's currently positive, can you put the amount left over at the end of each month into your fund?

☐ Set up an automatic payment for the money you can spare at the beginning of each month to make sure you keep adding to this account continuously.

☐ Look for other ways to add money to this fund even quicker: spare cash you have lying around that you can deposit, money that's in another account you're not using, selling stuff from your basement or attic that you no longer need, etc.

☐ When you reach your target, stop paying into this fund and move on to your next financial goal.

☐ Whenever you need to use this fund, carefully consider whether it really is an emergency worth depleting your fund for. A helpful guideline might be to judge whether something is affecting your day-to-day living (such as a broken washing machine) or whether you can reasonably live without something for a little longer (for example, a broken phone screen, if the phone still works but just looks bad). If it isn't a real emergency, try saving up for it over time first.

☐ Whenever you use money from this account for an emergency, set up a plan to replenish the account back to your target amount as soon as possible. Give the rebuilding of this fund enough priority to consistently grow it in order to be able to deal with the next emergency.

☐ Once a year, decide whether your target amount is still enough or whether you need to increase it—for example, if you have emergency payments cropping up regularly that you can't always cover for or to correct for inflation with time (for more on inflation, see Step 47).

Check Your Balances Daily

Change your life today. Don't gamble on the future, act now, without delay.

—SIMONE DE BEAUVOIR

DIFFICULTY LEVEL: Easy

OBJECTIVE: Set a habit to check your accounts daily to monitor your spending

REVIEW TIMES: Daily

It is unfortunately common for a lot of people to avoid checking their bank accounts regularly to monitor their balances. This is usually because they either have not made their finances a priority or because they are too scared of what they might find. But, the longer you leave it, the more likely it seems it could potentially be bad and the more scared you get, which makes you put it off even longer. This step will set you up so you will be checking your accounts regularly—if not daily—from now on.

The importance of checking your balances daily

On your way to financial independence, you'll want to be aware of what's happening to your bank accounts at all times, and in particular your checking accounts that likely have more day-to-day expenses coming out, to stay in control of your budget. In fact, checking your balances daily has many different benefits, including:

- You always know how you are doing financially and how much money you have at any moment.

- Although you have a budget and most expenses should not come as a surprise, some bills that are automated might come in earlier or later or can be substantially higher than predicted (energy bills, for example). Checking your balances daily means you can update your expenses immediately and adjust your budget if needed.

- You can check for any dubious payments—an incorrect amount or even an expense that's not yours and was charged to your account by mistake.

If you wait until the end of each month to check your spending, you will probably no longer remember whether the charge for a supermarket bill for the sixth of the month was correct or whether you even went to the supermarket on that day.

Checking your balances daily doesn't need to take very long. You simply check in with your accounts to make sure all is in order and that you're up to date.

Checking your balances makes everything much more "real": you see your accounts every day, instead of waiting until the end of the month. You'll also see things from this journey coming together quickly. You just need to get through the initial unpleasant feeling of seeing your money disappearing left, right, and center. . .

☑ STEP 29 ACTION PLAN

☐ Decide what balances you should check daily and which ones you don't need to. You'll want to review your regular checking account(s), but maybe you don't need to log in to your savings or investment accounts. Do you have more than one checking account you should log in to?

☐ Commit to checking these accounts daily. Don't just say, "I'll see how often I can do it," as that gives you an excuse to stop doing it after a short while.

☐ Think of a good time to check your accounts that will allow you to do it every day—maybe while brushing your teeth each morning, right after your lunch break, or just before going to bed.

☐ Mark this task in your calendar, add it to your journal, set an alarm, or put up a Post-it to remind yourself to execute this new habit. It takes a while to make a new habit automatic, so don't make it too easy for yourself to come up with the excuse that you "forgot."

☐ When you log in, check for the following:

- Are all the transactions correct? Check both outtakes as well as any money that might have come in.
- Are you not sure a bill is correct? Make a note of it and check it during your weekly money moment.

☐ Update your budget or spending tracker.

☐ Take note of anything else you notice that you would need to review, or anything you would like to change. Are you still paying a monthly subscription fee for a service you no longer use? This is a good time to write down a reminder to cancel the subscription during your next money moment.

☐ Stick to your habit, even if at first what you see is not very pleasant. With time, you'll feel more on top of your money flow, which will make you more motivated to take control over your finances, and you'll gradually see things improve.

Pay Yourself First

Financial freedom is a mental, emotional and educational process.

—ROBERT KIYOSAKI

DIFFICULTY LEVEL: Medium

OBJECTIVE: Prioritize payments toward your financial security over other expenses

REVIEW TIMES: Monthly

"Pay yourself first," one of the most well-known mottoes in the personal finance world, is a hugely empowering and motivating concept that stimulates you to keep your savings goals at the top of your list. Its origins are attributed to George Clason's famous book *The Richest Man in Babylon,* and although the book is nearly a century old, many of its lessons are still extremely valuable today.

Paying yourself first

You might object to the notion of paying yourself first with reasons such as, "But I'm not a business owner, so I can't pay myself." Or maybe you do own your own company but think, "I need to pay my people first before I can pay myself." Luckily for you, you are totally right in both cases. But that's not what this concept is about.

Pay yourself first has nothing to do with your salary and everything to do with priorities. You can be on a regular payroll and get paid by a boss but still pay yourself first. Or you can be a business owner and pay your employees and your creditors before anyone else but still pay yourself first.

Your monthly money path

Paying yourself first is about setting priorities for your finances. This becomes clearer if you picture the path your money follows each month. The cycle generally starts with payday, although even before you receive your wage, taxes are taken out of it, and you get whatever is left over. One of the first things you need to pay is probably the rent or mortgage. Then there's maybe a car you're paying off, insurance, utility and food bills, and you might be in desperate need of a new coat. On Friday you're joining your coworkers for an end-of-week drink after work, you need to get a present for your niece, you found an old dentist bill you forgot about, and of course there's that student loan or credit card debt you're still paying off. You likely have a few more expenses to add, so the list continues until there's hardly anything left at the end. Sound familiar?

Upon closer inspection, the people who were being paid here were many, but it certainly did not include you!

- Taxes are payments made to the city, state, or country
- Rent—that's your landlord getting paid
- Mortgage—that will go to your bank lender
- Car payments—another one for your lender or car dealer
- Insurance—the insurance company
- Water and electricity bills—your utility companies

- A new coat and the present —different stores
- Friday afternoon drink—the bar owner
- The dentist bill—your dentist
- The credit card loan—another bank charging you

For a moment, stop and find out where your payment is. Of course, you were able to buy yourself a roof over your head by paying down your mortgage or paying the rent, but that money is really being paid to somebody else. You're also able to buy food and clothes and financial security through your insurance, but while you're purchasing these items, somebody else is also benefiting. The one person who does not seem to be getting paid in any way here is YOU.

How to pay yourself first

It wouldn't be viable to say you should stop paying for any of these items in order to stop paying other people. You would probably not survive very long without food, shelter, and clothes, or you'd have a miserable life trying to make ends meet in another way. That's why this step is not called "Stop paying others." Our society and economy are based on exchanging goods and services for money; it's a key part of survival, enjoyment, and life itself. "Pay yourself first," however, encourages you to—before anything else—do exactly that: pay yourself first before you start giving away your money to others.

You might not be able to change so much about the fact that taxes are taken out of your pay first. (Although there are some retirement account funds that will let you invest tax-free; more on that in Part 7. More radically, you could consider moving to a lower-tax state or country.) However, you can make sure that as soon as you receive your net pay, you always pay yourself first.

How do you pay yourself first? The answer is as easy as the concept sounds: by first setting aside money at the start of the month for you to build a secure financial future, grow your capital and net worth, reduce debt, and improve your general financial situation so that you and your family, little by little, gain more financial security and freedom. By assigning part of your money to you, you give your future self an income. Instead of spending it all and giving it to others, you make sure that some of it comes back to you later.

Whenever you get paid, think about how to pay yourself first. Set aside money in a savings account, invest the money in a retirement account fund, or pay down your debt so that you free yourself of those monthly creditor payments before anything else. Make paying yourself a priority each month and only start budgeting whatever is left over after you've set aside money to improve your financial future. Don't allow yourself to come up with excuses like "I don't make enough" or "my bills are too high." Instead, find ways to reduce your expenses, increase your income (see Part 6), and remember that starting small is always better than not starting at all.

- -

Once you become familiar with the "pay yourself first" concept and internalize it, you'll discover the true power of this wisdom that will keep you focused on your mission to financial independence. We will look at several ways to pay yourself first in many steps to come on a practical level, starting with Step 31 on how to apply this to your next monthly budget.

☑ **STEP 30 ACTION PLAN**

☐ Go through the list of your fixed, variable, and discretionary expenses. Identify, one by one, who you are paying every time you make any of these payments. Go through the full exercise and write down the beneficiary for every single expense. See how many people are being paid before you?!

☐ Look at your savings expenses, the one expenses category that follows the "pay yourself first" adage, and see how much of your wage is assigned to this. Are these expenses prioritized, or do you only pay them at the end of the month with whatever is left over?

☐ Set yourself a target monthly contribution for how much to pay yourself each month.

☐ Make paying yourself first automatic by setting up a recurring monthly transfer for when you get paid. This can be to a savings account, toward paying off debt or anything else.

☐ Start your budget with what is left over after you've paid yourself first.

Use the 50/20/30 Rule

It's not your salary that makes you rich, it's your spending habits.
—CHARLES JAFFE

DIFFICULTY LEVEL: Medium

OBJECTIVE: Align your spending with your financial goals by creating your own budgeting rule

REVIEW TIMES: Monthly

When you were making your first budget in Step 22, you might have felt it was a bit of a stab in the dark. Maybe you would have appreciated some guidance on how to allocate your money—a formula that ensured you were assigning your money in a balanced way, taking into consideration both your daily life expenses as well as your long-term goals. Or maybe you were happy to rely on your own methods to start with but would now like to find out more about budgeting and how much to roughly allocate to each expense category. Especially now that you have found out about the importance of paying yourself first, you might feel uneasy about the amount you're setting aside each month for your future self.

The good news is, you've come to the right step! Here you're going to have a closer look at a very common guideline in budgeting, the so-called 50/20/30 rule: a formula that indicates how to assign your money. I like to think of it as a helpful guide more than a rule, as depending on your financial position and your goals, you will likely spend more on specific categories at certain moments in your life and less on others. I therefore strongly recommend you not simply adopt, but first adapt this guideline and adjust it to your own specific needs and circumstances.

So why did we not start budgeting with this rule from the very beginning? Why did I ask you to make your own budget first, if this formula existed all along? By making your own budget, you not only have set a budget that is based on your current expense patterns, you can now analyze how close your budget is to the 50/20/30 guideline. That will allow you to modify this rule to your own numbers in order to make it work for you instead of blindly taking over a rule that might be very far from your reality.

The 50/20/30 rule

Let's have a closer look at what the 50/20/30 rule is and then at how to make the rule work for you and your unique situation. In short, the 50/20/30 rule recommends the following distribution of your money when it comes to budgeting:

- 50% for essential costs: your fixed and variable expenses
- 20% for savings expenses
- 30% for discretionary expenses

Note that it's known as the 50/20/30 guideline, not the 50/30/20 guideline. The rule has assimilated the "pay yourself first" rule partially by recognizing the importance of allocating money to your savings expenses before assigning your discretionary expenses. Do it the other way around and you will likely not set aside enough money to meet your long-term goals that are achieved through your savings expenses. That's because whichever category is last in the list is prioritized least and will therefore always suffer from getting what is left over instead of the percentage it truly deserves. In fact, if it had taken on the importance of the "pay yourself first" concept completely, the rule would be 20(savings) / 50(essentials) / 30(discretionary).

How to adapt this rule

How, then, will this rule work for you? By taking the 50/20/30 as the base rule, you are going to work on finding your own ideal distribution of funds. You will need to adapt the rule, evaluate how things go, and with time find the best proportion to allocate your money to the various expense categories, whether that's 45/25/30, 55/15/30, or something completely different. It might even vary over time. As you go through some of the later steps of this journey, you might further want to adjust your rule, which is absolutely fine. See it as a continuous process. More time, more knowledge, as well as financial and personal changes will require you to keep on adapting this rule, so there's no need to find your one and only golden ratio that will work for the rest of your life. There likely isn't one.

It's amazing what you can achieve once you've decided on your own guideline. Finding out that your savings expenses only represent 10% of your total budget, for example, might be a very compelling reason to bump up the amount you set aside for those long-term savings goals.

☑ **STEP 31 ACTION PLAN**

☐ Start this step by looking at the totals of your various expenses from last month. Here's an example expense list:

- Fixed expenses: $750
- Variable expenses: $550
- Savings expenses: $300
- Discretionary expenses: $400
- Total expenses = $2,000

☐ Now take your fixed and variable expenses together ($1,300 in the example above) and divide this by the total monthly expenses ($2,000) to work out your essential expenses ratio. Do the same for your savings and discretionary expenses. That gives you the following distribution for the above example:

- Essential expenses (fixed + variable): 0.65 = 65%
- Savings expenses: 0.15 = 15%
- Discretionary expenses: 0.20 = 20%
- This translates into a distribution of 65/15/20

☐ If you have several months of expenses registered, repeat this for as many full months as you have so you can see how much these numbers fluctuate.

☐ Now the hard part: make the rule work for you and set yourself targets for these expense categories. Of course we know that influencing your fixed expenses is difficult, that your variable expenses might have some but generally not a lot of room for changes, and that if you cut down too much on your discretionary expenses, your life might become a bit unsatisfying. Finding the right balance between pursuing financial independence and living your day-to-day life is therefore the biggest challenge.

☐ Write down what you think would be your ideal distribution of funds, one to work toward long term.

☐ Then write down the distribution that, with a bit of effort, you can put in place next month that might not yet reflect your long-term distribution but at least gets you one step closer to it. Your rule of thumb does not have to be round figures. If you currently have a 65/15/20 distribution and you want to take down your 65 and increase your 15, do not push yourself for it to be 60/20/20 next month if that seems unrealistic. Start with just 1% difference, or even 0.5% if that makes it more achievable.

☐ Update your budget with the individual expenses within each categories. For example, if you've reduced the total money available for your discretionary expenses for next month from $350 to $300, then how much of that is coming from meals out, date nights, pedicures, etc.? Which categories are those $50 taken from?

☐ As always, keep track of your expenses, then at the end of the month see how you did and how close you were to your preset budgeting rule. Adjust your rule or tweak your budget further for next month until, little by little, this rule becomes yours and you get closer to your target distribution each time.

Get One Month Ahead

It is better to be unborn than untaught, for ignorance is the root of misfortune.

—PLATO

DIFFICULTY LEVEL: Medium

OBJECTIVE: Stop living paycheck to paycheck

REVIEW TIMES: Monthly

A hugely important improvement when getting control over your finances is moving away from living paycheck to paycheck and the constant worries of whether you'll make it to the end of the month. One effective way of doing this is working toward a situation in which you live on last month's income. We'll look at the advantages as well as a few possible disadvantages of this practice before exploring how you can implement this tactic.

The advantages of getting one month ahead

Being one month ahead with your finances essentially means you use last month's income for your current month's expenses and that you have an extra month's pay in your bank account. There are some major advantages of this tactic, such as:

- Timing of payments becomes less important: it doesn't matter if you get paid two or three days late or if a bill comes due earlier than expected.
- It's easier to be flexible if you need to spend a little bit more in one month and a little less

in the next month (think of birthday parties, outings with friends, or family days) provided you still keep a close eye on your budget and update it as needed.

- If a bill is larger than you expected, it allows you to use some of next month's money for it, giving you time to readjust your budget for next month instead of worrying how you'll be able to get the extra money together this month.
- Lastly, if you have a variable income, you won't be surprised by a lower-income month, in which case you can make any necessary adjustments to your spending.

Disadvantages of getting one month ahead

There are two main disadvantages when getting one month ahead of your finances:

- If you keep your extra month in your regular bank account, your money cannot work for you in the same way as if you had it in a savings or investment account. One could argue that having a full month waiting in your checking account is a wasted opportunity to generate interest.
- It can be tempting to use the extra money you have available in this month. If your monthly net wage is $2,000 and you get one month ahead, you'd have around $4,000 at the start of each month when you get paid (or around

$3,000 every two weeks if you get paid twice a month). You won't want to use the extra $2,000 since that's for next month, but it can be all too easy to do so anyway. To prevent this, it's very important to keep a close eye on your budget and stick to it.

Getting one month ahead versus building an emergency fund

At first blush, it might seem that getting one month ahead looks an awful lot like having another emergency fund for one month. But they're not the same, for two main reasons:

1. A very important difference is that an emergency fund is for emergencies, and your monthly budget is not. The buffer simply allows you to keep your money in your emergency fund for when an actual emergency happens, instead of using your emergency money for your regular monthly expenses you have but that you can't pay for at the end of the month.

2. Sometimes your budget encompasses more than one month—for example, a clothes shopping budget. If you set aside $50 a month and spend it all each month, you won't be able to pay for that nice pair of boots on sale for $100, because you'd never have saved up enough for them. If on the other hand you have access to both this month's and next month's money, you can

buy them using this month's $50 as well as the following month's—as long as you adjust your clothes budget for next month to $0.

How to get one month ahead

Just like when setting up your emergency fund, the method you use to get one month ahead depends entirely on how fast you want to achieve this and what your situation looks like. You might be able (and motivated enough) to achieve this in three months, but it might also take you a year or longer. Aiming to achieve this in around six to twelve months is a good goal. Here are just a few ideas on how to get the money together, but feel free to add your own:

- Cutting expenses
- Using a bonus
- Doing overtime
- Earning income on the side

- -

Getting a month ahead can take a while, but keep sight of your end goal, which is living stress-free on last month's income. It might take you more or less time than you had originally planned, but when you get there, it will be very much worth it!

☑ STEP 32 ACTION PLAN

☐ Determine how much you need to get one month ahead. This might be the same amount as your monthly income, or it might be an average or minimum needed if you have a variable income.

☐ Look back at your notes on how to put together an emergency fund to get some ideas for your plan of how to get this fund together. Do not leave it at a vague notion of "I will save money for the next six months" as that is likely *not* going to get you to your goal. Be specific in terms of when you want to achieve this goal and add it to your goals overview.

☐ Write down a plan on how to get one month ahead. Determine how much you want to save each month or week and what you will do to get there.

☐ If you have already saved up for your emergency fund from Step 28, you might have some extra money left over since you started cutting down your expenses and began keeping a budget. If you don't yet have your emergency fund together, consider completing that step before continuing with this one. Alternatively, you can get started on this step by simply allocating some of your monthly savings to getting one month ahead and direct the rest toward your emergency fund, even if that's 10% against 90%. That way, you're still prioritizing your emergency fund but you keep the momentum going by also making some progress to getting a month ahead.

☐ At the end of the month, during your monthly finance review (more on this in Step 35), analyze your plan, record your progress, and evaluate whether you need to make any further changes or adjustments.

Automate Your Payments

Habit is the intersection of knowledge (what to do), skill (how to do), and desire (want to do).
—STEPHEN COVEY

DIFFICULTY LEVEL: Easy

OBJECTIVE: Authorize automatic payments of your bills and reduce time, money and energy spent on manually paying your bills.

REVIEW TIMES: Monthly

Looking at all your expenses, you've probably become aware of how many different payments you have and to how many companies you regularly pay money. Bills do not just come in for utilities and groceries, but also for insurance, credit card payments, subscriptions, and many more! Over the course of a whole year, a lot of bills need attention.

Disadvantages of manual bill paying

A good amount of time can be spent on paying bills each month. Whereas there's an argument that manually paying your bills one by one is a good way to stay on top of how much you're spending and what you're spending on, there are two major disadvantages of paying bills in this way:

1. Time investment: going through the various bills, writing checks, or making payments online can be very time-consuming.
2. Extra costs: bills not paid on time often result in extra fees.

It might be easy to dismiss both reasons, thinking you pay your bills in just half an hour, or that you'll make sure never to miss a payment. But chances are there will be times you're too busy, away on vacation, or dealing with a family issue and you're just not able to pay those bills before their deadline. And even if "only half an hour" doesn't sound like much, what if instead you spent that half an hour managing your finances and planning how to meet your next financial goal?

Setting up automatic payments

To avoid extra costs and free up time so you can put it to better use, let's now go over how to set up automatic payments. Because you're tracking your expenses, you no longer need to worry that you don't know how much you spend on these various bills. Thanks to your expenses log, you'll budget for those payments regardless of the fact that they'll now be made automatically.

Once you have all your payments automated, you should never have to worry about scheduling time to pay bills or about paying extra fees for late payments. You can spend the time you save on improving your financial plans even more, and the money you save from not being charged late fees you can assign to particular goals.

☑ STEP 33 ACTION PLAN

- ☐ Look at your expenses list and check which of your bills already have automatic payments set up and which do not.

- ☐ Consult your money map to see how to best group your payments.

- ☐ For any bills you pay manually, contact the company or go to their website to request the necessary paperwork to automate your payment.

- ☐ Do this for as many payments as possible. Fill in the necessary forms and send them back to the company or to your bank.

- ☐ Register the automated expenses as recurring expenses in your expenses program or app if it allows you to do so. You might need to set it up with an estimated monthly amount and then adjust it every time your bill comes in if the amount varies from month to month.

- ☐ For any automated bill, request to receive a statement with the total you're charged each month, either by regular mail or electronically.

- ☐ At the end of the month, always make sure to double-check those statements against what you were charged to ensure the amount is right. Then update your records or clear the payment in your expenses app or program to confirm the payment has come through in your account and update the amount if needed before filing your statements.

- ☐ From now on for any bill that hasn't yet been automated, pay it and immediately take action to automate the payment for next time.

As I hope you can see, many of the steps we've covered up until now are beginning to build on each other. Their results should slowly be coming together now, which leads us to the next step of creating a yearly budget.

Make a Yearly Budget

Give me six hours to chop down a tree and I will spend the first four sharpening the axe.

—ABRAHAM LINCOLN

DIFFICULTY LEVEL: Medium

OBJECTIVE: Achieve your financial goals with a yearly budget

REVIEW TIMES: Monthly

Before moving away from your expenses, there are two last steps to complete that provide the bigger picture when it comes to your spending. The first one is putting together a yearly budget.

We have already discussed how without a budget it's easy to overspend and lose the big picture of where your money goes. You should by now have a monthly budget put in place where you carefully plan your expenses per category per month to ensure that you achieve your goals, both short term and long term. Although your budget might still need regular adjusting, it should provide you with an ever improving framework on how to spend your money from month to month.

A yearly budget

In addition to making a monthly budget, it's wise to also draw up a yearly budget in which you make a yearlong plan for your expenses. A yearly budget not only ensures that you remember to budget for infrequent expenses such as taxes or subscription fees, but also helps you make a better and more accurate plan for your expenses by bridging the gap between your long-term financial goals and your weekly, monthly, and daily spending patterns. Of course, having a monthly budget already gives you the opportunity to plan expenses far better than if you just spend without being fully aware of your spending patterns. But monthly planning will not give you very much insight into whether you're on your way to achieving your long-term financial goals that span several years or even decades.

How a yearly budget directs your monthly budget

Let's imagine you have a goal to save $30,000 in the next four years. Doing the math, you can work out that this is $7,500 a year or $625 per month that you need to set aside (ignoring inflation and interest for a moment). But the reality is you might not always achieve that goal. There might be months when your expenses increase, your income decreases, or you experience a financial setback that might require a withdrawal from your emergency fund. In that case, instead of continuing to save, you should look at replenishing that emergency fund back to its original value as soon as possible. In short, you just simply might not always be able to stash away $625 per month.

Instead of giving up and accepting defeat, a yearly budget will help you to readjust your monthly budgets for the months to come and will push you to still aim to set aside $7,500 a year even if in certain months you don't achieve the $625 target. If you only had a monthly budget, you wouldn't be able to do this. All you could say at the end of the month would be that you hadn't achieved your goal of $625 that month—and chances are good there would be another month when you'd be unable to achieve it and, who knows, even a third month. With this approach, you're unlikely to save the $30,000 in four years. And whereas a monthly budget will at least motivate you to try for the $625 again the next month, a yearly budget takes this a step further and pushes you to save extra to make up for what you didn't save in the previous month. For example, if you only managed to save $500 last month, a yearly budget will direct you to put away $750 in the next month. This will keep you on track for the $7,500 for this year and the $30,000 in four years.

Having a yearly budget and using it regularly will ensure that you stay on track for your long-term financial goals while simultaneously translating those goals into achievable monthly targets. It also keeps you motivated if you don't hit your targets in specific months because it quickly helps you to reevaluate and adapt to a new plan for next month. Life is never completely predictable, so you'll always need to find ways to navigate around setbacks and obstacles to get back on track quickly.

☑ STEP 34 ACTION PLAN

☐ Pull out your monthly budget and have a look at the various categories.

☐ Think about any categories you might still be missing that maybe do not come up monthly but only a few times a year. These could include fixed, variable, and discretionary expenses, such as:

- Taxes
- Bank charges
- Subscription fees
- Vacations or trips
- Holiday and birthday presents
- Events to attend—weddings, parties, etc.

☐ Determine your total yearly income that you have available to budget.

☐ Use your current budgeting guideline to set yourself yearly targets or predictions for each category based on your knowledge of your expenses up to now. Start with your savings expenses then go through your fixed, variable, and discretionary expenses and assign a yearly budget.

☐ Check your yearly budget against your current monthly one to make sure you're not too far off track each month to stay within your yearly budget.

☐ At the end of each month, when you analyze how well you did with your monthly budget and expenses, link it back to your yearly budget. Review how much you deviated from your yearly plan and determine how to adjust for this in the next few months.

☐ Update your upcoming monthly budgets accordingly and always keep an eye on your long-term goals to adjust where needed, or become more realistic if you realize your targets were a bit too ambitious.

STEP 35

Start a Monthly Finance Review

Believe you can and you're halfway there.

—THEODORE ROOSEVELT

DIFFICULTY LEVEL: Medium

OBJECTIVE: Review your monthly goals and progress and set targets for the next month

REVIEW TIMES: Monthly

In Step 24, you started a weekly money moment, which focused on implementing a weekly half hour to review your goals and make any adjustments to your budget while also updating your weekly spending.

Monthly finance review

Whereas the weekly money moment is incredibly useful to ensure you hit your monthly targets, the monthly review helps you achieve your longer term goals, be they quarterly, yearly, or even much longer term. Your monthly review will be the moment you look ahead and plan a little farther in the future. It gives you an opportunity to readjust your goals and spending patterns over extended periods.

There will of course be weeks when you can combine your weekly money moment with your monthly review, although for your monthly analysis you will need to set aside more time, as you will be analyzing more data compared to your weekly one. I recommend scheduling roughly an hour and a half every month to complete this step.

Since the monthly finance review is designed specifically to make sure you will achieve your goals over a longer period, you might notice at the end of some months that you want to update a goal or add in new goals. This is absolutely fine. Your goals are not supposed to be something that you set once and stick to forever. When situations and aspirations change, which they usually do, so should your goals.

☑ STEP 35 ACTION PLAN

☐ Find a time in your busy schedule for about an hour and a half to spend on this task. The most natural time to do this is usually during the last two or first two days of the month, but it can also be the first Saturday or the last Sunday of each month, for example. Decide what's best for you.

☐ During every monthly review, start again by scheduling your next review. Plan around birthdays, trips, work appointments, and so on. If later you have to move the appointment, then go ahead and do so, but at least if it's scheduled, it will serve as a reminder to do the review, even if it needs to be rescheduled.

☐ Go through the following points during your monthly review:

- If it coincides with your weekly money moment, start with that first to finish the week.
- Close out your budget from last month, making sure everything is correctly registered and that any outstanding bills have been paid, transfers have been made, and your expense log is fully up to date.
- Calculate your cash flow for last month, following the instructions from Step 19.
- Update the amounts for all of your debt.
- Update the value of your assets.
- Calculate your current net worth and register this in the right place.
- See how you're doing on your net worth goal that you set in Step 13 and adjust your goal or plans if needed, i.e., if you're falling behind or progressing faster than expected.
- Check how you did with your "limit one expense" challenge and calculate how much money you saved. Make sure to put that money toward your emergency fund.
- Decide which expense to limit next month. Can you take the same one from last month any further, or can you focus on a different expense? How much would you want to save? Or will you simply continue with the same expense and amount as last time?
- Check your progress in building up your emergency fund and adjust your plan if needed.
- Analyze how much you're on track to get one month ahead.
- If any bills have come in that still require you to pay them manually, or if new ones have been established this month, set up automatic payments now.
- Set a budget for next month, following the plan outlined in Steps 22 and 31, and check it against your yearly budget.
- Read through the financial goals you set in Step 8, again making sure your budget aligns with your goals. If not, make any necessary changes.

☐ Appendix A provides a further overview of steps and tasks to include in your monthly review, many of which will be discussed throughout the remainder of this book. Don't worry about these for now, but as you continue to go along, start incorporating these into your review.

Checklist Part 3

Use the following checklist to make sure you've done everything in Part 3 and are ready to continue with the next part:

☐ You've categorized your monthly expenses and have classified them into fixed, variable, discretionary, and savings expenses.

☐ You calculate your total costs in each of these expense categories at the end of each month and keep track of the average per month per category.

☐ You've calculated and registered your monthly cash flow and have set a reminder to update it at the end of each month.

☐ You've created a money map with a visual representation of how all your bank accounts are linked, which bills come out of your various accounts, and the percentages that each account represents.

☐ You have used your money map to further streamline your expenses and money flow, for example, by avoiding extra fees, keeping accounts active, or grouping certain expenses.

☐ You are aware of the impact of lifestyle inflation and have identified how you might have been affected or will be affected by this at various stages in your life. You use this awareness to your advantage and put long-term financial planning over the importance of short-term gratification.

☐ You have a monthly budget that guides your spending and you've adapted and adopted your version of the 50/20/30 rule to allocate your money to the various expense categories. You understand the importance of paying yourself first when creating your budget.

☐ You've set up a yearly budget that further helps you set a monthly budget based on your long-term goals.

☐ You've held your first financial check-in with your partner to discuss some of the main financial topics covered in the book up until now, to see if you're on the same page regarding your long-term goals and strategies.

☐ You schedule in some time once a week to go through your finances and update your spending and budget (your weekly money moment).

☐ You know your hourly rate and use that information to help you determine whether certain expenses are worth the time you invested to earn that money (that is, are worth the time costs).

☐ You've set yourself the challenge to reduce one expense a month, and you put the money you save on this toward a financial target.

☐ You've opened a new savings account for your emergency fund and have started building up this fund.

☐ You are checking your bank accounts regularly, ideally daily but at least once a week.

☐ You are working toward having one month's income in your bank account as a safety cushion.

☐ You have automated (most of) your bills and are working toward automating any pending ones during each monthly review.

☐ You've done your first monthly finance review and have scheduled one for next month.

💬 PERSONAL STORY: ESTHER

When I was a child, I could spend hours and hours reading through an atlas. I didn't want to become a flight attendant but a pilot, so that *I* could choose the destination of my next journey. Thirty years later, I'm not a pilot but spend my workweek in front of a computer screen. But the urge to explore the world and discover new places is still as strong.

Traveling is my biggest passion. It gives me the freedom to escape from work, but even more than that it stimulates my curiosity and appreciation. "Living" in a settlement in the middle of the Amazon or negotiating in a market in Uzbekistan: it is amazing to be part of a totally different world.

On average my partner and I go on a big three-week vacation once a year, usually to a different continent. Additionally we normally spend a week somewhere in Europe (we live in the Netherlands) and I also often manage to go on various city trips throughout the year. All in all I travel for roughly six weeks a year.

Of course, traveling is expensive. My partner and I both have a decent income but we are very careful about how we spend our money, so that we have enough to finance what we both love. To save more for our travels we try and reduce our fixed expenses as much as possible. We made a conscious decision not to take out a maximum mortgage and live a little smaller than we can afford. We also don't have a car, which means we not only save money but also feel less guilty about our carbon footprint from our flights. We try and always pay for our travels up front. This helps us feel in control over our finances.

Although my job is a way to finance my expensive hobby, last year I decided to reduce my work hours by half a day. I wanted more free time instead of more money, time I dedicate to my travel blog. I initially started this site to share my experiences and because I love writing. I have since been on a paid vacation as an assignment, though, so who knows: I might with time develop this into something more and make money with my travels!

—Esther van den Heuvel, The Netherlands
http://www.travelholic.nl

Your Debts

Now that you have put in place some major plans to get control over your expenses, it's time to start looking at an area of your finances that you likely feel nervous, scared, and dejected about at times: your debts. In order to become financially independent and in total control of your finances, it's important to understand how debt works, how to tackle it, and how even seemingly small debts, low monthly interest rates, and little extra debt repayments can make a tremendous difference to your long-term financial situation.

The good news is that a lot of the groundwork has already been done in Part 3 of this book that will help you avoid taking on more debt as you (started to) set up an emergency fund to avoid sliding back into debt when emergencies happen. You also started cutting costs so you can put the money you save toward certain goals instead of having to take out loans to fund some purchases. You began setting a budget that will help you allocate your money in a thoughtful way with your goals in mind. And last but not least, you became more aware of money concepts, such as lifestyle inflation and time costs, which will help you reduce your expenses even more to avoid accumulating more debt and to free up money to start paying down your outstanding loans.

Part 4 takes you through the necessary skills and knowledge needed to start paying off your debts so that by the end you'll be fully prepared to become debt-free.

Learn about Compound Interest

Time can be an enemy or a friend.

—JOSEPH BRODSKY

DIFFICULTY LEVEL: Medium

OBJECTIVE: Understand the effect of compound interest on your savings and debt

REVIEW TIMES: Yearly

You have probably heard about compound interest. Maybe you even learned about it in school. But because it's the key factor at play in some of the steps still to come and because the impact of compound interest over time can be huge, this entire step is dedicated to looking at how compound interest works. This is important to review first before we actually tackle your debt.

The good and bad of compound interest

In finance, compound interest is one of the most powerful factors at work. By using time as its catalyst, compound interest can do one of two things:

- Make you poorer when it comes to outstanding debts by increasing the amount you have to pay in interest
- Make you richer by generating more money with the money you already own

Let's look at how compound interest works over time.

Interest

When people or organizations borrow money, they are often charged interest on their loan. Say you borrow $1,000 from the bank. You will be required to pay the bank back the original $1,000 you borrowed, *in addition to* interest payments. Similarly, if you lend somebody your money, you likely receive interest on the money that you lent. (This is essentially what happens when you have a savings account with a bank: you are lending your money to the bank and therefore receive interest.)

The interest is a type of fee or risk payment that the borrower incurs for borrowing money in order to entice the lender to lend out their money despite the disadvantages involved. These disadvantages include the risk of losing all or some of the money (in case the borrower goes bankrupt and cannot pay it all back), inflation reducing the value of the money by the time it has been paid back, as well as the obvious problem of not having access to the money that has been lent out. By charging interest, lending money becomes more interesting despite the disadvantages because it allows somebody to make money with their money.

Compound interest

Compound interest is interest that is accumulated from interest on interest on interest on interest, and so on. In other words, interest charges on loans are not just calculated on the original amount, but also on any interest that has been added to the original loan since. The longer you have a loan, the more interest compounds—again showing the power of time.

An example of this is interest received in a savings account. Let's say you have an account that pays out interest every quarter. If you just leave your money in the account year after year, the balance of money in the account (which represents the loan given to the bank) increases a little at the end of each quarter when interest is paid out by your bank. As a consequence, the next time your bank pays out interest, it will be calculated over this higher amount, resulting in a slightly increased interest payout. When you're saving money, this compounding interest gives you more and more money the longer you have the account, as you'll see in the examples below. On the flip side, when you have debts, this compounding interest works against you as it keeps adding extra money to your outstanding balances every month.

Example 1: Simple compound interest

Let's look at an example to clarify this a little. Imagine you have $100 left over at the end of the month for which you open a savings account with an annual interest rate of 5%. That means that after one year of leaving your $100 in your account, you receive 5% interest on your $100, which, when added to the $100, makes a total of $100 + $5 = $105.

Now let's say you leave the money in that bank account for another year. After that second year, you again receive 5% interest. This time, you don't get 5% on $100, but on your current balance of $105. In essence, this means you get 5% on your original $100 and another 5% on the $5 you received last year as interest, or $5.25. At the end of the second year, then, you have $110.25 in your account.

That might not sound like a big deal, as you are only receiving an extra $.25 compared to the year before, but let's look at what happens after another few years if you just patiently leave your money in that account.

After a third year, you receive $5.51 in interest, and the year after $5.79. As you can see in Table 3, each year the amount you receive increases compared to the year before, as your balance also increases. After five years, the account would have over $127 in it thanks to the interest received. After the tenth year, it would be more than $162, and after twenty-five years, this amount would have grown to $338. Not bad if you think that all you did was put in $100 initially!

Table 3: Compounding interest

	Starting balance	Annual interest	End of year balance
Year 1	$100	$5	$105
Year 2	$105	$5.25	$110.25
Year 3	$110.25	$5.51	$115.76
Year 4	$115.76	$5.79	$121.55
Year 5	$121.55	$6.08	$127.63
Year 10	$155.13	$6.38	$162.89
Year 25	$322.51	$16.13	$338.64

Note: Calculations based on a $100 starting balance and a 5% annual interest paid out yearly.

Example 2: Saving and compound interest

Now, what if, apart from putting $100 in a savings account for twenty-five years for the interest to compound, you manage to add another $100 each year? After one year, the interest you receive would be the same as in the example above: you would get 5% interest or $5, making it a total of $105. At the start of the new year, you deposit another $100 in your bank, meaning you have a total of $205. At the end of that year when you get your 5% interest, you now get 5% on $205, which is $10.25, leading to a total of $215.25. You then add your extra $100, wait another year, and then receive almost $16 interest. If you continue doing this every year, after five years you would have a total of $580 in your account. After ten years this would have grown to $1,321, as shown in Table 4, and after twenty-five years the amount would be $5,011!

The true power of compound interest becomes visible if you think that in those twenty-five years, you have paid just $2,500 ($100 per year) into your account, but your capital has more than doubled to over $5,000.

Table 4: Compounding interest with extra yearly contributions

	Starting balance	Annual interest	End of year balance
Year 1	$100	$5	$105
Year 2	$205	$10.25	$215.25
Year 3	$315.25	$15.76	$331.01
Year 4	$431.01	$21.55	$452.56
Year 5	$552.56	$27.63	$580.19
Year 10	$1257.79	$62.89	$1320.68
Year 25	$4772.71	$238.64	$5011.35

Note: Calculations based on a $100 starting balance, 5% annual interest paid out yearly and an annual $100 contribution.

Compound interest over time

Because compound interest works best the more time it has to work, saving just a little more means you can grow your money by a lot more, as long as you give it enough time. If we take the above example to the next level and say that instead of paying $100 per year, you are able to save $100 per *month*, then after twenty-five years you would have paid in $30,000 but your balance would be more than $58,000! Set aside $200 a month, and the $60,000 you put aside will have grown to over $117,000.

As you can see, compound interest can be extremely beneficial when it works to your advantage, such as in a savings account. Now imagine the opposite: What if you *owe* $10,000 to the bank and you are charged interest? In the same way that compound interest can make you a substantial amount of money, it can also cost you a lot of money if you're the one paying it instead of receiving it.

The flaws

Unfortunately, the above money-growing scenarios are not always as rosy as they might sound at first, for two reasons. To start with, although interest rates of 5% for savings accounts were not uncommon for many years and would have even been considered low during some of the financial peak years in the seventies and eighties, at the time of this writing, rates are substantially lower and currently fall around 0.25%–0.50%. That is ten to twenty times less than the 5% used in the above examples. During financially healthy times, interest rates are usually higher, whereas during a recession or period of low financial growth, interest rates tend to drop significantly (more on this in Step 47).

This means that if you currently have your money in a savings account and are "lucky" enough to receive as much as 0.50%, after twenty-five years of saving, the numbers of the above examples change drastically (see Table 5). If you add $100 a month to your account, instead of seeing your $30,000 grow to $58,000, it would only reach $32,000. Hopefully we will soon see interest rates on everyday savings accounts rising again, but for now we are stuck with these historically low rates that have lost their power to compound significantly. (One way to get higher returns on your money is to invest some of it in the market via stocks or bonds, for example. More on this can be found in Part 8.)

A second factor that tones down the potential power of compound interest is inflation, which causes money to lose its value over time. Because of inflation, one can buy less for the same amount of money in the future (see also Step 47). With an inflation rate of 2%, after twenty-five years, the $58,000 mentioned above would only be worth $35,491. With a 3% annual inflation rate, it would be worth less than half that $58,000: $27,085.

That being said, even if the interest you receive on savings doesn't seem to make any substantial money, the power of compound interest is still a hugely important factor to understand and be aware of. Perhaps it's less of an issue for current savings accounts due to their low rates, but compound interest is a critical factor when it comes to debts, investments, and many other financial aspects that we'll be looking at in future steps. And hopefully, with time, those savings accounts will start making money again when interest rates go up. In the meantime, use this knowledge to your advantage and apply it to your financial strategy.

Table 5: Comparison of 5% versus 0.5% compounding interest after 25 years

	5% interest rate	0.5% interest rate
$100 initial payment only	$338	$113
$100 once per year	$5,011	$2,669
$100 once per month	$58,812	$31,957
$200 once per month	$117,624	$63,914

Note: Numbers rounded to nearest dollar. Exact amounts vary depending on specific calculation method used.

As you progress through the rest of the book you'll find that compound interest affects many different areas of your financial life. Don't worry about it too much for now, but come back to this step regularly and with time I'm sure you'll find it becomes easier to grasp.

☑ STEP 36 ACTION PLAN

- [ ] Look at all the debts you listed in Step 10 and check you have all the interest rates on each outstanding debt noted.

- [ ] Put together a list of any savings accounts you have and find out their current interest rates.

- [ ] If you have any other accounts that generate interest, such as investment accounts, work out the average annual interest you're currently receiving.

- [ ] Find an interest calculator on the Internet. Figure out how much money, in interest, you're receiving per year. Then see how this increases if you leave your money compounding for five, ten, or twenty-five years with current interest rates and the current amount of money you have in your savings account.

- [ ] Check how much compounding interest is costing you on outstanding debts where the interest keeps accumulating and adding to the overall cost of your debt long term.

- [ ] Once a year, check that interest rates are still the same. If they've changed, update them in your overview and calculate the impact of the change long term.

Stop Accumulating Debt

Every time you borrow money, you're robbing your future self.

—NATHAN MORRIS

DIFFICULTY LEVEL: Medium

OBJECTIVE: Become aware of the total costs of loans and commit to stop taking on more debt

REVIEW TIMES: Biannually

In Step 10, you listed all of your current outstanding debts, so you should have a good idea of how much money you owe and how much you're paying toward amortizing—i.e., paying off—these loans. Before implementing a plan on how to get rid of these once and for all, let's use the information from the previous step on compound interest and learn more about its effects on your debts and how much this is costing you. (Spoiler alert: this might be much more than you think!)

Long-term debt repayment

Let's say you decide to take out a loan of $3,000 against a yearly interest of 8% and for a duration of five years (sixty months). To keep your monthly costs down, you arrange to pay back the minimum monthly amount possible, which, rounded up, is $61 per month. Although low monthly payments sound pretty awesome, they are generally not your best bet long term, as you can see in Table 6: after those five years, due to the (compounding) interest and the total time you're paying money back, you would have paid a total of almost $3,650 back. That's $650 in interest payments, or more than 20% of the original loan.

Added to this, 8% is a relatively low percentage for a loan. Many loans range from somewhere between 11% up to 19% or even more. If you had $10,000 in outstanding debts against a 14% annual rate and a total of seven years to pay it back, your minimum monthly payment would be around $188 a month. At the end of those seven years, you would have paid back a total of just over $15,700, almost $6,000 more than what you borrowed!

Table 6: Total interest payments on two example loans

	Starting amount	Yearly interest	Duration of loan	Monthly pay	Total paid in interest
Loan 1	$3,000	8%	5 years	$61	$647
Loan 2	$10,000	14%	7 years	$188	$5,707

Note: Amounts rounded to nearest dollar. Exact amounts vary depending on specific calculation method used.

How is it possible that on a loan of $10,000, with an interest rate of 14%, you end up paying nearly 60% in interest rates over the course of seven years? You might have guessed the answer already: compound interest.

Compound interest on debt

For a moment, let's say your credit card offers a 1.5% monthly interest rate and a very "generous" payback scheme in which you only need to pay back 3% of the balance, with a minimum of $10 a month. If you carried a balance of $1,000 on that card, at the end of the first month you only need to pay back $30 (3% of $1,000). After the second month, your monthly repayment will be less than $30, as your outstanding debt decreased—you already paid off $30 last month after all—so 3% is calculated over a slightly lower amount. Every month your monthly payment will therefore decrease as your outstanding debt also decreases. Sounds too good to be true, right? Unfortunately, it is.

First of all, the 1.5% monthly interest rate quoted is, as it says, a monthly interest rate. That equals a yearly interest rate of 18%! Second, due to the low minimum monthly fee, you're giving the interest on your loan a *very* long time to compound. At the end of the first month, the bank charges you interest on your loan, so you owe $1,000 x 1.5% = $15 interest along with the $1,000 you borrowed, so a total of $1,015. You pay 3%, or $30.45, which means your loan is down to $984.55. (You might already see the problem: even though you paid $30, almost 50% of that amount was used to pay off the interest only.) After the second month, your bill is $984.55 + $14.77 (1.5% interest) = $999.32. You pay 3%, or $29.98, and the outstanding balance is then $969. Again, of your payment, roughly 50% was used to first pay off the interest of $14.77 that was just tacked on, before it was able to pay off some of the original debt. Since you are continuously charged interest each month, and therefore playing catch-up at the end of each month, it takes a long time for the principal to go down, and interest charges therefore remain high.

By the time you finish paying off your original $1,000 loan, as shown in Table 7, it'll be 118 (!) months down the road—almost ten years later! In that time, you have paid back $1,779, an extra $779, or almost 78% more than you originally borrowed.

As you can see, interest on interest on interest for almost ten years means that the true interest on that loan was closer to 78% in total instead of the very enticing 1.5% monthly rate the bank sold you on. Suddenly that offer does not seem so generous.

Now that you're aware of the hefty interest you're charged on these types of loans, let's decide to stop accumulating debt on your credit cards or any consumer loans in general, be that with the bank or any other lender from here on. Of course this is easier said than done, but in upcoming steps we'll be looking at ways to put a plan into action and achieve this.

To get control of your finances and become debt-free, be firm with yourself. Instead of the "buy, then repay" principle so often followed in our society, make "save, then buy" your new mantra.

Table 7: Total interest and time spent on paying off a $1,000 loan

Starting balance	Monthly interest	Yearly interest	Monthly payment	Total interest paid	Years to pay off loan
$1,000	1.5%	18%	3%	$1,779	9 years, 10 months

Note: Amounts rounded to nearest dollar. Exact amounts vary depending on specific calculation method used.

☑ STEP 37 ACTION PLAN

☐ From today on, stop using credit cards for any purchases you won't be able to pay back at the end of the month. In other words, only use your card if you can actually pay off the balance at the end of each month.

☐ Commit to not taking out any more loans at interest rates above 5%. Not. Ever. For anything (not a new car, your wedding, a vacation, a baby . . . nothing). From now on, make it a habit to first save the money before purchasing anything.

☐ Determine under which circumstances you would allow yourself to take out a loan at lower interest rates, such as only for assets (e.g., a house, a new business). For anything that won't make you any money and is really a liability (this includes cars), aim not to take out any more loans. If this sounds a little radical, feel free to adjust this rule as you deem necessary. But do give it some serious thought: Do you really want to take out another loan now that you know you're losing big money on each debt you have? Would you not rather experience the satisfaction of being able to pay the true price for a purchase instead of the price plus hundreds if not thousands of dollars extra on interest? Instead of buying a new car that only depreciates with time, consider saving up for a secondhand car as an alternative that is a) less expensive and b) possible to pay for in cash instead of having to finance with a loan.

☐ Refer to Step 49 in which you will set up various savings goals to start saving up for expenses such as a new car, a vacation, etc. This should make it easier to stop taking on any more debt.

☐ If you do take out a loan, calculate its true cost over time. There are many online calculators that will quickly show you how much you end up paying back over time depending on the amount of the principal and the interest rate. Use that information to decide whether you really want to spend that money.

☐ For each debt you have or loan you might still consider taking out, use your time-cost calculation to find out how long you need to work for each loan to be paid off.

☐ Twice a year, calculate how much interest you've paid out over your various loans and update how much longer you need to work, using your time-cost calculation, to pay off the remainder of your loans.

Credit Cards

Never spend your money before you have earned it.

—THOMAS JEFFERSON

DIFFICULTY LEVEL: Medium

OBJECTIVE: Understand the dynamics of credit cards and determine which of your cards to keep

REVIEW TIMES: Yearly

Credit cards seem to play an ever more important role in our lives. Although some people might be critical of the ease with which we swipe our cards without even thinking, there are also proponents of credit cards and the many advantages they offer. This step looks at both credit cards in more detail, and at the end you will need to decide for yourself what your personal approach toward credit cards will be for the next few months or years, taking into consideration your history of debt and your new commitment to stop accumulating more of it.

Credit cards and debt

Credit cards are incredibly attractive because they allow you to pay for something regardless of whether you have the actual money in your bank account, without having to apply for a loan each time. In reality, every time you use your credit card, you're taking out a (small or not so small) loan from your bank. At the end of the month, the bank will present you with the total amount charged on your card and you will be required to pay it back.

STAT BOX

More U.S. families had credit card debt (43.9%) than a debt secured by their primary residence or a mortgage (41.9%) in 2016 according to a federal study from 2017. The median outstanding credit card balance was $2,300.[12]

Up to here, there is, in theory, no problem. The problem arises if you don't have the money to pay your bank back, in which case the bank will take that as a cue to start charging you interest like with any loan. Of course, the bank will be eager to offer you a "generous deal" with a low monthly payback scheme like we saw before in Step 36, because the longer you have that outstanding balance, the longer they can charge interest, and the more money they earn (and you pay). Be aware that in addition to the interest you need to pay, you might also be charged a late payment fee every time you miss a payment.

Credit cards and bonuses

Although there are risks associated with credit cards, as they make it easy to overspend, credit cards also offer a number of advantages. This includes the building of credit scores (see the next step), automatic insurance on purchases, as well as cash-back and reward systems, in which you either get a small percentage of your money back or save for free extras. If you are able to use your credit card but not carry any outstanding balances and pay off your balances at the end of each month, these bonus features can of course be a huge advantage.

Whether you decide to keep all, some or none of your credit cards is completely up to you. There is no one "right" answer here. Instead do what you believe is best for your personal situation and history.

☑ STEP 38 ACTION PLAN

☐ Take out all your credit cards and put them on a table in front of you—not just credit cards from the bank, but any card you might have from a store or company. Count how many you have and determine which ones you use and which ones you do not. Check the following for each one and make sure to note this in your (digital) file:

- Credit limit
- Outstanding balance
- Interest rates and interest-free periods that are still valid
- Length of time you have had the card
- Rewards and cash-back offers

☐ Evaluate all of your cards by the criteria above and see which ones work best for you. Generally speaking, having two or three cards is probably more than enough, and some people prefer to keep it simple and just have one card.

☐ If you know you sometimes struggle to resist the temptation to use your credit cards, even when you don't have the money to pay them off at the end of each month, or if you currently have a substantial outstanding balance on your credit card, decide how to best stop accumulating more:

- keep them for now but make a firm agreement with yourself to only use them if you can pay off the money at the end of each month or in case of an emergency;
- give them to a trusted friend or your partner for safekeeping so that you don't have instant access to them; or
- get rid of them completely—bearing in mind this negatively affects your credit score for a while (see Step 39). Even if this might initially sound like a rather drastic decision, this could be the best course of action if your credit card debt is rather more than you'd like.

☐ If you decide to close any cards, you first need to pay off the balance. Consider rolling some debt into other cards if they're older (older cards increase your credit score—see the next step for more on this topic) or have lower interest rates, if that allows you to cancel some cards. For example, imagine you have the following three cards:

- A. Limit $1,000, outstanding balance $600, monthly interest rate 1.25% = yearly 15%
- B. Limit $2,000, outstanding balance $400, monthly interest rate 1.5% = yearly 18%
- C. Limit $1,500, outstanding balance $500, monthly interest rate 1.75% = yearly 21%

Because card C has the highest interest rate, you should aim to get rid of it as soon as possible. Use the first card to pay off $400 on the last card, then another $100 with the second card to close your third card. This utilizes the first card with its best interest rate to its maximum and cancels the card with the highest interest rate and therefore highest total cost.

☐ Avoid applying for new cards unless it's absolutely necessary. The fewer cards you have, the less the temptation to use them. Consider building up a decent credit score first (see Step 39 for more).

Credit Scores

Develop success from failures. Discouragement and failure are two of the surest stepping stones to success.

—DALE CARNEGIE

DIFFICULTY LEVEL: Medium

OBJECTIVE: Know your credit score and plan how to increase your score

REVIEW TIMES: Yearly

Credit scores

In Step 37, we discussed aiming to avoid taking out any unnecessary loans where possible and start saving up for a big expense before purchasing it to avoid extra costs and debt. This is generally a great guideline, but there are cases when you might need to consider taking out a loan, such as for a mortgage or business start-up.

When applying for such a loan or when trying to purchase other financial products (including insurance policies), your credit score can be of vital importance. A high credit score implies you are more reliable and responsible with your money.

Your credit score is made up of the following details:

- Your payment history and how reliably you have paid back your loans.
- Your credit utilization rate or the percentage of your available credit you use.
- How long you have had your credit.

A high credit score will give you the following advantages:

- Lower interest rates on loans and mortgages.
- Higher chance of being successful when applying for a rental property. Landlords tend to evaluate rental applications on credit scores. They believe that those with a higher credit score are less likely to default on their rent payment, i.e., not be able to pay it.
- Other financial products such as insurance policies as well as investment opportunities are sometimes only granted to those who have a sufficiently high credit score.
- Certain companies and employers do not hire people with low credit scores as they believe these people have less self-control and are less goal-oriented.
- Higher credit scores increase your chances of getting a higher credit limit. This, in turn, helps you decrease your credit utilization rate, which further increases your credit score again.

How to improve and maintain a good credit score

Having a good credit score is important, but how do you achieve this? Here are some tips to improve and maintain a good score:

- Do not default on a credit card payment. At the end of each month, make sure you pay off the minimum monthly required of any outstanding balance.
- Start paying off your debt as soon as possible. This shows you are a responsible person looking to reduce your debt instead of constantly living with outstanding amounts. (See also Step 41 on paying off debt.)
- Once you've paid off all outstanding credit card debt, from then on, make sure to pay off your credit card in full at the end of each month.
- Maintain a low credit utilization ratio, that is, the percentage of your credit limit you use. Try to keep it below 30%. For example, if you have credit card with a $2,000 limit, aim to use no more than $600.
- Do not apply for credit too often or for prolonged periods of time. A credit company will keep track of any inquiries they receive and if you've made lots of inquiries or over an extended period, your score will be negatively affected.
- While having (too) many cards also involves a certain risk of fraud, theft, or temptation to use more than you need, think carefully before you close any cards. Not only does this reduce your credit utilization rate, it also reduces the "age" of your credit (meaning you lose the years that you had the credit for) which furthermore negatively affects your credit score.

- That said, if the temptation is too big and you have a history of accumulating debt on your credit cards quickly, consider closing some or all of your cards. Your credit score will take a hit, but not building up any more debt will be more important, and you can bring your score back up again with some careful planning.
- Stop opening or accepting new cards you're offered and carefully compare credit cards on their interest rate and their rewards. Make sure to compare the interest over the same period of time, i.e., either compare the monthly interest rate or the annual interest rate.
- Keep track of your credit score regularly, ideally on a yearly basis, by requesting your credit score online via a credit reporting bureau. Set specific goals to increase your score.
- Start building your score early on. The longer you give it, the better your score.
- Apply for a credit increase. This means that your credit utilization ratio will be better as long as you do not increase the amount of credit you actually use.

- -

Keeping a good credit score is of great importance. Although having more cards with higher limits can improve your score, it is equally important to remember that this is only true if you use these cards wisely.

☑ STEP 39 ACTION PLAN

☐ Start by checking out your current credit score. Your credit card company, bank, or loan provider might state your credit score on your monthly statements or in your online account. Alternatively, you can contact a financial institution to find out what your score is—some will provide this for free, whereas others might charge you a fee. Register your score in your log and add this to your yearly list to check and update.

☐ Keep building your credit score slowly but steadily. It takes time to build up your score, but follow the guidelines above and you should start to see things improve. Remember that your credit score affects more than just the conditions you get on a loan, so even if you have committed to no longer taking on debt, it is important to keep improving your credit score.

☐ Check your credit score once a year and evaluate whether your credit cards and limits still meet your needs or whether you should make any changes.

The Impact of Extra Debt Payments

A person who never made a mistake, never tried anything new.
—ALBERT EINSTEIN

DIFFICULTY LEVEL: Medium

OBJECTIVE: Find out how small extra payments toward a loan can save huge amounts of time and money

REVIEW TIMES: Every three months

After reading some rather depressing news to do with debt, interest, and total debt payments in Steps 36 and 37, it's time for some uplifting information—in particular, how effective it can be to put extra money toward paying off a loan and how much it reduces not just the time spent paying back the money, but also the total amount paid back. I hope this will inspire you to find ways of making extra payments toward reducing your debts. Even small extra contributions—thanks again to our friend compound interest—will have a huge effect.

Paying off debt

The money you pay off on any loan consists of two parts: the principal amount (or the part of the original amount borrowed you're paying back) and the interest (or the percentage that you get charged as a "fee" for borrowing the money).

While normal debt payments include both a principal payment and an interest payment, any extra payments you make toward your debt should pay off your principal amount directly, meaning you do not pay off any interest with this. This is an advantage as it means the outstanding amount goes down quicker and next time interest is charged, the amount on which to charge this will have reduced, resulting in less interest to pay, too. Some lenders don't like you making extra payments, however, so always check that the extra money is put toward the principal and not seen as an early next payment, in which case it will be used to pay interest as well (and you benefit less from making these extra contributions).

Making extra payments

Let's go back to one of the examples from Step 37. In that step, we looked at an outstanding debt of $1,000 at a 1.5% monthly interest rate and a payback rate of 3% with a minimum of $10 a month. But let's make one change: this time you make an extra payment of $25 on top of the minimum amount per month.

You might say this is a small difference, but the impact will be huge as two things now happen: not only are you reducing your debt faster, meaning you will be tied to those monthly payments a lot less time, but because your outstanding balance is lower every month compared to if you had just paid back the minimum, the interest that you keep accumulating is less each time as well. Remember the power of compound interest, which comes from interest on interest on interest; 118 months (the amount of time you need to pay off this theoretical loan with just making minimal payments) is a long time for compounding to take place! So the faster you reduce the debt, the less time it has to exert that power.

Long-term results

Like before, the first month you're charged 3% of the $1,015 debt you have at the end of the month, so you will need to pay back $30.45. This time, however, you add an extra $25 on top of that, so you pay a total of $55.45. Whereas before you were left with $984 in outstanding debt at the end of the first month, with the extra payment, your balance is now $959. The second month you originally accumulated around $29.50 in interest, but this time it will only be $28.80. These are all small differences at first sight, but let's continue our calculations.

Remember that in the previous example in Step 37 it took you 118 months to pay back your loan and you ended up paying an extra $779 back on the $1,000 you borrowed.

If you continue to pay an extra $25 each month on top of the minimum required payment—and here comes the really shocking news—it only takes you 31 months to pay back your loan, as shown in Table 8! That is just under three years, compared to the ten years it would take you with just the minimum payment. Also, guess what happens with the interest you pay? It goes down to $221, instead of $779, a difference of more than $500. Once again, even if you're just making a small extra contribution, this can have a big impact over time.

Aim for even bigger results

If instead of working off a 3% payment (which means that each month you pay just a little less back as your balance decreases), you keep up with your original first payment of $55.45 per month, the effects are even bigger. In that case it would take you just 22 (!) months, and a mere $175 extra to pay it all off. As you can see, this is a tremendous difference to the original ten years it was going to take you if you had just gone for what your lender had proposed.

- -

The most important lesson of this step is that there is a way out if you feel you are controlled by your debts at the moment. As you might have guessed, the next step will be all about putting in place an action plan to start paying off one of your debts faster!

Table 8: Long-term effects of extra debt payments

	Minimum amount	Minimum + $25	Same monthly payment
Monthly payment	Max $30.45 (3%)	Max $55.45 (3% + $25)	$55.45
Time to pay off	118 months	31 months	22 months
Total interest paid	$779	$221	$175

Note: Amounts rounded to closest dollar. Exact amounts vary depending on specific calculation method used.

☑ STEP 40 ACTION PLAN

- [ ] Get out the details of all of your debts. You need to know the starting balance, your current balance, your interest rate, and how much you're paying back monthly.

- [ ] Do a search online for "debt consolidation calculator" or "debt payoff calculator." You'll likely get hundreds of options; just select the one that seems easiest to use. Depending on your debt, you might have a fixed monthly payment, or a minimum payment percentage (as the one used in the examples above), so find a calculator that allows you to select whichever is applicable to you.

- [ ] Put in the numbers for each of your debts pretending that you have not yet paid anything back, i.e., as if you were about to make your very first payment on each. Write down the total amount of months it would take you to pay off each debt as well as the total amount of interest. This might not be a pretty sight, but it's important to be aware of how much each debt will have cost you at the end of its life span.

- [ ] Of course you can't make any extra monthly payments for the months you have already paid back each debt, so to see the effect of extra payments, you need to put in a new calculation. For each debt, now put in the amount that is your current outstanding balance (not the original starting amount), and see how many more months or years it will take to pay off the balance.

- [ ] In the calculator, select the option of "making extra monthly payments" and start by adding in an extra payment as low as $10, then slowly increase to $25 and $50 a month. Again, all of these payments might sound small, but look at the impact over time.

- [ ] See what these extra payments can do and the effect they have over time. Notice how much money you might be able to save by paying back your debts more aggressively. In your file note down the difference in total time and money spent with these extra monthly contributions.

- [ ] Review your outstanding debts and extra payments every three months and evaluate how further contributions can have even bigger impacts.

Start Paying Off One Debt

The only person you are destined to become is the person you decide to be.

—RALPH WALDO EMERSON

DIFFICULTY LEVEL: Medium

OBJECTIVE: Pick one debt and prioritize paying it off

REVIEW TIMES: Every three months

From the previous step you should now be up to speed about the positive effect of extra payments on outstanding debts. That leads us to the current step: start paying off a debt. Of course, if you have outstanding debts you're probably already paying these off, but the point here is that you're going to pay down debt *faster* by making higher monthly contributions than the minimum required.

The advantages of paying off faster

When you pay off a debt faster than scheduled, a few things happen:

- You end up paying less interest, as there's less money and less time for the interest to compound.
- You reduce the time it takes to pay back the loan.
- Psychologically it's a great relief to have paid off a debt: one less thing to worry and think about.
- It increases your motivation by giving you positive reinforcement and showing you that you *can* achieve your goals.
- The moment you pay off a debt, the monthly amount you poured into this debt all of a sudden

✔ MAKE IT FUN!

Paying off debt isn't particularly fun, especially not if it seems like an endless journey. Make it more interesting by finding a buddy (friend, partner, colleague) who's also looking to pay off their debt. Race each other: see who can pay off the most each month, either in dollars or, if your income or expense patterns are very different, in percentage of the total debt

becomes available, which you can then use in its entirety to pay off another debt. This not only keeps up the momentum, it also means that the more debt you pay off, the faster you'll pay off your next debt as you free up more and more money.

How to pay down debt faster

When you decide on your first debt to pay off faster, there are a few things to bear in mind:

- Commit to pay off *one* debt faster. Do not start paying off all debts at the same time, as not only will you not see any clear results for years, it also will not give you the advantage of freeing up money at an early stage to then help you with the other debts.

- When you start focusing on paying off your one debt, make sure to keep making the minimum monthly payments for all of your other debts. You don't want to incur extra fees due to missing payments on those debts you haven't prioritized, or all the hard work you put in on one end will just be erased on the other end.
- Decide which debt to pay off aggressively first using one of the following techniques:
- Debt snowball method: Start with the debt with the lowest outstanding balance first and gradually work your way up. The advantage of this method is that it gives you results faster at the beginning, which will hopefully create more stimulus and keep your motivation up.

- Debt avalanche method: Start with the loan with the highest interest rate and work your way down, ending with the loan with the lowest interest rate. The benefit of this approach is that over time you save a lot more money as you avoid that high interest rate from compounding for longer than needed.

This step will likely take you a good amount of time to complete, so it's only normal if it's a little slow at first. With time, you'll get there! But even the (small) extra amounts you pay off will help you reach your target, little by little.

☑ STEP 41 ACTION PLAN

This is where the real action happens, so get ready to make some serious progress with this subsequent plan:

- ☐ I recommend you do not start paying down any debt until you've put together the emergency fund from Step 28. There isn't much point in paying down debt if you wouldn't be able to deal with an unexpected $600 emergency repair, as it will just rack up more debt again. So best to first build your emergency fund and get that one out of the way before moving on to paying down debt.

- ☐ Once you've got that fund together, look at your list of debts.

- ☐ Decide which debt to attack first. Do you feel more likely to keep up this step using the debt snowball or the debt avalanche method? Pick whichever is best for you depending on your situation and the character of your loans.

- ☐ Look at your budget and figure out how much money you can free up to pay down your debt faster. Determine how much money you've been saving with the "limit one expense" challenge and take the average monthly amount as a good starting amount to pay monthly on the debt you want to pay down first. Is there any other money you might be able to save? What adjustments to your budget do you need to make?

- ☐ Once you have decided how much extra money in total you can pay back each month, go back to the online calculator to find out about the effects of extra payments. Check how much money and time you'll be able to save on your first debt by adding in those extra $10, $25, or $50.

- ☐ Now that you've decided how much money to put in and where the money will be coming from, include this in your budget, adding in a category for extra loan repayments.

- ☐ Contact your loan provider for details on how to make the extra contribution and ensure there are no charges for making extra payments. If there are, try to negotiate these or consider moving on to your second debt instead.

- ☐ Keep up the extra payments until you've paid down the debt completely.

- ☐ All the while, strive to keep making minimum contributions to all of your other debts.

- ☐ Once you have paid off your first debt, move on to the next one on your list.

- ☐ Update your outstanding debt amount at the end of each month. Evaluate how much extra money you were able to pay toward your debt and whether you'll be able to make the same contribution next month.

Keep 50% of Any Extra Money

We are what we repeatedly do. Excellence, therefore, is not an act but a habit.

—ARISTOTLE

DIFFICULTY LEVEL: Easy

OBJECTIVE: Commit to always using 50% of any windfall for one of your long-term financial goals

REVIEW TIMES: Yearly

This step focuses on how to save money faster with a simple idea. Although this habit can help you to pay down debt more quickly, it's not meant to be just a one-off. When applied over time, this will help you progress toward other new financial targets that you might be setting yourself later on.

The current step—save 50% of any extra money—is easy to understand, yet (as is often the case when it comes to money) difficult to implement because it requires you to resist the temptation of instant gratification and instead forces you to focus on the long-term advantages of self-control.

Extra money

There will be times when you get a financial windfall and receive some extra money. Maybe you were given some extra cash by your family for your birthday, received a holiday bonus from your employer, or got a tax return. Just as you are likely to be faced with unexpected expenses now and again for emergencies, the opposite scenario can also happen from time to time (although unfortunately this usually happens less).

Pay raises

Apart from these one-off moments when you get extra money, you might also get a more structured or long-term increase in money, such as in the form of a pay raise. Although a pay raise is generally higher income from work, try to see "pay raise" in a broad sense and think of it as an increase in your monthly cash flow in general, which can come about for many different reasons. Apart from higher pay from your employer, it could also be a little side income you might be getting from doing extra work, a lower mortgage payment, or some other favorable reduction in your expenses, resulting in a little extra money left over at the end of each month.

Build your financial security

It's tempting to spend any extra money you get immediately, whether you were expecting to get that money or not. You might feel you have worked hard for it, or maybe you have been going through some rough times and just want extra cash to spend on yourself and enjoy it while you can.

I'm not going to tell you that you should live like a puritan and not spend any of that money on something you want or feel you have earned. Sometimes the best thing you can do is to use it for a relaxing vacation, take your partner or family out for dinner, get some new clothes, or do whatever else you feel like doing.

But now that you understand the power of small steps and compound interest, it shouldn't come as a surprise that putting away even just half of that money will give you so much more in the long run than using and spending it all in one go. Making wise decisions beforehand on how to deal with extra money and setting the guideline to always keep 50% and allow yourself to use and freely spend the other 50% can help you fast-track paying down debt, building up your savings or reaching some of your other financial targets and reaping the benefits of this increase in money beyond the present moment. Invest it, use it to make an extra debt payment, or put it in a savings account to build up a three-months-expenses fund (Step 45) and you'll likely appreciate the money even more than if you were to spend it all now.

Budgets and extra money

A note of warning here: Whether or not you're expecting any extra money, make sure you never budget for this, so that when this money comes in, it really is *extra* money. In that way, you are truly able to enjoy its benefits. Another reason it's safer not to budget for it is that at the end of the day you might not know for sure that you'll be getting the extra money, nor the exact amount of it. Maybe your great-aunt forgets or can no longer afford to give you money this year, your employer might need to cut costs and forgo that holiday bonus or delay your promotion, or you might no longer be entitled to the tax return you have become used to getting.

Saving 50% of your raise and compound interest

Remember the example we used in Step 36 to highlight the power of compound interest? There we saw that if you were able to pay $100 per month for twenty-five years into a savings or investment account that earned 5% interest, your balance after those twenty-five years would have grown to over $58,000. Now imagine that in addition to that scenario, every five years you get a pay raise of $200 a month, of which you allocate half, so $100, into your monthly investment plan. Instead of paying in $100 year after year for twenty-five years, you are now, after five years, able to put in $200 a month. After ten years, you again get a pay increase of $200 a month, so you put in another $100 extra on top of the existing monthly payment. You continue doing this every five years until for the last five years you manage to save $500 a month.

Following this strategy, after twenty-five years your account would be worth two and a half times as much as the $60,000 you would get if you stuck to paying $100 a month: you end up with almost $150,000, having paid in "just" $90,000. That means you earned $60,000 in interest in this account over those twenty-five years. (Note, however, that tax increases and inflation have not been corrected for.)

- -

Implementing this step every time—and as soon as—you get a windfall or raise will guarantee that an increase in earnings doesn't automatically result in an increase in spending, but instead ensures your money gets put to good use long term.

☑ STEP 42 ACTION PLAN

☐ Review your budget and double-check you are not relying on any extra but nonguaranteed money. If you are, rebudget and pretend that extra money doesn't exist.

☐ Have a quick think about how likely it is for you to get a pay raise anytime soon. When did you last get one? How often can you expect a raise in your industry or company? Is there anything you can do to get one sooner, such as renegotiate your salary, take a training course to become a more valuable team member, or start a new business on the side?

☐ Do you foresee that any recurring costs will go down anytime soon? Can you renegotiate your mortgage or can your utility bills go down thanks to a new offer you might qualify for? If so, how much extra money would you have available each month?

☐ Decide what you would do with any extra money and write it down so that if/when it comes in, you can simply follow your plan. For now, this might still be building your emergency fund, getting one month ahead, or paying down a high interest debt. Later on in your journey, this will likely change and might move to investing or other savings goals.

☐ Determine how much you would want to keep of any extra money, whether it's a one-off payment or a structured increase in your cash flow. Even though this step mentions 50%, maybe you're happy to only spend 40% and keep 60%, or the reverse. Again, write this down so it's a commitment with yourself.

☐ Every time you get any extra money or a pay raise, make sure to immediately set up an automatic transfer from your checking account into your savings account, investment account, toward paying off your debts, or any other financial goal that you have, so you actually will stick to your plan. Then take the remaining amount and spend it however you want. Make sure to thoroughly enjoy it, knowing that you are sticking to a sensible balance between spending some money while at the same time investing in your future.

Become Debt-Free

Don't let the perfect be the enemy of the good.

—UNKNOWN

DIFFICULTY LEVEL: Medium

OBJECTIVE: Set target dates for when to pay off all your debts

REVIEW TIMES: Monthly

Becoming debt-free might or might not have been a goal you identified when you put together your financial goals in Step 4. Whether this was the case or not, you hopefully have by now realized that becoming debt-free will work greatly in your interest if you want to avoid paying the huge extra costs of outstanding loans over the years. Becoming debt-free might take you three, ten, or twenty years, but it will be a tremendous achievement in the long run.

Becoming debt-free

In Step 41, you set yourself the goal of paying off one debt. But it will not stop at just one. As soon as you have paid off that one debt, the next step on your journey is to set goals to pay off all your debts.

In this step, you will put together a definitive plan with accompanying dates of when you will be paying off each debt in turn, and when you will ultimately finally be debt-free.

Just consider for a moment how exciting and liberating that feeling will be when you have finally paid it all off: no more debts, no more interest to pay, and no more monthly payments taken out of

your paycheck for an expense that you made months or even years ago. . . .

Setting target dates

The plan you put together today will have target dates assigned to each debt, to make your goals more specific. You might not be sure how to accurately predict every single date on which you'll pay off a debt, and more likely than not your prediction will not be completely correct, but you shouldn't see these goals as being set in stone. After all, your situation will change over time. You might have a windfall or an unexpected situation that forces you to cut down on your monthly debt payments. Or you might become so motivated by seeing the first results that you manage to find even more money to put toward paying down your debts. Whatever it is, the dates you set are targets for the moment, so remain open to the idea that they can and most likely will change. Nevertheless, you are always more likely to achieve a goal that you regularly update and adjust than a goal that has not been set at all.

Becoming debt-free will be something to look forward to and to celebrate when it finally arrives. It might seem as if this isn't going to happen anytime soon, but once you get started, you might be surprised how often you will manage to pay off a debt ahead of your target date.

☑ **STEP 43 ACTION PLAN**

☐ Look at the debt you identified in Step 41 as the first debt to pay off. With the outstanding amount and the total monthly payment you will soon be making, how many months will it take you to pay it off?

☐ Do you expect to be able to make any extra payments during the year? Any holiday or birthday money coming in? A potential bonus? Part of a pay raise? Can any of that be put toward this debt?

☐ Determine the date when your first debt will be entirely paid off. Put that date down as a target for this debt, add it to your financial goals, mark it in your calendar, or start a countdown. That will be your debt repayment milestone number 1!

☐ Now decide on the second debt you want to pay off. Remember that while paying off your first debt, you should continue to make the minimum monthly payments on your other debts. Use your online calculator to see how much the outstanding balance on the second debt will be by the time you have paid down your first debt.

- For example, let's say you have a debt of $2,000 that you want to pay off first and another of $5,000 that you want to pay off after, as it has a lower interest rate. You decide to make extra payments on the first debt in order to pay it off in eighteen months. In the meantime, you keep making the minimum contribution to your other debt, which let's say is $50 per month. After eighteen months when you pay off your first debt, the outstanding balance on the second debt will no longer be $5,000 but just over $4,530 (assuming a 6% interest rate). Therefore, in eighteen months you only need to figure out how to pay off $4,530, not $5,000.

☐ Calculate how many months it would take to pay off your second debt if you added the monthly amount you were paying on your first debt to the minimum you're already paying on your second debt. With that, calculate the date when you will be paying off this second debt completely and again add that date to your goals.

☐ To continue with the above example: Once you pay off your first debt, you have not just $50 a month available to pay off your remaining $4,530 balance, but also whatever money you were spending on the first debt (say, for example, $130). So now you have $180 per month available to put toward the balance.

☐ Continue the same process for any other debts you have until you determine the date when you finally pay off your very last debt (excluding your mortgage for now, for more on this see the next step). Note the target date for each debt and make an ever bigger note for the date you pay down your final debt, i.e., when you become debt-free!

☐ During your monthly finance review, check how you are doing with your debt payoff plan and adjust any dates or plans as needed

STEP 44

Pay Off Your Mortgage

If you pay off your mortgage before retirement, you take a huge financial load off your shoulders.
—SUZE ORMAN

DIFFICULTY LEVEL: Medium

OBJECTIVE: Determine your target date to make the last payment on your mortgage

REVIEW TIMES: Biannually

Part of becoming a true financial independence winner is becoming debt-free, as per the previous step. Paying off your mortgage merits its own step, however, because it tends to be different from most other debts, in several ways. Although most people agree that paying off your debts as fast as possible is key to becoming financially independent, opinions differ when it comes to paying off your mortgage.

This step will look at both sides so you can decide for yourself which course to take with your mortgage (provided you have one—otherwise you can skip this step). Whether you consider yourself debt-free only when you have paid off all of your loans—including your mortgage—or whether you don't include your mortgage in this is up to you. There is no consensus over the exact definition of "debt-free."

Reasons NOT to fast-track paying off your mortgage

There are several arguments in favor of not paying off your mortgage aggressively and just sticking to the minimum monthly payments:

- A mortgage is a type of investment because it's used to purchase an asset that will (hopefully) increase in value over time.
- The interest rate on a mortgage is generally a lot lower than other types of debt. Instead of paying off your mortgage faster, it might be more lucrative to invest that extra money, over time potentially giving you bigger returns compared to the interest you would have saved by paying off your mortgage.

Reasons to speed up paying off your mortgage

Arguments in favor of paying off your mortgage as fast as you can include the following:

- A house is not in the same assets class as, for example, stocks and bonds, the latter of which you can easily sell to get money. If you need extra cash or want to use your assets as part of your retirement provision, you are unlikely to simply sell your house to free up some money, something you can do a lot easier with investments such as stocks and bonds. (We will look at this in more detail in Part 8.) You never know when you can sell your house; after all, some houses are on the market for years. Added to that, you can sell as big or small a part of your investment portfolio each time you want to, whereas with your house it's all or nothing (you don't first sell your roof, then your kitchen, and then your basement).

- There are no guarantees that your house will truly increase in value over time or that it will have increased in value by the time you need or want to sell. During the recent housing market crash, many houses were sold below their original purchase price because people simply had to sell.
- Regardless of your house being an investment or not, you are losing money in the form of interest payments. Pay off faster and you stop the money leak of interest on interest on interest being charged on your original loan.
- Finally, with a mortgage you're tied to paying back money all the time. Until you pay off your mortgage, you have a financial obligation that not only might be a psychological commitment, but also means you have less financial freedom.

Paying off a mortgage

One point of caution when it comes to paying off your mortgage: most providers are not so eager for a mortgage to be paid off faster and might include this in the original mortgage agreement. If this is the case you will likely be charged a fee for speeding up paying off your mortgage, meaning it might cost you money to pay off faster. If you decide to pay off your mortgage aggressively, make sure to calculate the fees you'll be charged and how this measures up against the money you'd save by reducing the life span of your mortgage. Consider switching to a different lender that doesn't charge fees to avoid these extra charges, although there will likely be other costs involved for remortgaging, such as exit, valuation, and conveyance fees. Make sure it's worth the extra costs, time, and energy that you spend on this process.

- -

Although you might decide not to pay off your mortgage faster than needed, there is no doubt that as soon as you no longer need to pay your monthly mortgage fees, your monthly expenses will be reduced substantially.

☑ STEP 44 ACTION PLAN

☐ Open up a new spreadsheet in Excel or a similar program or start a new page in your financial notebook. Label it "mortgage overview."

☐ Find your last mortgage statement along with the following details and copy them into the first column of your document. (If you can't find your statement or if it doesn't have all the details, contact your mortgage provider.)

- your starting balance or loan amount
- your annual interest rate
- the date of your first payment
- the total length of time of your mortgage (in years)
- the current balance or amount you still owe

☐ At the top of the second column, write the current month and year and complete each category from the first column with the information.

☐ Find an online mortgage calculator and fill in the specific details of your mortgage. The online mortgage calculator may give you some extra information that you might like to add to your mortgage overview, such as:

- total interest paid until present date
- total principal paid until present date
- expected total interest paid at end of mortgage date
- total interest paid at the end of the mortgage date (This one in particular might be a bit of a shock! This is ultimately one of the ways banks make money.)

☐ Find the option of "making extra payments" in the mortgage calculator and fill in how much you could possibly get together each month or couple of months to throw at your mortgage. If your mortgage is at a low interest rate, this particular loan might be the last one you're tackling anyway. If that's the case, you will have freed up considerable amounts of monthly contributions from your other loans already. Note what happens to your end date and your total interest paid and by how much they go down.

☐ Add this information to your spreadsheet, i.e., in a new column add: "extra monthly/quarterly/annual payment." Write $100 in—we'll start with $100 for now—then create the categories "months saved" and "interest saved," and add the information corresponding to the $100 extra payment.

☐ Repeat this procedure with a higher amount (say $200 or whatever figure you feel might be feasible) and again note down in your spreadsheet or notebook what effect this would have on your mortgage and payments.

☐ Lastly, find and read through the conditions and stipulations of your mortgage, or contact your provider, to find out if there's a fee or forfeit for making extra payments toward your mortgage. Add this information to your spreadsheet. If there is, check whether this fee is significantly more or less than the interest you would save. This will help you decide whether it's worth paying off your mortgage faster.

☐ If you decide to go ahead, schedule an appointment with your bank to discuss details, such as whether you can decide how much extra to pay, how to make the extra payment (transfer, automatic standing order, etc.), and double-checking whether there are any fees involved.

☐ Review this step and the target date once a month to make sure you are on track if and when you start paying down your mortgage faster. If you are not speeding up paying back (yet), you can review this just twice a year.

Checklist Part 4

Use the following checklist to make sure you have done everything in Part 4 and are ready to continue with the next part:

☐ You understand the power of compound interest and have calculated the effects of long-term interest on your savings and your debt.

☐ You know that low monthly payback schemes are a disadvantage long term as they make you pay back for a very long time and also lead to extra interest paid.

☐ You have made a commitment to stop taking on any more debt with a high interest rate (above 5%) and have set guidelines for yourself in which scenarios you can still take out a loan.

☐ You know your credit score and have devised a plan to increase your score.

☐ You have evaluated your credit cards and their outstanding balances, limits, ages, and reward schemes and have decided whether you want to close any cards in order to reduce the temptation or avoid risk of fraud.

☐ You have calculated the effects that extra contributions can have in time and money spent on your loans.

☐ You have decided which debt to start paying off first, based on either the avalanche or snowball method. If you already have your emergency fund saved, you are now making extra payments toward paying off one of your debts, while keeping up minimum payments for your other debts.

☐ You have made a commitment to always save half (or your own specific percentage) of any extra money you receive, be that a one-off in the form of a bonus or tax return, or a more structured influx of funds, such as in the case of a pay increase.

☐ You have set yourself target dates of when you will pay off each individual loan. You know when you're planning on paying off your last loan and thereby becoming completely debt-free.

☐ If you have a mortgage, you have analyzed what a difference extra payments can make on your mortgage costs long term and you've made a decision as to when to pay off your mortgage.

For me, like I think for so many other people, having debt was always a given part of adult life. Everybody I know has debt, mainly from student loans, but a lot of my friends also have car loans and credit card debt. It just seems to be a standard thing in life for most people.

I had no idea how much these loans were costing me. It's a funny thing that if you accept something as normal, you don't make the effort to actually understand it.

Once I worked out how much I am paying in interest, I've made paying off my debts one of my top priorities for this year. I won't be able to pay everything off in just one year, but it has certainly motivated me to find new ways to pay off as fast as I can. I don't want to be tied to these debts for many years to come, as I feel it weighs on me and stops me from becoming financially free.

I've still got a long way to go but now that I've started it keeps getting easier. It really helps to keep track of how much I've paid off as that works as a great motivation to keep it up, even if I feel I'd rather spend my money on something else. A few weeks after I started I created a count down jar: it's a picture of a big jar that fills up a little more every time I make another contribution to my debt. At first I had it on a piece of paper on my wardrobe, but one afternoon I decided to buy chalkboard paint and turn the inside of my bedroom door into a big chalkboard so I could have a huge chalk picture of the jug on it. Now I am reminded of my progress pretty much first thing in the morning and last thing before I go to sleep!

If there's one thing I know for sure, it's that I don't want to take on such huge loans anymore. I'd rather save up first. The only problem I have is that I'll want to buy a house within the next two years, so that will probably mean I'll have to take out a mortgage. But for anything else I purchase, I don't want to borrow any more money!

—Sue Thomas, UK

PART 5

Your Savings

Now that you've started to pay down debt, you probably have become more aware of the need to save up money first before making some purchases, as well as the importance of setting money aside in order to reach your bigger goal of becoming financially independent. Added to that, identifying savings goals can make you feel excited about growing your money, especially if you start picturing what you'll do with that money once you've saved up enough.

In Part 5 of this book, we'll take a closer look at your savings and you'll set some specific savings goals. Some of these will be for the near future while others will be more focussed on establishing more financial security long term. With the help of some practical ideas, you'll be able to set up a solid plan to start saving up for these goals sooner than you think!

STEP 45

Build a
Three-Months-Expenses Fund

*Successful people save in prosperous times so they have
a financial cushion in times of recession.*

—BRIAN TRACY

DIFFICULTY LEVEL: Medium

OBJECTIVE: Build up a cushion worth three
months of expenses to cover a possible
loss of income

REVIEW TIMES: Monthly

 **STAT BOX**

Women in the US have a median of
$2,000 in emergency savings against
$10,000 for men, according to the
2016 Annual Transamerica Retirement
Survey by Transamerica Center.[13]

Once you've built your emergency fund of $1,000
for unexpected or emergency expenses and have
made substantial progress toward paying down
your debts, it's time to continue with a new savings
goal in line with your commitment to reach financial independence. This step looks at the why's and
how's of a three-months-expenses fund, after which
you'll start putting this together.

You can start saving up for this fund when you
have only started paying down your debts, pay off
all your loans completely before saving for this fund,
or find a middle ground such as after paying off your
high-interest debts over 5%.—The right approach
depends on what you feel comfortable with. Factors
such as how likely you are to need a three-months-
expenses fund soon as well as how much interest
you're paying on outstanding loans are some to bear
in mind when making this decision.

A three-months-expenses fund

The rationale behind a three-months-expenses fund
is that it would cover your basic living expenses for
a few months if, for whatever reason, you stopped
receiving an income. This could be because you lost
your job, were unable to work for a certain amount
of time, or voluntarily decided to take time off from
work, perhaps to care for your children or an elderly
parent or because you want to focus on something
else. A three-months-expenses fund would function
as a safety net that tides you over for a couple of
months, after which you hopefully can go back to
work, find a new job, or start generating an income
in a different way.

A three-months fund is a good minimum amount to strive for that will give you enough of a cushion to deal with a loss of income in the short-term, although it would be wise to consider building it up further to a six-months-expenses fund for even more financial security. Considering, however, that getting together enough to even cover three months will probably take you quite a while, I suggest you work toward three months first, then get the rest of your savings and finances sorted before expanding it.

Building up a three-months-expenses fund will likely take you a while. Have another look at some of the ideas mentioned in Step 28 on saving up for an emergency fund. In Part 6, we'll look at different ways to increase your income so you can get this money together faster.

☑ STEP 45 ACTION PLAN

☐ Open a new savings account that is fee-free to keep this money separate from any other savings you have, including your emergency fund.

☐ Decide how fast you'd like to get this fund together: if you have a secure job and income and have no plans to take a break anytime soon, the need to work on this step might be far less urgent than if you're planning to take a few months off work soon or if you fear for the security of your job. Of course you cannot always predict life and a curveball can be thrown your way, so building up this fund in a reasonable amount of time will nearly always be a good idea.

☐ Clarify your target amount for this fund. There are different goals you can set yourself:

- Save three months of essential expenses (i.e., all of the expenses that you could not or would not want to give up).
- Save three months of all your expenses, including any discretionary and savings expenses.
- Save three months of both your own and your partner's expenses or income, in case both of you end up without an income.

☐ Look at your expenses critically: Is there any money you can set aside to allocate to this fund on a regular basis? How are you doing with the cut-down-one-expense challenge? If you've finished building up your emergency fund, your one-month cushion in your regular account, and have paid down some of your main debts, have you freed up any money that can be directed this way?

☐ As before, don't worry if your current contribution is low, even if it's just $10/month. All small things make a difference in the long term. Most times it's better to start even with a very small amount (especially if you're still paying down some high-interest debt) to at least begin.

☐ Keep track of how you're doing on this new goal regularly and review your accomplishments and plan during your monthly review to stay on track.

☐ Work toward building a three-months fund for now, but keep in mind that at a later point you should consider to aim to get to six months, to provide even more security.

Start a Piggy Bank

Try to save something while your salary is small, it's impossible to save after you begin to earn more.
—JACK BENNY

DIFFICULTY LEVEL: Easy

OBJECTIVE: Find a coins jar and regularly deposit spare change to use for savings goal

REVIEW TIMES: Daily / weekly

You might have had a piggy bank at some point in the past, possibly when you were a child, and like most children you might have looked at it in anticipation every time you put in a coin, hoping that single penny would somehow magically fill up the piggy bank to the top . . . or at least get you to your savings goal in order to buy that new toy or video game. As a child, it can be highly enjoyable seeing the stack of coins grow every time.

Yet when we're adults, a piggy bank seems to lose its value, as we now have a bank account to keep our money in, which we might not look at with the same excitement. With our expenses being substantially bigger compared to when we were children, it furthermore seems unlikely that some loose change will get us anywhere close to our financial goals.

The benefits of a piggy bank

Although a piggy bank will indeed not likely make you rich, there are two advantages to having one:

✔ MAKE IT FUN!

Do a fifty-two-week savings challenge. Save $1 in week 1, $2 in week 2, and so on until you save $52 in the last week of the year. Alternately, adapt this to different amounts or challenges. (Try it backward: start saving $52 in week 1 all the way down to $1 in week 52.)

- It builds up a habit of thinking about money: with every coin you put in, you reinforce your determination to get to the goal you're working toward and you reiterate that you're in control.
- It brings you one (however small) step closer to your goal. (And since we like taking small steps here, that idea very much resonates with this journey!)

Maybe your piggy bank will never get you to that goal of hitting $10,000 in your savings account. Nevertheless, every coin you drop in reminds you of that goal and keeps you going. Regardless of how much you save in your piggy, even if it's less than 1% of your target, it will encourage you to find the remaining 99% in other ways.

Set your own contribution rules

The awesome thing with a piggy bank, or basket or mason jar or whatever you fancy using, is that you can decide on the contribution rules yourself. Do you want to empty out your wallet and pockets at the end of each day? Save all $1 bills as soon as you get one handed back in change? Would putting in a daily amount work better for you? Can you use it as your reduce-one-expense-challenge bucket? Or will you come up with your own formula to grow this money?

Deposit your money

If you regularly deposit the money from your piggy bank into your savings account or use it to directly pay down debt or invest in the market, you will see the fruits of your labor paying off as you go. True, it can be a little disappointing having to start all over again every time you empty your piggy bank, but it can also work as a motivation to start again, maybe with an adapted contribution rule.

If you're still putting together your emergency fund, that would be an obvious goal to start with, so when your piggy bank is full, take the money to the bank and deposit it in your account. Or you might be saving for your three-months-expenses fund or something else, be that a vacation, an extra debt payment, or a down payment on a house. Make sure you're clear on what the money will be used for and don't be tempted to use it on a Friday night when you're going out for pizza. . . .

✔ MAKE IT FUN

Spice up your jar and decorate it with ribbons, stickers, spray paint, small photos, or whatever else you can think of to turn it into a beautiful container.

☑ STEP 46 ACTION PLAN

☐ Find an old piggy bank, jar, bucket, tumbler, or anything you can use for this step. Anything will do, so best not to spend $10 on a pretty mason jar if something old that you still have in the kitchen or attic would be totally fine.

☐ Put your container in a prominent place, maybe next to the front door, so that you can see it and are reminded to complete this step as you walk through the door at the end of each day.

☐ Decide what you want to do: Put in $1 every day? Or maybe put in $5 at the end of the week? Alternately, you can decide that you'll put in *any* dollar bills you have at the end of each day, maybe with a maximum daily amount, or to dump in all your pennies, nickels, and quarters daily or weekly.

☐ Figure out what works best for you, playing around with the amount and frequency. You might find you have lots of coins every day and that you're putting in a little bit too much money to keep up with this. Or it might be a little too slow, in which case you could combine two rules: $1 every day and at the weekend any extra dollar bills you still have.

☐ Determine when to empty your container: when you get to $100, after three months, or simply when it's completely full.

☐ Write your goal on a sticker and put it on your piggy bank. Remind yourself with each coin you put in what you're working toward and why. And remember that even if you are still $999,999 away from a million, you just made your first contribution. And every contribution means you're one step closer!

On Inflation and Interest Rates

Inflation is taxation without legislation.

—MILTON FRIEDMAN

DIFFICULTY LEVEL: Difficult

OBJECTIVE: Correct your long-term financial targets for inflation to keep your buying power

REVIEW TIMES: Yearly

We mentioned inflation in some earlier steps and it will come up a few more times in later ones, so it's time to have a closer look at this economic phenomenon. What effect does it have on the economy in general and your personal finances specifically? Let's find out.

Inflation

Inflation is an increase in the prices of goods and services over time, leading to a decrease in the relative value of money. Inflation leads to a situation in which people can buy less for the same amount of money. For example, if you have $1,000, you can buy ten items that cost $100 each today. But if the item's price goes up over the next few years to $110, the $1,000 will only buy you nine items in the future.

Deflation

The opposite of inflation is deflation, with prices dropping and therefore our money increasing in value. Although this might initially sound pretty appealing, a period of deflation is normally a sign of economic recession. Any recession can have a significant impact on your personal finances. When customers know that prices will go down with time and that their money will be worth more tomorrow than today, they hold off on making new purchases or investments. This can lead to a vicious cycle as interest rates on loans drop (see further down as to why), which especially affects big purchases for which people take out loans, such as mortgages. The more people postpone purchases, the more prices drop, and the more interesting it becomes to wait even longer. When people spend less, businesses generate less revenue, and they likely need to cut bonuses, wages, or even jobs. And with employees receiving less money or no longer having a (stable) job, they're less likely to spend.

With less money being spent and more people in unemployment, less tax revenue comes in for the governments but they need more money to pay out in unemployment benefits. This can then lead to a time of austerity, resulting in even less money for the people. When money is no longer flowing, the economy soon becomes unhealthy and stagnant. Nearly everybody will be affected by such a situation as jobs disappear, investment portfolios drop in value, houses sell at lower prices, interest on savings accounts drops, and wages and retirement benefits are frozen.

Effects of inflation

An economy experiencing small inflation levels is usually a sign of a healthy and growing economy. Therefore, economists normally welcome a yearly inflation rate of just under 2%. A relatively stable inflation rate means less insecurity and a solidly growing economy. During times of healthy inflation rates, prices go up slightly each year, meaning it is more interesting to buy today than next year when that new purchase is more expensive. People are happy to spend, businesses can create more jobs, and with that, more money becomes available to be spent again. Governments collect more in taxes and need to spend less on unemployment benefits, meaning more money becomes available to spend again on infrastructure, health care, and education, among others.

In other words, even if it means the value of your money goes down a little each month, inflation at a low rate usually implies a continuously growing, healthy economy.

Additionally, inflation has a small positive effect on the value of debts. An outstanding balance of $10,000 today is more now than in five years when that $10,000 will have experienced value loss and will be worth less in today's money. That said, if the interest rate on the debt is higher than the inflation rate—which will nearly always be the case for most loans—you still want to aim to pay off these debts as soon as possible. The longer you wait with paying off your debts, the more interest accumulates.

Interest rates

Interest rates and inflation are closely connected. By modifying interest rates, inflation can be kept under control. When the economy does well and is growing at a healthy pace, central banks often increase the interest rate. Whenever interest rates increase, it becomes more expensive to borrow money as loans will have higher interest on them, which leads to people borrowing less and therefore spending less money. When they spend less, prices increase less quickly, thereby keeping inflation in check.

But when the economy is not doing so well, banks will often decrease interest rates, making borrowing money more interesting and thereby encouraging people to spend more to get money rolling again. As soon as people start spending again, prices will go up with time, which in turn leads to minimal inflation. This is why even though central banks do not have a direct influence on prices, their control of interest rates allows them to indirectly influence inflation rates to avoid deflation and hyperinflation and stimulate the economy.

Inflation and your money

As mentioned before, economists generally welcome an inflation rate around 2%, although often inflation rates in a healthy economy can be somewhere between 2% and 3%. With a 2% inflation rate, it takes thirty-five years for money to lose half of its buying power, meaning that $10,000 today will be worth the equivalent of $5,000 in thirty-five years. With a 3% inflation rate, it takes just twenty-three years for money to lose 50% of its buying power, and at a 4% inflation rate, this time is reduced to seventeen years. Since inflation rates of a growing economy are usually between 2 and 3%, a good rule of thumb is that money on average loses half its buying power in approximately thirty years.

- -

Inflation rates are difficult to predict, with some years seeing higher and other years lower rates, so your calculations will never be 100% accurate. Having at least some corrections made for inflation is what's most important here. Then, as always, you can keep correcting for this as you continue along your journey to financial freedom.

☑ STEP 47 ACTION PLAN

☐ Pull out your current net worth and net worth targets. You're going to readjust your net worth target for inflation, so you know what your real goals are. Inflation rates change and can never be predicted, but assuming a rate of 2.5–3% is generally safe.

☐ To calculate what your real targets should be by correcting for inflation, take the inflation percentage (say 2.5%), divide it by 100, and subtract that from 1. So for 2.5%, the number will be 0.975. Multiply this number by itself the number of years you're looking into the future. For example, say you want to look twenty-five years into the future. Calculate 0.975^{25}, so 0.975 x 0.975 x 0.975 (until you have that number twenty-five times). You can use your phone's or computer's calculator by activating the advanced options which will likely show the x^y function. Type in 0.975 first, then hit x^y followed by 25 to get the calculation. Alternatively, you can even type into your search engine: "0.975 to the 25th power" to get the answer.

☐ Now divide your target amount by that number to find out how much your target really should be.

   • For example, if your target is to get to a net worth of $500,000 in twenty-five years, correcting for an inflation of 2.5%, the equivalent would be $500,000 / $(0.975)^{25}$= $500,000 / 0.531 = just over $941,000 in twenty-five years. If you didn't correct for inflation and just stuck to the $500,000 you set out to get initially, that money would be worth just over $265,000 in twenty-five years. So even if you reached your target of getting half a million together, it would be worth just over half of what it's worth today.

☐ To make a more conservative estimation, use 3% instead of 2.5%.

☐ Repeat these steps for any other long-term targets you have such as savings, three-months-expenses fund, etc.

☐ When you go through the remaining sections of this book on investments and retirement accounts, remember to also apply this inflation correction when setting your goals.

☐ Look at any monthly contributions you're making at the moment for specific targets and bear in mind you should also increase these contributions in line with the inflation rate in order to stay on track every year. So if you contribute $100 a month to a specific target and the inflation rate is 3%, next year you should look to contribute at least $103 a month.

☐ Any savings such as emergency and three-months-expenses funds you should adjust with inflation at the end of each year, too. Make sure to check the past year's inflation rate and make any contributions to your funds to keep those on par with the current value of your money. If you have an emergency fund of $1,000 and inflation is 3%, then top up your fund with $30 at the end of the year so that it doesn't lose its purchasing power.

Your Savings Rate

Do not save what is left after spending; instead spend what is left after saving.

—WARREN BUFFETT

DIFFICULTY LEVEL: Medium

OBJECTIVE: Calculate your savings rate and set monthly and yearly targets

REVIEW TIMES: Monthly

Why do so many people still have debt, not enough money in their retirement accounts, or no financial plan for their future? Ask anybody you know and a vast majority will say that they just do not make enough money to pay off their debt or to throw at their retirement fund. But even when those same people get a pay raise, chances are they still will not be using that extra money to pay off their debt, nor will they tuck it away and use it to save for later. They will simply spend it on new things and without even realizing it, their lifestyle will gradually inflate to a new level.

Increase your savings

It's easy to focus on finding excuses for not saving enough: "I don't make enough money," "If only I earned another $1,000 a month . . . ," "It's so much easier for my neighbor because he earns a lot more than I do," "I wish I didn't have such a big mortgage, it's a huge expense each month," "I came out of college with a $50,000 debt," "I have two young children—do you know how expensive they are?" . . . and the list goes on.

Instead of waiting for that miraculous moment when you suddenly earn more, spend less, and are in no other way hindered to invest in your financial future, this step will let you take the reins to speed up your savings goals. (These goals are not just savings in a savings account, but can also include investments, contributions to your retirement account, or your debt reduction payments.)

Your savings rate

While your level of income and your expenses are without a doubt important factors in your path to financial independence and other financial goals, there is a third combined factor that is arguably even more important: your savings rate.

Your savings rate is the proportional amount of your income that you're able to save monthly, i.e., your savings expenses divided by your total income. If you make $2,000 and manage to save $200 per month, your savings rate is 10%.

Interestingly, if you earn more, you might not necessarily be saving more. If your neighbor makes twice as much money and takes home $4,000 per month but only saves $200, his savings rate is only 5%. You would be surprised at how often people with higher incomes have shockingly low savings rates. Why? Because of lifestyle inflation (see Step 21). They earn more so they buy a bigger house, a bigger car, go on a more luxurious vacation, and get more expensive clothes and gadgets for their kids.

Now guess who has the financial advantage

between you and your neighbor? All other factors—such as debt and the availability of an emergency fund—being equal, it would be you, of course. Imagine you both lost your jobs and had the same $20,000 in savings to tide you over until you found a new job. Because you are used to spending far less than your neighbor, you would last a lot longer. Without changing your expenses, the $20,000 would last you eleven months (at $1,800 a month), as you can see in Table 9, whereas your neighbor would see the end of those $20,000 after just over five months, as he currently spends $3,600 a month.

The double advantage of your savings rate

The good news about your savings rate is that by focusing on improving it, two major things happen:

1. you stash away more money, meaning you reach your savings goal faster;
2. you need less to live off, meaning your savings goal can be lower.

If we go back to the example where you earn $2,000 and manage to hit a 10% savings rate, it means that you spend $1,800 each month and save (or invest) $200. Now let's imagine that for the next year you aim to get to a 20% monthly savings rate. Instead of spending $1,800, you now manage to live off only $1,600 per month, and you have doubled your monthly savings from $200 to $400!

Assume that you're going to set up your own company and that you're building a six-months-expenses fund to function as a financial cushion in case you don't bring in any money for the first half year.

- If you had continued to live off $1,800 a month, you would have needed $1,800 x 6 = $10,800 in your six-month fund. By setting aside $200 monthly, this would take you fifty-four months or four and a half years, as you can see in Table 10.
- With your new goal to spend just $1,600, your six-months fund would need less money: $1,600

✔ **MAKE IT FUN**

One way to increase your savings is by doing a "Save the Change" challenge. Round up any purchase you make to the nearest dollar and save the difference. For example, if you buy something for $2.39, round up to $3, then set aside the remaining $0.61. There are even apps such as Acorns, Digit, or Chime Bank's app that can directly transfer the difference into a savings or investment account.

x 6 = $9,600. Setting aside $400/month, twice as much money as before, it takes you only two years (twenty-four months) to get this money together, i.e., less than half the amount of time!

You might have realized by now that your savings rate as calculated by savings expenses divided by income is essentially the 20 (or whatever number you adjusted it to) in the 50/20/30 budgeting rule (see Step 31). By increasing your savings rate, you reduce the amount of time needed to achieve your goal—first because you set aside more money, and second because you simply need less to live on and therefore have a lower target to work toward.

Becoming aware of your savings rate will greatly improve your financial situation and speed up your savings goals over the next few years. Remember that the more you set aside, the less you need to live off, and the less you need to set aside to reach financial independence!

Table 9: How long a $20,000 fund would last at different savings rates

	Monthly earning	Savings rate	Monthly savings	Monthly spending	Time $20,000 would last
You	$2,000	10%	$200	$1,800	11 months
Neighbor	$4,000	5%	$200	$3,800	5 months

Table 10: Building a six-months-expenses fund at different savings rates

	Monthly saving	Monthly spending	Six-months fund	Time to build fund
10% SR	$200	$1,800	$10,800	54 months
20% SR	$400	$1,600	$9,600	24 months

Note: SR = savings rate.

☑ STEP 48 ACTION PLAN

☐ You can calculate your savings rate in different ways, so you need to carefully decide what you see as your real savings for each month. If you're simply looking at the amount of money you did not spend this month, you might get a disfigured picture. What if those $20 you have left over this month you simply spend on the first day of next month? Was that a real saving or a delayed expense?

☐ Look carefully at your money and budget and decide which dollars to include in your calculation, such as:

- Retirement account contributions
- Mortgage and debt payments
- Investments
- Savings account contributions

☐ It can also be arbitrary whether or not to include your savings account contributions if (some of) that money is already earmarked for a very specific short-term goal, such as a vacation or new laptop. It doesn't really matter whether you include this as long as you're consistent whenever you calculate your savings rate.

☐ Total the amounts for any contributions you make to saving accounts, debt payments, and any other strategy to grow your money, then divide that by your total monthly income to get your savings rate for that particular month.

☐ Continue calculating for a few months back if you have full expense patterns to see how much it fluctuates over time.

☐ Calculate your savings rate at the end of each month to closely monitor this rate over time.

☐ Now that you know the importance of your savings rate and how increasing it can benefit you in two ways, set yourself an overall yearly savings rate target to get to by next year (aiming to gradually increase your rate) and add this to your yearly budget.

☐ Now set yourself a target for your savings rate for the next month based on this yearly target and adjust your budget if needed.

☐ Calculate how different savings rates affect your savings goals differently. Start with your three-months-expenses fund and calculate how a higher savings rate would reduce your total annual expenses and therefore reduce the capital needed for this fund. Do the same for any other goals you might have set yourself.

☐ Work out how much longer or shorter it would take you to get to that capital depending on different savings rates, although remember that both inflation and interest will affect these calculations in the long run.

Set Your Savings Goals

One way to keep momentum going is to have constantly greater goals.
—MICHAEL KORDA

DIFFICULTY LEVEL: Medium

OBJECTIVE: Set your savings goals and start contributing toward them

REVIEW TIMES: Monthly

In addition to the savings goal of putting together a three-months-expenses fund, you will probably want to set yourself some other savings targets, whether you start working toward them now or at some point in the future when you have reached some of your earlier financial objectives. At the beginning of this book in Step 4, you might have set yourself some savings goals that you can look at here to adapt or incorporate into your long-term savings plan.

Setting savings goals

When setting yourself savings goals, you likely end up identifying different goals with different time frames. I recommend identifying goals in the following categories:

- Short-term goals. Examples include saving up for a vacation, a new phone, or your wedding. These goals usually take around one to two years to achieve.
- Midterm goals. This category includes saving up for buying a new (secondhand?) car or a down

payment on a house, or planning ahead for future children, for example. These goals take roughly three to ten years to achieve depending on the amount you need and how much you manage to set aside each month.
- Long-term goals. Any savings goal that takes more than ten years falls into this category. Think of saving up money to fund your child's college or for your retirement.

How to prioritize goals

Whether you will be contributing to these goals at the same time or whether you want to first complete one goal before moving on to the next depends entirely on you and how important each savings goal is for you. Any long-term goals of course benefit more from compounding interest the sooner you start making contributions, so even if you're able to assign just a small amount of money to these goals on a regular basis, they'll start growing more and more with time. Consider setting up a yearly guideline for your savings in which you divide your savings budget between your various targets. For example, you could assign 45% for short-term goals, 30% for midterm goals, and 25% for long-term goals.

Having your goals written out can be exciting, especially once you see your money beginning to grow with every contribution you and the bank—through interest payments—make. Most likely, once you become more serious about your savings goals, there will be times you wish you had more money available to assign to your goals to speed up the process. To help with that, the next part of this book will look at your income in closer detail and identify ways to start making more money.

☑ **STEP 49 ACTION PLAN**

☐ Brainstorm savings goals in all three categories (short, mid, and long term). You might come up with way too many of them, which is okay. For now just write them all down even if you will not be able to work on them all.

☐ Once you have all your ideas down on paper, look back at your notes from Step 8 and identify any you can add to your list. Or, if you no longer see them as important, leave them out.

☐ Identify your most important goals: Which ones do you definitely need or want to set? Which ones are nonessential ones, i.e., great if you manage to save up for, but not absolutely needed?

☐ For your most important goals, assign a timeline or number of years in which you would like to get the money together.

☐ Estimate how much you need to save for each of your essential goals.

☐ Determine how many goals you want to work on at the same time. This might be anything from all of them to none of them if you are still making major debt repayments or contributions to your emergency or three-months-expenses fund.

☐ Decide how much of your monthly savings contributions you can assign to each goal. This could be a set amount or a percentage of the monthly savings amount you have available.

☐ Remind yourself of your savings goals and add ways to keep track of your progress, such as adding your goal to a Post-it you see every day or creating a track-your-progress poster.

☐ Set up a new savings account for each goal or alternatively earmark your money in your savings account clearly so you know exactly how much money you have available for each.

☐ As part of your monthly finance review, check how much money you contributed and update your log or tracker.

☐ Twice a year, review your goals to make sure they're up to date, and adjust amounts and also monthly contribution targets. If needed, add new goals to start saving up for, and set dates for when you'd like to start these in your calendar.

STEP 50

Save and Spend on YOU

> *You can only become truly accomplished at something you love. Don't make money your goal. Instead, pursue the things you love doing, and then do them so well that people can't take their eyes off you.*
> —MAYA ANGELOU

DIFFICULTY LEVEL: Easy

OBJECTIVE: Identify a small personal reward and start saving up for it

REVIEW TIMES: Every two–three months

Unlike the rest of the 100 steps, this step advocates a little extra spending—on yourself in particular—instead of cutting down your expenses. Although some of it might sound as if it takes you away from your ultimate goal of a secure financial future, it is indeed a very important step on your journey. The habit of budgeting and saving to spend on *you* leads to small rewards that remind you of what's important and why you're going through the hassle of the other steps.

Budgeting and frugality

Once you really get into personal finance and see the advantages of building up savings and investing, it can become very tempting to try to cut down all of your expenses as much as possible, skimping and saving and living a life of extreme frugality. Of course, there's nothing wrong with being frugal and some people get real satisfaction out of it—but others end up taking it to an extreme level, making themselves unhappy in the process. They eventually

end up giving up on their journey to financial independence, or they become unhappy and disgruntled as they feel they can no longer enjoy life and instead are only thinking about "tomorrow," "a secure financial future," and "being cheap" instead of living in the now and enjoying life as it is.

Spend on YOU

To reward yourself for your hard work and keep the enjoyment of life at the center of your quest, you are going to do some carefully planned spending on yourself from now on as a compulsory part of your savings budget. The journey to financial independence should be fun! This step is meant to keep your motivation up, experience short-term results, and simply reward yourself now and again. Budgeting and spending on yourself, ideally on something you otherwise would not purchase or do, is a great way to achieve all of the above.

Some examples of how you can spend a little extra on yourself might include:

- A lunch out in a restaurant that is special to you
- A new magazine or book
- A new accessory or gadget
- A special item of clothing that's outside of your clothing budget
- Luxury bath or shower products or makeup
- A new plant or some flowers for your home

- A massage or beauty treatment
- An afternoon on your own or with a friend to have a coffee, go to the movies, or visit a museum

It can be anything that gives you some special joy and happiness and that feels like a little splurge. You're looking for something you'd like to buy for yourself but that you don't normally do. Plan on two or three months to put that money together, so you really feel you have earned it and built up anticipation. It should be something relatively common and easy to acquire. It's not a savings goal in itself; it's more like a kitty with some money you set aside each month so you can buy something with it every so often.

Just one warning: Whatever you buy, it should be something for *you*. Buying your child a new toy or your partner a surprise present might make you happy, but that does not qualify as spending on you. Some people find it difficult to spend a little extra on themselves, but the whole point of this step is to allow *you* to indulge a little and appreciate the progress *you* have made. If you can't resist the urge to buy something for somebody else, then budget accordingly now and again and buy them something, too. But never buy for others instead of for yourself.

Don't feel guilty for spending this money. Life is to be lived, and the small pleasures in life form an important part in this. So don't avoid spending this money just because it's a luxury. You have worked hard enough to earn and save this money—you're allowed something extra! Then when you purchase and use the item, simply enjoy it, feel proud of your progress, and celebrate your journey to financial independence and how far you have already come.

☑ STEP 50 ACTION PLAN

☐ Brainstorm ideas on your ideal reward, something that would give you pleasure and a sense of achievement every time you were able to use it or purchase it. Ideally it would be:

- something that's not a long-term savings goal, as the whole point here is that you get more regular small rewards; and
- something for which you can set aside $5–20 each month and be able to buy after two or three months of saving.

☐ Create a separate kitty, find a nice jewelry box, or be creative and make your own container where you put the money (if you decide to set aside cash). Alternatively, assign the money to this category in your budget and withdraw it from your regular account when you need it.

☐ As soon as you have enough to buy something, go out and buy it! You want to see the advantages of setting money aside and planning your budget, but without having to wait twenty years to collect your prize.

Checklist Part 5

Use the following checklist to make sure you've done everything in Part 5 and are ready to continue with the next part:

☐ You have opened another new savings account to start building a three-months-expenses fund. You have started making (small) contributions toward this fund.

☐ You have an old jar, box, or tin (a piggy bank) in which you regularly deposit spare coins or change and that will be used for a specific savings goals.

☐ You have corrected your long-term financial goals for inflation rates and made any adjustments at the end of each year, such as adding a little extra to your emergency fund, to ensure it doesn't lose purchasing power.

☐ You understand how increasing your savings rate speeds up your journey to financial independence and you have reviewed your current savings rate and set yourself targets.

☐ You have set yourself short-term, mid-term, and long-term savings goals and are making (small) contributions to those you've prioritized, or you know when you'll be able to start working toward them depending on other financial targets you're focusing on.

☐ You have several ideas on how to spend some money on yourself and are working toward implementing one of these ideas in the next two to three months.

I've always saved money, but my usual way of saving has been to put money away without really knowing what I was saving for. Because I was saving without goals, I'd find myself feeling guilty any time I dipped in to use my savings, even if it was something I thought I should use my savings for.

I wanted to change this and so have been trying to save for specific goals, while also putting a smaller amount away that is to be left untouched, for future unknown savings needs. This is especially important for me as an Irish person living in Spain, as any trip to see family and friends is a considerable expense with travel and costs, and needs to be saved for. I didn't want my reluctance to use my savings to stop me from spending time with my loved ones—nor did I want it to prevent me from taking full advantage of life in a sunny, beautiful country!

Because when I save for specific goals I can see clearly how my savings are helping to impact my life in a positive way (holidays, spending quality time doing events, meals, etc., with friends and family), I don't feel guilty when I use it. Whereas before, I would be reluctant to use my savings for anything, saving for specific things has really encouraged me to have a better attitude toward money. I've realized that having two ways of saving, for both the long run to be kept untouched and short-term goals to use as I see fit, has a much more positive impact on my life, and attitude to finances.

—Jenny Galligan, Ireland/Spain

PART 6

Your Income

Until now, you've made great progress in the areas of your savings, your debt, and reducing your spending in order to increase your cash flow and net worth on your way to financial independence. By putting extra money toward your long-term financial goals, you are slowly but steadily building a secure financial future.

We are now moving away from the areas of debt and savings to focus on something completely different: your income. By analyzing your income and identifying opportunities to increase this, you can speed up the journey to financial independence even more.

In this part of the book you'll learn more about the different possible income streams that exist and you'll be guided through the process of formulating an income plan to further increase your earnings.

STEP 51

Multiple Income Streams

Invest in yourself. Your career is the engine of your wealth.
—PAUL CLITHEROE

DIFFICULTY LEVEL: Medium

OBJECTIVE: Learn about the seven income streams and calculate how much you currently generate from each

REVIEW TIMES: Biannually

The vast majority of people see income as the money they get from their job. While this is generally a relatively secure way to guarantee a steady and satisfactory income, it does not have to be your only way of bringing in money.

The seven types of income

There are in fact seven (!) different types of income. While each source has its own benefits and disadvantages, there is a strong argument for building so-called multiple income streams over time. This not only gives greater security and protection against financial adversity, but can also provide more long-term satisfaction, as it gives you an opportunity to generate additional income in areas you feel particularly passionate about.

Here are the seven different income streams:

1. EARNED INCOME FROM A JOB

Earnings from working either in your own company or for someone else. This income stream is generally based on getting paid for your time.

2. PROFIT

Money you make by selling products or services as part of a business activity at a higher price than the cost price.

3. INTEREST INCOME

Income you get from lending money to others, such as to a bank, the government, or through investments like crowdfunding.

4. CAPITAL GAINS

Money you receive as a result of selling something that you acquired at a much cheaper price than what you are selling it for.

5. DIVIDEND INCOME

Income from stocks if the company whose shares you own makes a profit they can pay out.

6. ROYALTIES

Money you receive on products you've made or from franchises of your brand.

7. RENTAL INCOME

The money you collect from renting out assets that you own (usually property).

Most people consider the first type of income—a wage from a job—as the main and only source of income they will ever acquire or can rely on sufficiently. Very few people look beyond this stream of income as a possible way of building more earnings.

Trading time for money

The key feature of earned income is "trading your time for money." Incidentally, this is also one of the main reasons why people get dissatisfied with their jobs and start looking for financial independence: they want to stop giving up their time in exchange for money and instead free up time without having to worry about money. They have come to realize that while you cannot make more time, you can always make more money, and they are therefore looking for ways to move away from relying solely on income stream 1 to other sources of income in which they might need to invest less time to generate the same income, thereby creating a passive income stream.

Pursuing other income streams

Of course, you don't need to pursue all streams of income, but what's especially useful is the realization that money doesn't have to come from just your job and that there are many ways to supplement (and with time maybe even replace) your income.

Some of these streams are easier to achieve, either in time, risk, or start-up capital. Some are an active income source, others are a passive stream, and some are in between (where you put in a lot of time at first but hardly any after a while). Some have a nearly limitless income (think of famous pop stars and the royalties they receive) and others a limited amount (there's unfortunately an upper limit to the time you have available to trade in for money because there are only so many hours in a week).

In the next few steps, we're going to look at all of the above-mentioned income streams in detail to find out more about each stream and to identify whether these might be a possible income for you to work toward. We'll start simple and create an overview of all that you already receive in each of these areas.

- -

In all likelihood, there will be quite a few categories on which you score a whopping $0. If that is the case, don't worry! In fact, I hope this is the case because it means the next seven steps will still be relevant to you and will show you where you might want to develop more income (which most likely is not from all seven of them anyway!).

☑ **STEP 51 ACTION PLAN**

☐ Get your notepad out or open your Excel spreadsheet or Evernote document and list the seven income categories.

☐ Next to each category, indicate your current monthly (average) income.

☐ Once you start actively building one or more new income streams, update these numbers every six months to register your progress.

STEP 52

Income Stream 1: Earned Income

Opportunity is missed by most people because it is dressed in overalls and looks like work.

—THOMAS EDISON

DIFFICULTY LEVEL: Medium

OBJECTIVE: Analyze the likelihood of earning more through your earned income

REVIEW TIMES: Yearly

In these next seven steps, we're going to look at each of the seven income streams in turn to analyze opportunities to further develop each possible source of income. You shouldn't feel that you need to take action in all seven areas, though. Instead, the main purpose is to make you aware of each income source so you can decide whether to focus on any of these to make some additional money.

Earned income from a job

The first income stream is your earned income. Most people get this from working for somebody else either salaried or as a freelancer, although if you are an entrepreneur you might also receive a regular wage if you're on your own company's payroll.

A key feature of earned income is nearly always that you're paid for your time, be that time you spend in the office, working from home, networking at conferences, traveling to meetings with clients,

or whatever your job requires you to do. Generally speaking, the more you work, the more you get paid: if you go from part-time to full-time, if you work extra hours, or if you take on a management role that requires more time (as well as extra responsibilities, experience, and whatever else), you usually get paid more, while the opposite is true if you cut your hours.

Relying on earned income as your main source of income tends to give you financial security (up to a certain extent, of course, as one can always lose their job due to various reasons) as well as financial comfort to pay for your expenses. Added to that, jobs can give a sense of satisfaction as your professional rewards feed a passion or feeling of commitment. In the action plan following, we're going to look at how to earn even more money through your job.

Before doing anything with the answers and thoughts following the action plan below, the next few steps will first go through the other six income streams before deciding which of these possible extra income generators will get your definitive attention for now.

According to the U.S. Bureau of Labor Statistics, the median gross weekly earning of full-time workers in the US was $876 in the second quarter of 2018. Divided by gender, this was $780 for women and $959 for men.[14]

☑ STEP 52 ACTION PLAN

If you have your own company, when completing the steps below, you should only look at the salaried wage you receive—for example, if you're paid a set monthly rate each month. If you have (additional) earnings from your company from profits (based purely on the month's or quarter's sales) or from shares that you have in that company, leave those out here as they'll come up in subsequent steps. If you are getting both a salary *and* a profit income, then only take your salary into account here and leave the profit analysis until later.

Similarly, if you have more than one wage—for example, if you're working more than one job—consider each separately for the questions below, as they might generate different answers.

With any big changes when working toward an increase in salary, always ask yourself the question, Would it be worth it? Think about this not just in terms of money (i.e., you might earn an extra $100 per month if you took a class to become more qualified), but also the invest-ment required: How much does the course cost? How much time would you need to put in before even getting the raise? What would you have to sacrifice to do the class, and is that time you currently spend on your family, friends, hobbies, sports? Would it affect your job satisfaction? Nothing comes for free, so if you took a class, it would likely have an effect on other areas of your life. Ask yourself the same if you're looking to earn more through a pro-motion. Would you need to work more hours? Would it be worth sacrificing even just a little bit of your relationship with your significant other, friends, children, and so on for this promo-tion and extra wage?

Now grab a pen and paper or access your digital file and write down your answers or thoughts on the following points. (If you don't currently have a job, answer these questions for your ideal job and/or your last job, then use that to decide on the type of job you might want to pursue.)

☐ How much do you earn a month? If your income varies: What is your average and your minimum monthly wage?

☐ How do you think your wage will develop over time?

☐ Do you get a pay raise every year? If so, how much?

☐ Do you get any bonuses? If so, how much?

☐ Have your raises or bonuses recently increased or decreased? Might your raises or bonuses be affected by recent company developments (from growths, cuts, or merging companies or departments)?

☐ Do you think you'll start working more or less hours in the near future?

☐ Is your company laying off people? Might you lose your job?

☐ Are you likely to get or are you working toward a promotion? How would that affect your salary? Would that be worth it? (Bear in mind the extra time you might be expected to put in, travels you might have to make, training or conference commitments that might be involved, etc.)

☐ How happy are you with what you earn? Most people will nearly always say they want to make more money, but do you really? Why? What would you do with it? Or are you already comfortable enough with what you get? If you'd like to earn more, how much would you want that to be?

☐ Is there anything you can do to increase your salary?

- Can you take classes or complete a course to learn specific skills or knowledge? Would it be worth it?
- Can you talk to your manager to discuss a pay raise? Have you formulated strong reasons to back up your request?
- Can you do something that would make you more valuable and indispensable to the company so you can start building a case for a pay raise? Would that course of action be worth it?

☐ Do you want to consider looking for a job in a different department/company to increase your wage? Would it be worth it?

☐ Are you considering a completely different career path and corresponding salary? What would you need to do to achieve this?

☐ Can you start something on the side to supplement your salary, i.e., take up some extra hours once a week in a different job?

Income Stream 2: Profit Income

I'm a great believer in luck and I find the harder I work the more I have of it.
—THOMAS JEFFERSON

DIFFICULTY LEVEL: Medium

OBJECTIVE: Analyze the possibility of earning extra money through setting up your own company

REVIEW TIMES: Yearly

A profit income is the money you get if you have a company (which can be anything from an Etsy shop where you sell handmade crafts to a multinational company) or sell your products or services above the cost price and take (some of) the profits as personal earnings (which is not your regular wage; see Step 52). A profit income is often based on the amount of profit made during a certain time period, and is the total amount of money that's come in minus your total amount of expenses.

Having your own company

Many people dream about having their own company, and although this often sounds like a fantasy situation, being an entrepreneur also requires a lot of hard work, and it can take a substantial amount of time before a company starts making a profit. It also involves learning many new skills, a considerable amount of risk, and a lot of perseverance, so the life of an entrepreneur is not always as rosy as it might seem. Therefore, making a profit income is not nearly as straightforward as it sounds.

But if and when you do manage to make your company successful, apart from the satisfaction and sense of achievement, it might also mean you can take (part of) the profits as an extra income. With time, you might even be able to step out a little bit from the day-to-day functioning of the business, if that's what you want (although you might not want to!) and let others do the work for a salary while you take some of the profits as an income—turning it more into a passive income.

Depending on the type of company you have, how much profit is actually being made, and the number of owners and employees, this can be more or less straightforward—although, again, it is neither guaranteed nor easily achieved. But all in all, having your own business is certainly a possible way of making (extra) money that can provide higher future earnings than a regular job.

Do you want to be an entrepreneur?

Though many people might say they want to have their own business, maybe this isn't actually something that *you* want? It's beyond the scope of this book to talk about the ins and outs of setting up and running your own company, but from a practical point of view, you first need to know whether having your own (side) business is something that attracts you in order to supplement or replace your current income.

There are many different types of companies one can have, from a one-person part-time operation to a much bigger company, though the latter is not necessarily better or more effective at giving you a higher or more stable income and more satisfaction. Let's weigh your options.

I'm not advocating setting up your own company, as this definitely is not for *everybody and the income might take years to start coming in. That said, and regardless of the enjoyment of being able to shape the course of your own company, it can certainly be a good way to make a living, whether that income is coming solely from your company or it's to supplement current income from your paid job.*

☑ STEP 53 ACTION PLAN

If you consider starting your own company and feel this might be something you want to do—to be your own boss and in control of decisions as well as your income stream—then think about some of the following:

☐ Do you like crafting, or do you have other creative skills? Could you potentially open an online shop on Etsy or somewhere else? This could be anything from jewelry to clothes, dolls, art, decoration, pet supplies, furniture, etc.

☐ Do you have any particular skill you can make profitable by setting up your own company? Think about selling your services online, tutoring, or designing courses.

☐ Would you want to set up a specific company that markets a particular service? Think about a dog-walking service, a design company, a restaurant, or a software company.

☐ Let your creative ideas flow and think of possibilities based on your skills, experience, and interest. Is there anything else you can make or deliver that you can turn into a successful venture?

Income Stream 3: Interest Income

A penny saved is a penny earned.
—BENJAMIN FRANKLIN

DIFFICULTY LEVEL: Medium

OBJECTIVE: Find out the possibility to increase the amount of interest income you generate

REVIEW TIMES: Yearly

In the previous two steps, you thought about your first income stream, which was a salary coming from a paid job, as well as the possibilities of a second income stream in the form of profit income. For most people, either of these might be their main and only income stream and they might never have thought of the option of developing other sources of income. Yet there are five more possible ways to generate an income. Even though you don't need to pursue them all, there might be one or two that could supplement your earnings and profits.

Interest from savings

A third income stream is interest from money lent out. Whenever you borrow money, this generally costs money, as we saw in previous steps, in the form of interest. Similarly, you might also be lending money out through a savings account. By parking your money at the bank, you are lending this

money out to the bank for them to use. That's why the bank is paying you interest on your money. Now you might wonder why your bank would care about the measly $1,000 or even less that you have in your account. The answer is simple: you're not the only person with savings at the bank. If there are twenty people like you, that makes $20,000 for the bank to use. And for two thousand people with savings like yours, the bank suddenly has access to $2,000,000! The interest the bank pays you on this money is far lower than what they'd pay if they borrowed that same amount from the central bank, yet with that $2,000,000 they can provide many a lender with loans at 14% or higher interest rates. So even if each of their customers only has a small amount of savings, as you can see, every little bit helps!

Bonds

Another way of lending out money is through bonds. We'll be looking at this in more detail in Part 8, but as an overview: with bonds, you lend money to an entity (organization or government) in exchange for interest. Bonds tend to have higher interest rates than savings accounts as the risk of losing some of that money is higher with bonds. So in order to reward you for the extra risk, you receive more interest, which makes bonds an attractive way to generate interest income.

Crowdfunding

In recent years, crowdfunding initiatives have become increasingly popular as an alternative way to raise money for a new business idea. With a crowdfunding project, ordinary people contribute money, from relatively small sums of $50 or even less, against an interest rate to help fund a start-up or business idea. Depending on the conditions, interest payments to the company's investors might not start until two years later, or until the company starts making a certain profit, so the income from this source might not be as straightforward. Not all start-ups make it till the end of their first year, however, meaning you might never see (part of) your money back. But due to all these increased risks, the interest rate on crowdfunding opportunities is again generally higher than in a regular savings account. We'll look at crowdfunding in more detail in Step 79.

Interest income

Now to go back to having savings money in the bank: unfortunately that $1,000 you have at the current 0.5% interest rate is never going to make you big bucks. It will give you exactly $5 gross on a yearly basis. Depending on where you live and how much you earn, you will likely need to pay income tax on this, too, so you'll end up with about $3–4 a year. That certainly won't make you rich, especially not once inflation catches up and indeed overtakes the interest rate.

But this step is not so much about using this stream to become rich, but to review interest as a possible way of generating more income. For a moment, imagine that instead of $1,000 you have $1,000,000 in your bank account (a big jump, I know, but just play along for now!). Instead of getting $5 gross in interest, you would be receiving $5,000. That is suddenly a bit more interesting (although I admit when you have a million dollars, $5,000 might not seem like much). Let's assume now that the 0.5% interest rate goes up to 3% in a few years. That would suddenly bump up the interest received to $30,000 gross a year, which is the equivalent of a monthly gross income of $2,500. Not so bad now!

Long-term potential

Although with the current low interest rates, you'd need a *lot* of money to get any worthwhile earnings on your savings, and although this income is very unpredictable due to the fluctuation of those interest rates, it is certainly worth remembering that interest income is another possible way to make some money, especially if you let it compound over the years. Average bond returns are often around 4%, and crowdfunding interest ranges between 3% and 8%—so you can see that interest income has a potential to generate an income if you lend out your money in this way.

Another big advantage of interest income is that it's a passive income stream, i.e., you don't have to do much to get the money, apart from your regular checks on your savings, bonds, or crowdfunding investments and setting up (automatic) payments into your savings plans.

Whether you have a big interest income or not (yet), remember that instead of taking these earnings out of your account, a much more powerful way of building up even more money is to leave it where it is and let it accumulate through compounding interest. In that way, the money grows even more over time, giving you bigger savings and ultimately even more income.

☑ STEP 54 ACTION PLAN

☐ Review how much you're currently earning in interest from:
- Your savings account
- Bonds and CDs (credit deposits)
- Crowdfunding

☐ How much money are you able to deposit into your savings account every month, and how does this affect your interest generated?

☐ Calculate a few years ahead (use an online calculator) to see how much interest you'll receive if you keep up with your current monthly payments. What if you were able to increase these contributions? Of course, you don't know how interest rates will develop over time, but since this is a relatively safe way of making some money, how much (if any) might you want to add to your interest-generating assets and investments?

☐ After finding out more about bonds in Steps 68 and 69, come back to this step and determine your strategy when it comes to investing in bonds.

☐ Once you've read more about crowdfunding in Step 79, look into this as a possible way of lending out (more) money to get interest in return. Determine whether this might be something for you.

Income Stream 4: Capital Gains

Formal education will make you a living, self-education will make you a fortune

—JIM ROHN

DIFFICULTY LEVEL: Medium

OBJECTIVE: Discover whether pursuing capital gains might be a possible income generator

REVIEW TIMES: Yearly

The fourth type of income stream is income from capital gains, which can turn into a key source of income, although in many cases one needs substantial amounts of time to develop this type of earnings.

Capital gains

Capital gains are the profits one makes when selling assets at a higher price than the original purchase price. This is especially common with real estate; for example, if you bought your house for $200,000 and sold it for $220,000, this would result in a $20,000 capital gain. Other assets such as antiques, art, and stocks can increase greatly in value over time and provide the seller with capital gains. Interestingly, most legislation also recognizes the profit made from the sale of gifted and inherited items as capital gains in the same way, even if you were not the one who paid for them originally.

Although income from capital gains and income from profit can seem very similar, the difference between these two is that profit income comes from products or services you produced, created, or offered over substantial periods as part of your regular business activity, whereas a capital gain generally is not the result of normal business, but rather involves an original investment that increased in value.

Capital losses

Whereas capital gains involve an increase in the value of an asset, conversely there is also something known as capital losses, when something is sold for less than the original price. This is unfortunately not uncommon, especially when there's a market crash and people sell their assets, particularly stocks, at bargain prices. Similarly, this can also happen on the housing market. In recent years, we've seen that the once popular belief that a house is always a good investment and can only ever increase in value is not always a reality, as many have experienced firsthand.

Capital gains and time

Generally speaking, assets do not normally appreciate (or increase) in value overnight. A key factor needed for capital gains to develop is time (with the exception being assets purchased cheaply, renovating or fixing them, and then selling them at a profit). One important aspect of a capital gain, therefore, is to analyze whether it was worth the time, money, original investment, and risk or insecurity that came with it. Not all capital gains are equal.

Assuming you sell your house at a price that's $30,000 above the price that was paid for it (which on paper sounds pretty awesome), let's also take into consideration the following possible factors:

- You already moved to your new house several months ago, meaning you've been paying two mortgages at the same time. Maybe you even had to take out a higher mortgage for your second house than your original plan, as you didn't yet have the money from your other house available to use as a down payment, or maybe you had to eat into your savings to get the money together.
- The $30,000 most likely will not be cash in hand as you probably will be charged capital gains taxes on this.
- What if you bought the house thirty years ago? That $30,000 profit you made is not actually the same if you take into consideration inflation and the fact that money loses approximately half its value every thirty years.
- What about the emotional side of the sale? You and your family might have been quite worried about this house in the last few months: What if it took another year to sell? Did you have to take down the price from your original asking price? Were you worried about having to pay for it for another year or even more?

The potential of capital gains

All of these notes of caution aside, capital gains can definitely provide a great and fairly passive way to make money, be that with real estate, antiques, or on the stock market. There are years when the stock market goes up more than 10%. A long-term average of 7–8% is a good rough estimation, which is an appealing (though absolutely not guaranteed) income source for those who are able and willing to put some money in. With these rates, it only takes roughly ten years for your investments to double in value, and if you have even more time than that, you'll likely see your investments grow significantly, giving you a great source of income in the form of capital gains when you sell. (For more on investing, refer to Part 8.)

All in all, capital gains are an attractive way to make money, but whether that's through property, stocks, or other assets, it's never risk-free, because you can't predict how time will affect the value of your investments. For every person who tells you they made a lot of money on the stock market or housing market, you can likely find somebody who has experienced the opposite.

Generating income through capital gains can be a profitable way to make money, although it can also be very unreliable and is not without risk. As the assets require time to increase in value, it's difficult to plan too far into the future, as one never really knows what tomorrow will bring and sometimes you can actually sustain a capital loss. Relying on making money in this way is therefore unpredictable. At the same time, it has a lot of potential, making it attractive for many.

☑ STEP 55 ACTION PLAN

☐ If you already have assets you might be able to sell at a higher price than what you bought them for, make a list and see how much more you expect to sell them for and what percentage this would be of the original price. For example, if you invested $1,000 in the stock market and your assets are currently worth $1,100, then the increase is 10%.

☐ Are you currently investing in assets with the idea of selling them in time? Can you contribute anything extra to these investments? Or are you first focusing on other financial goals such as debt repayment or regular savings?

☐ If you don't have any investments that might give you capital gains, start thinking about whether this is an income stream you might want to pursue further. We'll look at investing in the stock market later on, but in the meantime, start opening your mind to this source of income.

☐ Think about what assets you could potentially focus on that fit in with your lifestyle and/or interests.

☐ Property can be a very profitable business, especially if you have an eye for opportunities and know when and what to sell. It requires a lot of start-up capital or a second mortgage, however, so this might not be something you can or want to pursue at the moment. There are options to combine buying a property with generating a rental income by renting out your property (see Step 58) with the possibility of making a capital gain on it in a few years. The rent received can offset (part of) the mortgage until the property might be worth a lot more to sell again.

☐ Other asset classes such as art, jewelry, antiques, stocks, and even bonds are also possible investments that can appreciate over time and give you a possible income stream from capital gains.

☐ Think of other ideas and options, talk to people, read up on the various possibilities on the Internet, or find a podcast on the topic of multiple income streams or side hustles and then decide whether any of these options sound doable.

Income Stream 5: Dividend Income

To get rich you have to be making money while you're asleep.

—DAVID BAILEY

DIFFICULTY LEVEL: Medium

OBJECTIVE: Find out how dividend can become a possible income stream

REVIEW TIMES: Yearly

Our fifth possible income stream is dividend income, an investment-linked money stream. This type of income is based on company profits paid out to the shareholders of that company. Before you dismiss this type of income as not your thing, read on and then jump to the investing steps later in this book. You might find that investing can be done in a less-risky way than you thought.

Dividend income

If you possess shares (stocks) of a specific company, you essentially own a tiny part of that company. Whenever that company makes a profit, they will likely pay out some of that profit to the owners of that company, i.e., its shareholders. These profits are called dividends.

Of course, investing is not without risk, and a regular dividend income stream is not guaranteed. For example, if the company doesn't make a profit, the shareholders won't get any dividends. Worse

still, the company might go under altogether, in which case those shares would lose their entire value and be worth nothing. This would be particularly unfortunate because not only would you no longer receive dividend payments anymore, but you would also lose your investment (the money you paid to buy the shares).

Reinvesting dividends

Despite the possible risks associated with stocks, dividend income is a great example of a passive income: you don't need to do very much to earn that income, apart from selecting the right stocks and deciding how much to invest. When you get dividends from your stocks, you can automatically reinvest them straight into the stock market again, meaning you buy another small part of a company. The more you own of a company, the more you get when dividends are paid out (which is based on the percentage you own), and the more you can reinvest again into the same or another company. Therefore, when they're reinvested, dividends end up following the same principle of compounding as interest on savings.

Dividends versus savings

So why not just stick with savings and play it safe, given that with investments, you might not get anything if the company doesn't make a profit, and in addition you run the risk of losing your starting capital? There are two main reasons why investing can be more advantageous than saving:

1. Dividend payments are generally higher than the interest rate you get on your savings account.
2. Shares do not only offer the possibility of dividend income but also of capital gains. On average and over prolonged periods, stocks can appreciate a lot in value, so the additional option of being able to sell them at a profit in the future is what makes investing in stocks even more attractive.

Investing is never without risk, but it can be a decent income provider, so you want to make sure you have a good understanding of both the risks and advantages before stepping into the stock market. Skip to Part 8 to look at the ins and outs of investing in greater detail.

☑ STEP 56 ACTION PLAN

We'll be looking at stocks and the stock market in Part 8, so you don't need to suddenly go out and buy stocks if you don't want to. But if you have in the past felt that investing was "not your thing" and is only for people who have a lot more money than you, here are some small steps to get you started with this possible source of income:

☐ Ask people you know whether they have any investments. Obviously you have to feel comfortable asking, so think about friends, family, and colleagues who don't mind discussing finances with you. Think of the following questions to ask:

- How long have you been investing?
- What is your experience with your investments?
- Would you recommend that others invest? Why or why not?

☐ In later steps, you'll discover there are different ways of investing money, some carrying more risk than others, so don't worry if you get conflicting advice. In fact, if you get only positive or only negative responses, keep looking until you find somebody who gives you a different opinion. If later on you do decide to start investing, you want to have at least one or two people you might be able to ask for tips and help, so knowing who has experience investing and is happy to talk to you about it will prove beneficial.

☐ If you already have some investments, how much money are you currently adding to your investment account every month, and how does this affect the amount of dividends you hope to receive in the long term?

Income Stream 6: Royalties

If you want your income to grow, you too must grow.

—IDOWU KOYENIKAN

DIFFICULTY LEVEL: Medium

OBJECTIVE: Brainstorm ways to earn royalties as an extra income

REVIEW TIMES: Yearly

If you're like most people, you probably think of famous pop stars and writers when you hear the word *royalties* and discard it as a serious option for extra income. Since you probably are not a famous singer or author, this is not something that would be attainable for you, right?

Royalties

Turns out, royalties are not only for the (already) rich and famous. They are, in fact, paid to whoever creates or invents something that gets sold or used by others, and more often than not, that can be a not-so-famous book, a patented product or invention, or an artwork that gets produced and sold en masse on postcards or posters.

Royalties are payments you get from people using your ideas or your products. After you have created, invented, or put together your product, other people will then market, promote, and sell it, and while those others are likely the ones working hard to make the product successful, you get a (small) percentage of the profit of each sale.

A second type of royalties exists for franchises

of famous companies; think about a Starbucks or McDonald's franchise, where the mother company gets paid for the franchise's use of the logo, concepts, and marketing strategies.

Royalties versus profit income

Before we continue, it's worth quickly looking at what royalties are not. As said above, royalties are based on other people using your products in order to make money with them either directly (for example a publishing house selling your book—this is a direct sale) or indirectly (in case of a radio station playing your song on the radio—this is not a direct sale; they just hope to attract more listeners and thereby more advertisers).

If you're an artist and open your own store on Etsy, or have an income from a blog, you don't get any royalties, however. Nobody is selling anything for you; it will be you putting in all the hard work of getting your brand out. Any income you make in these cases will likely be profit income.

If, on the other hand, your art gets used for a new line of greeting cards by a big brand, you most likely *will* receive royalties on the cards sold by somebody else. The key is whether you're selling your idea or product to somebody else in order for them to use and sell products with it, or whether you're selling your own products or ideas directly to customers.

Passive income through active work

Getting an income from royalties is not exactly

passive, as you need to create something first. But once it's been created, patented, and successfully pitched to potential sellers of your product, it can become a (semi)passive income stream, and as long as your royalties will keep coming in. But you need to invest a lot of hard work and time into setting this up first, which requires skill, perseverance, and a unique idea or execution—a bit like setting up your own company.

Royalties are an interesting way to build a side hustle, as it allows you to develop something you're truly passionate about. At the end of the day, it's completely up to you to decide in what to create!

☑ STEP 57 ACTION PLAN

I hope this step has made you at least aware of royalties as a possible side income for not just famous pop stars, but anybody who can develop a marketable idea or product. Below are points that allow you to investigate a little more to find out whether this might be something you could develop for yourself. Have a look at the following questions, without judgment of whether this is possible in the sense of time, knowledge, or money needed. For now, just consider the options. Nobody ever got rich by saying, "I don't have time to do this," so keep an open mind.

- ☐ Are you crafty or into art? Artwork royalties can be paid on items such as greeting cards, linen and towels, posters, plates and cups, and many more. . . .

- ☐ If you're skilled with photographs and/or design, you can look to sell some of your work. The copyright will pay you royalties for each purchase.

- ☐ Do you feel you have a book in you, be that fiction or nonfiction, and that you might be able to get it published?

- ☐ Have you got a good idea for a game you might be able to develop and sell to a big games company?

- ☐ Do you have a successful business or can you set up a successful business that you could franchise?

- ☐ Are you good with computers and can you find a gap in the market for a new software to patent?

- ☐ Think of other options you could develop or create. There are so many options, from knitting patterns you can offer big yarn stores to resell, to ringtones, computer games . . . you name it. The sky's the limit!

Income Stream 7: Rental Income

> *Things may come to those who wait, but only the things left by those who hustle.*
> —UNKNOWN

DIFFICULTY LEVEL: Medium

OBJECTIVE: Understand the possibilities of earning extra income through renting

REVIEW TIMES: Yearly

We have arrived at the last of the seven different income streams: rental income. As with some of the previous steps, keep an open mind about this source of income, even if you currently feel that you wouldn't want to go down this road anytime soon.

Rental income

Rental income can come from any asset you own and let others use in exchange for money. The most obvious and well-known form of rental income is the renting out of a building, such as a house or apartment. It can be for private use (having tenants living on your property) or for commercial use, such as the renting out of an office space or shop. Whereas renting out a property is the most well-known option to create a (steady) rental income, it also needs the most start-up capital.

The risks of rental property

If you have a property, however big or small, from a storage area or garage to an apartment or house, that you rent out, you can create extra income that's relatively passive and can supply you with a decent amount of extra cash. But renting out your property is not without risks and costs.

- First of all, acquiring a property means you most likely have to take a mortgage (maybe in addition to one you already have for your own house), meaning there are the extra monthly costs of paying off this second mortgage. Having a mortgage is not necessarily a big problem, as long as you're able to rent out your property during (most of) the year. If you are, you might almost have your renter paying off your mortgage with the rent you're receiving. If you don't manage to get a renter in for most or part of the year, however, or if they don't always pay their rent, the situation can become more problematic as it would mean that you have the set monthly cost of your second mortgage, but not the income to cover it.
- Another potential risk with rental property is that you might not be able to get back the initial capital invested into the building if the market value drops below the original purchasing price at the time you look to sell it. In recent years, the property market has fluctuated heavily,

demonstrating that any property can decrease significantly in value over time even if you expect it to go up.

- A third risk associated with rental property is the time you need to invest in developing this income: you need to look for, buy, and manage the house, decorate and furnish it, find renters, keep up with maintenance tasks, collect rent, find new renters when old ones leave, etc. As such, it's not always easy money. You might not find renters easily, or only for short amounts of time, or there may be a lot of maintenance tasks that creep up. In the end, you might have to spend a lot of time (and money!) on this income source.

That said, if you do have a place that's easily rentable for which you can find good, long-term renters who hopefully don't trash your place, and if you can keep up with the maintenance, a property for rent can be a highly profitable way of making extra money.

Other types of rental income

Rental income is not limited to the rent of a building. You can also rent out other possessions, as proved by the recent increase in local initiatives such as rent-my-lawn-mower or rent-my-toolbox-for-a-day. People are generally happy to pay a small price for something they cannot or do not want to buy themselves, either because of financial reasons, space issues, or a desire for minimalism (living with less). Ultimately, if you only use a drill two or three times a year, is there really a point in buying one yourself? Although with these types of rental income you will likely receive far less money and on a less regular basis than on an apartment you rent out, you might have a variety of objects you can rent out to others who would like to borrow them from you at a small price. And as we've seen time and again, little contributions can make a big difference over time.

- -

Of course, you probably don't have money lying around to just buy an apartment to rent out, and maybe you won't be pursuing this income stream for another ten or even twenty years (if at all). But if you want to get into the rental income industry at some point, you have to take it up in your financial planning. So start thinking ahead now and consider the options!

☑ STEP 58 ACTION PLAN

☐ Brainstorm a list of possible things you could rent out: from tools and other objects to a house, your garage, a storage area, kids' supplies, etc.

☐ Have a look online to find out more about local initiatives for rental services, and see what other people are renting out, what prices they ask, and how they organize and advertise.

☐ If long term you might consider buying a property for rental income, talk to people you know (think beyond your family and friends to colleagues, friends of friends, etc.) who rent out an apartment. Ask them about the different aspects involved.

☐ Try to speak to people who have both positive and negative experiences so that you're well informed about the various risks and opportunities.

☐ Browse the Web for property for sale in your town or state to see what's on the market in various price ranges and areas. Get a rough idea of how much money you would need for a down payment, what the mortgage would be, how much it would initially cost to refurbish, how much you could charge for rent, and how rentable the property would be.

☐ Decide whether you might be able and willing to pursue this income stream at this point in your life. If not, come back to this step in a year when your situation might have changed.

In the next step, we're going to wrap up the income theme by coming up with a plan of action to steadily increase your monthly income.

Plan Your Income

> *It does not matter how slowly you go, as long as you do not stop.*
>
> —CONFUCIUS

DIFFICULTY LEVEL: Difficult

OBJECTIVE: Put together a plan on how to increase your income

REVIEW TIMES: Biannually

In the past eight steps, we have looked at different income sources and you've analyzed each one in detail, looking at your own situation to determine whether any of these might be possible avenues for you to pursue. That leaves just one last thing to do before moving on to yet another topic: making a plan to put into practice what you just learned.

If you truly want to take control of your income, thinking and talking about it is all very nice, but nothing much will happen unless you make a plan, follow it as best you can, and then adapt it continuously. Taking action is what will ultimately determine whether anything will change, or whether it will just remain a fantasy.

So now that you have looked at each possible income stream, brainstormed ideas, and even considered whether some of these ideas would be worth the extra time or money, it's time to draw some conclusions.

Are you currently happy with the income you receive or do you want to get more control over your overall income? Would you like to pursue any of the ideas you came up with? And if so, which one are you going after first? How are you going to do this? What is your end goal? When are you going to start? And what do you need to get started?

There are many possibilities to grow your income. Take matters into your own hands and start working toward the income you want.

☑ STEP 59 ACTION PLAN

In this action plan, you are going to start with a goal, then work all the way back to today to see how to actually get there. Get out your notebook or open your digital file and let's get started with the following questions:

☐ Start with setting a clear goal: What is your income target in five years? How much would you like to be making by then? Five years is a long enough period to work toward and make real changes, while not being so long that there's no urgency to it.

☐ Set yourself a target that excites you but also scares you a little, whether that's earning 50% as much as you do now, three times as much, or maybe even ten times as much. Be honest with yourself, however, and think about how much you really want and need to earn. Bear in mind that the extra money will not just materialize in front of you; you will need to work hard to get it. If you need to put in eighty hours a week to make ten times as much, is it worth it?

☐ Write down the date in five years' time along with your target income and set it as a deadline.

☐ Look at the seven income streams individually and go through every single answer and idea that you came up with. Consider the following questions:

- How much time would you need to invest weekly into developing this income stream, and how long would it take to achieve this?
- How much money would you need to implement this idea?
- How much would this idea add to your monthly wage in five years?
- How likely is it that this idea will lead to your desired outcome?
- How motivated do you feel to pursue this? Is this something you could enjoy doing, or is it mainly an idea that sounds great but that you would not want to actually do?
- What sacrifices would you need to make to pursue this idea?
- When would you be able to start this?
- What skills or information would you need to pursue this income?

☐ Draw up a chart or matrix. In the rows, put the different ideas for income, and in the columns, put the questions/categories mentioned above. This will help you easily compare the various options, as shown in Table 11 (see next page).

☐ Your chart can have as many ideas as you want—three, twenty, or a hundred. Go through every single one of them and answer the questions above, and any other questions or points you might wish to add.

☐ Give each cell in the chart a grading of 1 through 5, or a plus or minus, to compare the pros and cons of each. For example, if your first idea doesn't need any start-up capital, give that one five points (that being the most ideal option). But if that same idea would require a lot of personal

Table 11: Comparison chart to test chance of success of various ideas

	Time and effort required	Money needed	Monthly wage increase	Success likelihood	Motiva-tion	Sacrifice	Starting Date	Skills and infor-mation needed
Idea 1								
Idea 2								
Idea 3								
Idea 4								
Idea 5								

sacrifices—such as working an extra twenty hours a week and needing to travel on weekends, thereby missing a lot of family time—you might want to give it just one point (least ideal).

☐ When you're finished, look at your matrix and compare each idea against the other ones to determine which to pursue first. The winner might not be the one that generates the highest income or needs the least amount of time. Decide which of the factors are most important to you. For example, you might not want to take on a project that you did not rate with a minimum of 4 out of 5 for motivation or enjoyment, even if that project has the potential to generate the most extra income. What is your critical factor? Determine the minimum score you'd need on each question individually for an idea to be a winner.

☐ Try and narrow it down to one or maybe two top projects. Avoid taking on more than two new projects at once so you can focus and not spread your funds, and time, too thin.

☐ Once you have your new potential project to increase your income, determine the first step you need to take. What can you do *today* that will make you start this project, so that from now on, every day, you can work toward achieving your new goal? Write down your first step, then write down a second and third step. Schedule them into your calendar.

☐ Every day, work your plan. Every time you complete a step, determine the next step and schedule it into your calendar. Remember that with every step, however small, you get a little closer to your goal.

☐ Twice a year, analyze your income to review your plan and see whether you're on track and what adjustments you need to make to get to your five-year target.

Checklist Part 6

Use the following checklist to make sure you've done everything in Part 6 and are ready to continue with the next part:

☐ You're familiar with the seven different income streams and have calculated how much you generate from each on average on a monthly basis.

☐ You have analyzed the likelihood of earning more through your job in various ways and the potential effect a job or career change might have on your income.

☐ You have analyzed the possibility of earning more money through setting up your own company to create profit income.

☐ You understand the power of passive income in the form of interest when interest rates are high through savings accounts and know there are other ways to receive interest income, such as through bonds and crowdfunding. You've calculated how much interest you should receive each year based on your current contributions to interest-generating accounts.

☐ You have analyzed the possibility of pursuing capital gains as a possible income stream.

☐ You have investigated dividend income and how this can become a possible income stream for you.

☐ You have thought about ideas or products you might develop that you can sell to bigger companies in order to generate an extra income from royalties.

☐ You understand the possible advantages of renting out property and have looked at how much you would need in start-up capital and mortgage to finance a property and get it ready to rent out. You have also looked into options to generate rental income by renting out items or equipment you own.

☐ You have compared various ideas on how to create a new income stream in all of the seven possible streams and you have decided which idea to pursue first.

When I left school, I didn't know what I wanted to be when I grew up. But I did know that I wanted to travel (and I didn't want to get into a huge debt!). I saved some money and three months after I finished my final school exams, I flew to the UK where I stayed for almost a year. I lived off some minor savings and managed the money I was earning to fund small travels.

On my return I went to university, studying remotely via correspondence while working full-time in retail and retail management. I had some other jobs on the side, one based around retail and event photography with an experiential marketing business.

When I finished studying, I still didn't know what I wanted to do, but the love of travel reignited, so I did a course on how to teach English, and for the next seven to eight years I alternated between working three months a year teaching English in Spain and seven months a year in Australia with the event photography business, which had developed into an operations and management role.

This was a great way to be able to travel the world in the time off in between and build my skill set in each role. Both jobs continued to complement the other as I developed my skill set and capability, which helped me excel and progress through promotions in both businesses through the years.

Throughout this time, I had always been sensible with my money. I had never had or wanted a credit card as I never wanted to be tempted to spend beyond my means. I always saved what I needed and worked to support myself and my travels while I was away.

In Spain, I progressed through as a teacher to a teaching coordinator to assisting with training and then working as a director of one of the summer campuses. In Australia, I progressed from a store manager to a multisite manager to training manager and into HR and learning. By this time, my passion for learning/training and management/leadership had become quite well rounded. So at the age of twenty-nine, I finally worked out what I wanted to do—and that was to become an expert in the field of L&D (learning and development) within adult education.

Back in Australia, I did a more in-depth course in training design, delivery, and assessment to develop these skills. I knew that by completing this training course, I would be able to negotiate job responsibilities and salary with my current employer in Australia, as well as make myself a more desirable candidate for future positions I may want to pursue in this field.

I secured full-time work with the event photography business as it grew, doing exactly this. Once I stopped the travelling lifestyle, I finally got a credit card for the sole purpose of gaining some credit history to hopefully purchase an investment property at some stage in the future, which I was able to do at the age of thirty-two. At thirty-three, I had finally paid off my study loan, too.

I still travel, however, only for a few weeks a year. I now work as a subject matter expert in learning and instructional design within a very large organization in Australia where there are further opportunities to grow and develop—in terms of both my skill set and my salary! Because I have my investment property as well, I take great comfort in knowing I will have financial security and independence later in life. Now it's just time to think about how to pave the way to secure investment property number two!

—Kylie Watson, Australia

PART 7

Your Retirement Plan

Retirement accounts form the foundation of most welfare states and allow people to stop working when they reach a certain age while continuing to receive a monthly income. Although your retirement might still be many years or decades away, retirement planning is absolutely key to financial independence. You need a guarantee that you can retire and live off the retirement provision you have built up over the years and not need to continue working well past your retirement age (unless of course you want to).

Retirement payouts generally kick in at a certain age, so if you're looking to retire early as part of your path to financial independence, then a retirement account will probably not be of much use until you reach that specific age. Until your official retirement age, you'll need to find other ways to provide for yourself and your family. But once you reach that age, your retirement account can take over from your other funds and start giving you a monthly income, as long as you've saved up enough.

In Part 7 you'll increase your knowledge of different retirement accounts and the roles they might play in your retirement provision. At the end of this part you will put together a strategy to ensure a comfortable retirement.

An Introduction to Retirement Accounts

Retirement: It's nice to get out of the rat race but you have to learn to get along with less cheese.

—GENE PERRET

DIFFICULTY LEVEL: Medium

OBJECTIVE: Find out what types of retirement accounts you are entitled to

REVIEW TIMES: Yearly

Retirement. It's a word dreaded by many, not just because they might not like the idea of being old and having nothing but time on their hands. Many people simply don't have a clue what their retirement income will look like and fear that they might never actually be able to retire properly, due to (nearly) empty retirement funds or the absence of a decent retirement plan altogether.

Taking control of your retirement accounts

Be that as it may, ignoring your retirement plan is not going to do you any good, and considering the many changes that retirement accounts are going through at the moment in many countries, it's wise to learn more about them and especially to understand your own retirement projection better so you can put together a sensible plan. It might be tough, unpleasant, or tedious at first, but once the bulk of

the work has been done, you can sit back knowing you might still be a long way from where you want to be, but you now have a plan to get you there.

Although retirement account options vary widely from one country to the next, from industry to industry, and among different employers, there are some common characteristics of retirement benefits that we'll be looking at. This step starts with some of the retirement basics before moving on to the various plans and their own advantages and disadvantages in the next couple of steps.

What are retirement accounts?

Retirement accounts are, in essence, a fund into which the state, an organization, and/or an employee pays money in order to finance retirement. This allows people to stop working when they are older, while still being able to have access to a monthly income or, alternatively, a lump sum that has been saved over the years. Although many countries have retirement accounts as a compulsory part of an employee's benefits that must be paid monthly, there are others for which this might not be the case, leaving those who don't arrange a retirement account themselves in danger of financial insecurity and problems later in life. Even those who do have a retirement plan often don't realize how much (or little) they will get when they actually retire. Others might find themselves with a retirement savings gap in which they won't get enough from their retirement funds to meet their basic needs. This can happen, for example, if they stayed at home for some years or if they were self-employed but didn't set up a retirement account plan.

Types of retirement accounts

Retirement account plans can generally be divided into three different types. Each type can have different characteristics depending on the country, state, or industry you are in.

- **Social Security:** Also called a state pension in some countries, this is a retirement contribution paid by the government when somebody reaches retirement age. It's normally financed by the employee and/or employer during the employee's active working life through monthly taxes taken out of the employee's wage and/ or by the employer's compulsory Social Security contributions. Employees generally build up a state retirement account in the country/ countries they live and work in, provided they have worked for a certain minimum number of years. Once retired, some countries will pay out the same monthly amount to everybody, regardless of how much the employee previously earned, whereas in other countries, the amount might depend on the wage received over the last number of years.

- **Workplace retirement accounts:** These are retirement accounts provided by an employer, union, or work sector into which the employee makes a monthly payment. Common examples of this type of account in the US include 401(k) and 403(b) plans. Other names for these retirement account include "company retirement accounts" or "occupational accounts." Participating in a workplace retirement account

is often voluntary and not all companies offer this option. In some cases, employers also make contributions to this account for their employees in addition to the payments the employees make into this fund.

- **Personal retirement account:** A personal retirement account is a private retirement account set up by individuals via banks, insurance companies, or retirement account plan providers. These are commonly referred to as IRAs (individual retirement accounts) in the US and are a good alternative for those who don't have access to a workplace retirement account or who have reached the maximum contribution on that workplace retirement account and want to top off their retirement funds.

An employee could therefore essentially receive retirement payments from various sources, depending on where they have contributed to a retirement account. Once you start withdrawing from your retirement funds, regardless of which type of account you have, your withdrawals are considered income, meaning you are usually taxed on that money. The exception to this is if you have set up a retirement account plan that works off after-tax payments made into the fund (more on tax advantages for retirement accounts in Step 62).

- -

The information you collect now will help you in the next three steps when we look at each type of retirement account in detail, before moving on to putting together your own retirement plan in Step 65. Even if you don't like to think about retirement accounts because they sound complicated, boring, or scary, remember that by taking one step at a time, you can achieve anything you set your mind to. Even funding your retirement accounts.

☑ STEP 60 ACTION PLAN

We will be looking at each type of retirement accounts in detail in the next few steps, but for now let's start with an easy exercise to get an idea of what your retirement situation will be like.

☐ Check whether you're entitled to a Social Security or a state pension upon retiring, and if so, how much the current payout is per week or month.

☐ Find out whether you're enrolled in a workplace retirement account and, if not, whether your company offers any options to do so. Request account details and an overview of your contributions if applicable, and find out how much you currently have in this fund.

☐ If you have a personal retirement account outside of your employer's scheme, find details of payments, your status, and specifications.

Social Security Benefits or State Pensions

The trouble with retirement is that you never get a day off.

—ABE LEMONS

DIFFICULTY LEVEL: Medium

OBJECTIVE: Learn how much your (projected) monthly Social Security benefits or state pension will be

REVIEW TIMES: Yearly

⇌ STAT BOX

In December 2017, the average monthly Social Security payment in the US was $1,404 for retirees.[17]

After the basic introduction to retirement accounts from the previous step, this step will be looking at Social Security or state pensions[16] (depending on where you live) in more detail. Retirement accounts vary greatly from one country to the next, if a government-funded option even exists at all. In most countries, you might receive benefits at retirement age if you have been employed for a certain number of years, but the circumstances change from country to country. Be sure to research the situation in your country or state.

Social Security or state pensions

Social Security or state pensions are income given to retirees that's paid by the national or federal government from funds to which employees and/or employers contribute during an employee's active work life. If you're entitled to this type of benefit, it would normally be regardless of any workplace or private retirement accounts you might also have. Most Social Security and state pension payouts are not exactly a fortune and are designed to provide for your basic needs only. They are characterized by various factors, which we will look at below.

Funded vs. unfunded accounts

As we've seen before, money loses its value over time due to inflation. So when a country or state collects money for retirement benefits, it will be worth significantly less if it's just left sitting in a bank account waiting for you to start drawing on them.

Retirement account programs need to therefore manage contributions in such a way that the money doesn't become worthless by the time it's paid out to the retiree. This can be done in two ways: setting up a funded account or setting up an unfunded account.

- In **unfunded retirement account** plans, any Social Security and state pension contributions made today by employees, employers, and from taxes is used to pay current retirement accounts. Younger generations pay the older generations' pension, so your own retirement account will (in theory) be paid by future generations. In this way, retirement payouts are set based on the value of today's money and money paid into the fund will not have lost its value by the time it's paid out.
- In **funded retirement account** plans, all contributions made are invested, with the idea being for the money to (hopefully) grow enough over time to minimally beat inflation, and ideally do even better than that by the time the money needs to be taken out to pay benefits. For obvious reasons, this option is slightly more risky, but it can also give better results, i.e., generate more money over time.

You can't normally choose whether to set up a funded or unfunded retirement account. In most cases, the Social Security accounts or pensions of national governments are either unfunded or partially unfunded, whereas most private and workplace retirements are funded.

Inflation

Social Security and state pension benefits are nearly always corrected for inflation. Although this doesn't mean they always keep up exactly with inflation, if inflation is 2% this year, you can reasonably expect the retirement accounts to go up somewhere between 1 and 2%, too. However, this might not be true if a government needs to make cuts or the economy is in recession, in which case benefits can sometimes be "frozen," i.e., they're not adjusted to keep up with inflation.

Changing demographics

A huge challenge for retirement plans is that we live longer and longer with each generation. Whereas

retirement accounts were once implemented to support people for just a few years after retirement age, nowadays many of us end up relying on these benefits for several decades. This results in retirement accounts becoming more expensive as they need to pay out and support people for a longer period.

As we live longer, the relative percentage of people receiving a Social Security or state pension benefit also increases compared to the number of people paying in to them. For unfunded retirement account plans especially, this can pose a big problem as the proportion of people contributing relative to the people withdrawing from these funds decreases. In addition, many countries are also experiencing a drop in birth rates, which will amount to fewer people being able to support the benefit needs of the retired population.

Retirement age

To combat the problem of changing demographics described above, many countries are increasing their official retirement age in order to make sure that retirement accounts continue to have enough funds. This is achieved in two ways: people work longer, thereby making contributions to the retirement account for longer, while at the same time they start drawing benefits later and therefore will be receiving Social Security or state pension payments during less time overall. Most countries have already made steps to move away from their traditional retirement age, so you, too, might find you will need to work longer than the traditional retirement age in your country.

In some countries, you can decide to retire before the official retirement age, although it generally means you receive less money. In the US, for example, you can choose to retire at 62 and receive just 75% of your Social Security benefits.

Years worked

In many countries, you need to have worked a minimum number of years to be entitled to the full state pension or Social Security. This is to ensure sufficient contributions to the retirement fund are made. In the US, this is generally based on a minimum of ten years of work, with the total pay based on the average of your wage during the thirty-five years in which you earned the most. Other countries require a minimum of thirty-five to forty years of employment to qualify for a state pension, and in some countries, the monthly amount retirees receive might be the same for everybody, regardless of their wages while working. If you haven't worked for the minimum number of years required, you either might not qualify for Social Security at all, or you might be penalized with a deduction for each year you didn't work. This situation is also called a "retirement gap."

Assume you need to work a minimum of thirty-eight years to receive the full state pension and that for every year you didn't work (and therefore didn't contribute), 2% of your monthly pension gets deducted. If you only worked twenty-eight years instead of thirty-eight or more, you get ten times 2% less, so in this case you would receive 80% of the maximum state pension you would be entitled to.

In some countries and states, time out of work might not affect your retirement account if that was time you took off to look after children younger than a certain age. Some countries furthermore allow people to compensate retirement gaps with their partner's retirement account, if they have worked more than the minimum number of years needed to collect the full retirement account. All of this varies widely across the world, so make sure to check the situation in your country.

Deferring retirement accounts

Some retirement accounts give you the option to defer your payment, which means that if you decide to take your retirement benefits later than at the official retirement account age, the annual payment you receive once you start receiving your pension increases. Because you're not withdrawing, and are in fact still paying a contribution to Social Security or state pensions if you continue to work, this is very beneficial for governments. Because of this, they seek to reward people by paying them slightly more later on. To use the US as an example again, any retiree delaying retirement might get as much as 8% more for every extra year worked beyond the legal retirement age, up to a maximum of 24% after three years.

In most countries with Social Security or state pensions there will likely be changes in the next few years and decades in order to keep up with changing demographics. Make sure to inform yourself well of new developments regularly to avoid unpleasant surprises later on!

☑ STEP 61 ACTION PLAN

As mentioned before, Social Security or state pensions vary hugely from one country to the next, if you are lucky enough to be entitled to one in the first place, so make sure you do your research well. Remember that if your retirement age is still many years if not decades away, many things can change between now and then, but that should never give you a reason not to at least familiarize yourself with the current situation and use that as a base to plan from. You can always update your plan as needed as things change and as you get closer to retirement each year.

☐ Look up what the current state pension amount is per month in your state or country or how monthly Social Security benefits are calculated. Remember that most retirement withdrawals are taxed, just like a regular income, so check the gross amount along with the tax percentage you would be liable for.

☐ Find out what the current official retirement age is and whether this is changing over the next few years. Many countries used to have 65 as the legal retirement account age but are increasing this to 67 or 68 over the next few years, with some eventually raising it up to 70.

☐ What is the minimum number of years you need to have worked to be entitled to the full retirement fund?

☐ If you don't reach the minimum number of years required, what are the consequences per year not worked?

☐ Look into the current options of deferring a retirement account. Would you be paid more? How much extra per year would you be paid if you decided to hold off withdrawing from your retirement account at the official retirement age? Check whether this is likely to change anytime soon.

☐ Lastly, based on the current monthly retirement provisions, calculate how much of your monthly expenses would be covered by Social Security or state pension benefits.

☐ Once a year, check the amounts and update your records along with any (projected) changes in the official national retirement age.

Workplace Retirement Accounts

The secret of getting ahead is getting started.
—MARK TWAIN

DIFFICULTY LEVEL: Medium

OBJECTIVE: Discover how much your (projected) monthly workplace retirement account will be by the time you retire

REVIEW TIMES: Yearly

A workplace retirement account—in the US often known as a 401(k) or 403(b) account—can be offered to employees by an employer or a work sector and contributions are usually made monthly directly from employee paychecks. Although many of the characteristics discussed in the previous step about Social Security or state pensions are also applicable to workplace retirement accounts, the latter often have many additional features. Let's look at those now.

Automatic or opt-in

Employees can either be enrolled in their workplace retirement accounts automatically or be required to opt in. If you don't know whether you're currently participating in your workplace retirement account, find out as soon as possible.

Monthly contributions

You can determine your monthly contribution to your workplace retirement account. There is usually both a minimum and maximum contribution you can make, and although it might sound tempting to just pay the bare minimum, if you budget well and set aside enough money, you might find you can pay in more than just the minimum, thereby building up your funds quicker. Remember that the more you contribute now, the more you'll have by the time you retire, not just from your monthly payments but also from the compounded interest.

Employer's contribution

In addition to your own monthly payments, your employer might also contribute to your retirement account. If this is the case, then that's a huge advantage of your workplace retirement account that none of the other retirement account plans offer. It is, in essence, free extra money. The amount of your employer's contribution often depends on your own payments. For example, your employer might pay 50% of whatever you pay in up to a maximum of 5% of your monthly salary.

Even though you're getting this extra money from your employer, the state doesn't count it as part of your income, so it won't affect your current taxes. Maxing out your employer's contribution (i.e., making sure you pay in the amount needed to get your employer's maximum supplement) is nearly always worth pursuing. In the example above, that would be paying in 10% of your salary so that you get the full 5% extra added on by your employer.

Tax advantages

Most retirement account plans offer a tax advantage in one of two ways: when you pay in (this is common for workplace retirement account schemes) or when you withdraw (usually more applicable to individual retirement accounts like the ones described in the next step).

- **Tax advantages when you pay in:** Retirement account plans that offer tax advantages when you pay in, let you make contributions to your retirement account over your gross income, so, before your money is taxed. To illustrate the difference between paying taxes before or after making a retirement account contribution, let's start with a scenario in which you *don't* get tax advantages when paying in. We'll assume you earn $2,000 gross per month and pay 15% in income taxes, meaning you take home $1,700 net. If you decide to contribute 6% of your salary toward your retirement account, it would be calculated based on your after-tax income,

or on $1,700. That comes to $102 that you're paying in per month, as shown in Table 12, leaving you with $1,598 to spend per month.

If, on the contrary, you decide to contribute to your retirement account with pretax money, instead of calculating the 6% over your net pay, it would be taken from your gross pay of $2,000, which comes to $120. You will only be taxed *after* you have paid into your plan. As shown in Table 13, of the $1,880 you have left, you pay 15% taxes, which leaves you $1,598.

As you can see, you end up with the same net amount, but your retirement account did a lot better when you used pretax money. A great extra advantage of this type of retirement contribution is that if the retirement contribution is taken out of your gross wage, you don't even see it in your bank account, which means you are less likely to even miss it. Note, however, that in this case you will be charged income taxes when you start withdrawing from your retirement account.

- **Tax advantages upon withdrawing.** This is a different type of plan in which you get a tax advantage when you withdraw money from your retirement account instead of when making contributions. In this scenario, you can only

Table 12: Retirement account contributions made after paying taxes

Gross pay	Taxes	Net pay	6% to retirement account	Left over
$2,000	$300	$1,700	$102	$1,598

Table 13: Retirement account contributions made with pretax money

Gross pay	6% to retirement account	Pretax pay	Taxes	Left over
$2,000	$120	$1,880	$282	$1,598

contribute to your retirement account after paying your taxes. Normally, retirement withdrawals are regarded as a type of income, which means that upon receiving your funds each month, you are required to pay taxes. But in the case of a retirement account with tax advantages upon withdrawing, the state acknowledges that you already paid taxes on your money when you paid your contributions (because they came out of after-tax income). You therefore do not need to pay taxes when you start withdrawing from this type of retirement account.

Differences between the tax advantages

You might wonder what the difference is between these two types of tax advantages. Simply put, you either pay taxes now, when contributing, or once retired, when withdrawing. The first option (tax advantages when contributing) allows you to pay in more money and therefore gives your retirement account pot more money and time to grow and accumulate interest, which likely results in a bigger retirement account by the time you retire. The second option, however, might be more attractive if you expect your tax rate to go up—for example, if you think you might be earning a lot more in a few years, or because you think you will have a big retirement account income by the time you retire. If by the time you start withdrawing your tax rate is a lot higher and you pay more taxes, you would have possibly done better taking advantage of a lower tax rate now instead of paying the higher tax rate when you withdraw.

Apart from your expected tax rate evolution, another difference between the two types of tax advantages is the maximum allowed yearly contribution: there is likely a cap on what you can put in each year, so you might need to switch from one fund to the other if you reach the annual limit.

Types of contributions

Traditionally employer-sponsored retirement accounts offered a defined benefit scheme, although nowadays more are moving toward defined contribution plans. The difference between these two types are the following:

- **Defined benefit.** With this type of account, the monthly amount you will receive is determined beforehand and will depend on your salary and how long you have worked, not on how well your investments have done by the time you retire. Regardless of the total amount you have in your retirement account pot, you will receive what was agreed on. Two common ways your monthly retirement payout is determined in a defined benefit plan is a) based on your final salary, or b) based on your average lifetime salary. Defined benefit retirement accounts are very expensive for employers and are therefore declining in popularity rapidly, since investments are not always giving the returns they hoped for.
- **Defined contribution.** With this type of retirement account, you know how much you're contributing, but you don't know how much you'll be able to withdraw from it by the time you retire. Your contributions to your retirement account are invested by your retirement account provider, and depending on how your investments do over time, there will be more or less available in your retirement account pot, and the amount you can withdraw from it changes accordingly. Most plans are currently based on this type of plan.

Employer-sponsored retirement account plans offer a huge advantage over other retirement accounts because of the fact that your employer often contributes to it, essentially giving you free money. If, however, you're not entitled to a workplace retirement account, simply move on to the next step, where we look at private retirement account options in greater detail.

☑ STEP 62 ACTION PLAN

☐ If you have a workplace retirement account or if you can sign up for one, you would have in theory requested details of your company's workplace retirement account policy in Step 60. Find out the following information and specifics:

- How much you have contributed up to now
- The current value of your retirement account portfolio
- The maximum you can contribute (usually indicated on a yearly basis)
- Whether your employer matches your contributions and, if so, how much
- The tax advantages you are eligible for
- How much flexibility there is to choose how to invest your money
- Whether you are on a defined contribution or defined benefit plan

☐ If needed, speak to human resources to make sure you have all the information clear.

☐ Once a year, check your projected workplace retirement account and update your records to adjust your plans.

Private Retirement Accounts

The question isn't at what age I want to retire, it's at what income.
—GEORGE FOREMAN

DIFFICULTY LEVEL: Medium

OBJECTIVE: Compare condition of various private retirement account funds and determine whether to open an account

REVIEW TIMES: Yearly

If you're not enrolled in a workplace retirement account and/or don't have the option to join one at your company, or if you're self-employed or unemployed, you might want to open a private retirement account. In addition, even if you have a retirement provision offered by your employer, you may want to look into private retirement accounts, either as an alternative to or in addition to your workplace retirement account, to supplement your retirement savings even more.

Private retirement accounts

A private retirement account works in very much the same way as a workplace retirement account, with the following exceptions:

- A private retirement account is often not set up through your workplace, so you have to choose your own plan.
- Your employer will not be making any contribution to this account.
- The tax advantage you get in a private retirement account might be different from what you get in a workplace retirement account, depending on the laws in your state or country.

Choosing a private retirement account

One huge feature of a private retirement account is that you need to arrange everything yourself. Not only do you have to choose a retirement account provider, you also need to choose among different packages, conditions, and investment options.

Choosing your own retirement account plan means you have more flexibility to find one that meets your specific needs (or what you predict these to be down the road). This can also be a disadvantage, however, as not only will you likely need to spend a substantial amount of time comparing options, but you are also far more likely to be affected by news, hypes, and market scares, resulting in emotional decisions that are not always in the interest of your retirement account in the long run. (For more on this, see the steps on investing in Part 8.)

Below is a list of some of the most important factors to look at when comparing retirement account offers:

- **Minimum payment.** Check if the account has a minimum monthly contribution. How much is this per month? Can you afford this? Is it a fixed contribution or can you vary the amount if you're tight for money or if you have a variable monthly income?

- **Maximum contribution.** Many plans have an upper limit of monthly or yearly contributions one can make. How much are you looking to pay in? Is that possible or do you need a higher cutoff point?

- **Costs.** What are the annual maintenance fees, transaction fees, administration fees, management fees, and late fees (the costs come under a variety of names)? Even if the costs sound small to you now, they might add up to a lot over time.

- **Tax advantages.** Like with the workplace retirement plans, individual retirement accounts (IRAs) often offer either a tax advantage when you contribute (such as with Traditional IRAs in the US) or when you withdraw from your account (in the US, Roth IRAs fall into this category).

- **Penalties.** Pretty much all retirement account funds will have a penalty if you decide to take your retirement account out earlier than what is agreed to, so make sure to check how much this is and whether it changes depending on how close to the agreed retirement age you are.

- **Investment options.** Your money can be invested in a variety of ways, so you want to make sure that you feel content with how your money is managed. Investments can have more or less risk associated with them, depending on the mix of stocks, bonds, and other assets. Since this is your retirement account we're talking about, you want to be confident about how your money is allocated. In later steps, we'll look at the different investment options and how both growth potential and risk shift based on the various alternatives.

- **Investment influence.** How much can you influence the investments with time? Many retirement accounts offer a lifestyle investment option, in which, as you get closer to your retirement age, your investments are moved to lower-risk assets such as bonds or savings. Others keep your portfolio allocation the same from beginning to end. Check whether you can change investments with time to better suit your needs and risk tolerance.

- **Withdrawals.** How can you withdraw from this fund? When you get to retirement age, there are different ways to start drawing an income, including: lump sums (either taking all of it in one go, or choosing a partial lump sum), a set monthly income or annuity, a flexible income (where you take out a variable income depending on your needs), or a combination of the above. Each withdrawal option has its own advantages and disadvantages including tax consequences and possible risks, such as protection against inflation and the possibility your money might run out before "the end."

A private retirement account gives you the flexibility to prepare for your retirement the way you want and is a great alternative or supplement to the other two types of retirement accounts described earlier. Make sure to give it enough time and thought so you can make the right decision for you.

☑ STEP 63 ACTION PLAN

☐ Look for private retirement account options and find the following key features to compare them. Usually insurance companies offer a variety of options, but also look at other entities such as banks or specific individual retirement account providers.

- Minimum monthly payment
- Maximum yearly contribution
- Fees
- Tax advantages
- Penalties
- Investment options
- Investment influence
- Withdrawal options

☐ If you already have a private retirement account, pull out the paperwork and check the conditions mentioned above.

☐ Ask friends, family, and colleagues for recommendations or to tell you their experiences.

☐ Think about what basic requirements you have for a retirement account by going through the checklist above. What are absolute key elements that you are minimally looking for? How much flexibility do each of the options offer you? Can you make changes with time?

☐ Compare the various retirement account options, and consider making a chart with the pros and cons. (Take a look at Step 59 for an example chart to compare various options.)

☐ Once a year, go through the individual retirement account options and update the projected monthly income you would be able to rely on by the time you retire.

Annuities

> *You can be young without money but you can't be old without it.*
> —TENNESSEE WILLIAMS

DIFFICULTY LEVEL: Medium

OBJECTIVE: Learn how annuities could supplement your retirement account

REVIEW TIMES: Yearly

Before we move on to making a retirement account plan in the next step, there is one more retirement option to discuss: annuities. They might sound like something complex (and they certainly can be when they want to be!), but this step will break down their characteristics, benefits, and disadvantages so you can decide whether to include them in your retirement plan.

What are annuities?

Annuities are a financial product somewhere between insurance and investments. You can buy annuities to insure yourself against living too long. Yes, you read that right. Whereas a life insurance insures against dying too early, an annuity insures you against living too long. It essentially provides you with a set monthly income that you get for a set amount of time or even for the rest of your life after a certain age. If you're fearful that you might outlive your other retirement provisions, i.e., that you might withdraw too much from your investment and retirement accounts or that these accounts won't end up being as hefty as you hoped for, a set monthly income might be the right solution.

When you buy an annuity, your money gets invested into the stock market to allow it to grow over time. You can buy an annuity with all of your retirement savings just before you retire, or you can buy several smaller annuities over time.

Types of annuities

Annuities differ in the way they're set up. Some of the key variables include:

- Fixed versus market-dependable variable monthly income
- Payment for life versus payment for a fixed number of years guarantee
- Flat-rate versus inflation or cost-corrected payments that are adjusted each year
- Individual vs. joint annuity for both partners that keeps paying out even if one of the partners passes away (though usually less)
- A guarantee that protects the principal (or original amount) you pay in even if the market crashes

Of course, the more guarantees or security, the higher the price you generally pay for the annuity.

Advantages of annuities

Annuities offer many advantages as well as disadvantages. Let's start with the advantages.

- Buying an annuity is a very simple way to guarantee a monthly income: you pay a lump sum to start with and later get a set monthly income.

- You are covered for life (or at least you can choose to take this option) so you don't need to worry about outliving your retirement account or investments.
- It offers a good alternative or supplement to a retirement account if you don't have enough money in your retirement funds.
- You can decide to buy various smaller annuities over time instead of committing all your money to just one option.
- On a fixed monthly payment annuity, even if the market drops significantly, you can continue to count on the same monthly income. This is a far better scenario than having to sell your own investments at sales prices if the market drops—something you would likely be forced to do if your retirement account was all tied up in a privately managed investment portfolio.
- Some annuities let you defer payout, so the money has more time to grow. The later you start withdrawing from your annuity, the higher the monthly payout.

Disadvantages of annuities

Annuities also have some major drawbacks, including the following:

- They lock in your money for a long period of time (i.e., as long as you live).
- Once you have made a decision on an annuity, it can be nearly impossible to change it.

- The way rates and fees are calculated are often not very transparent.
- Annuities will not make you much money. Even though your money gets invested in the stock market, due to the fees and profit margins charged by the company who sells you the annuity, it won't grow spectacularly. If you are still quite a bit away from retirement, you might want to invest that money directly into the market so that it can grow and fully utilize the power of compounding interest. See also Part 8 on investing for more information about this.
- Annuity income is generally taxed at the regular income tax rates in most countries and states, so there's no tax advantage.

Annuities in recent years have lost some of their popularity due to the disadvantages described above, yet they can offer considerable financial security later on in life. As always, only you can decide whether they're right for you—but remember that you are signing away your money for a long (and I mean long . . .) time, so make sure you read the small print before you sign anything. If you are still a while away from retirement, don't make any rushed decisions. Take the time to investigate and potentially consult a financial expert to help you.

☑ STEP 64 ACTION PLAN

More than with any other financial concept we have discussed up to now, whether an annuity is the type of investment you should pursue depends completely on your risk tolerance, personal situation, and retirement forecast.

☐ First of all, sit down and look at the advantages and disadvantages stated above. Per bullet point, indicate how important this is to you.

☐ Even if you are still (many) years away from retirement, it's always useful to know what you can choose from. You can normally buy an annuity from an insurance company, retirement account provider, or broker, so check out some reputable annuity providers. Compare prices, fees, and guarantees.

☐ Consider whether you want to have the financial security (and potentially lower price) now by buying an annuity early or if you would rather leave it until later (and potentially only a few weeks before your retirement, or even after it's begun) when you have a better picture of your retirement needs and funds available.

☐ Make sure to familiarize yourself with the information on investments first in Part 8 before deciding to take out an annuity.

☐ Come back to this step once a year to reevaluate your situation and decide whether to buy (another) annuity.

Make a Retirement Plan

You cannot escape the responsibility of tomorrow by evading it today.

—ABRAHAM LINCOLN

DIFFICULTY LEVEL: Difficult

OBJECTIVE: Put together a plan to ensure your retirement accounts will allow you to retire comfortably

REVIEW TIMES: Yearly

Although it's nearly impossible to predict how your retirement account will develop over time and how much retirement options might change, especially if you're still years or decades away from retirement, calculating your retirement savings regularly and setting goals is a key habit to develop if you don't want to be taken by surprise when you finally get to retirement age and need to rely on these payments to live on.

Retirement planning

It's tempting to think that our retirement will work out for us and that we'll be able to retire comfortably after forty, forty-five, or maybe fifty years of working. Yet with fewer and fewer young people carrying the burden of paying for an ever-increasing aging population, not just in numbers but also in years living after retirement, we simply don't know exactly how retirement accounts will develop. Already many countries are increasing their state retirement age, and this might happen again in a decade or two.

STAT BOX

Both men and women (36%) expect their self-funded retirement accounts (IRAs, 401(k)s) to be their primary source of income in retirement. Just over a quarter (27%) of women expect Social Security to be their primary source of income compared to 23% of men. Another 14% of women and 15% of men expect to rely on "working."[19]

Knowing where you are and making a decent plan for your retirement provision, no matter how far away in the future it might seem, is essential to get as close to your financial retirement goal as possible. Because retirement accounts are not as guaranteed as they once were and their future development is uncertain, the only way to take full control over your future finances is by putting together a retirement plan and taking the necessary steps now. Added to that, the earlier you start, the more time you have to your advantage, allowing you to make the most of compounding returns of your savings or investments.

Can you really live off less?

You might expect to be able to do with less money by the time you retire, what with not having any work-related expenses such as travel and work clothes, your mortgage having been paid off, your children no longer needing any financial support, etc. But the truth is, being retired is more expensive than you probably think. Look at the people you know who are retired or ask friends about their retired parents. Now that they no longer work, chances are they suddenly have plenty of time to do other things, such as taking golf classes, going on vacations, or maybe spending a lot of time with their children and grandchildren who live far away and taking them out for trips or meals.

Even understanding all the information presented in this part of the book, retirement accounts are complex, and every state or country has their own systems, taxes, and regulations. Do yourself a favor and become thoroughly informed to ensure you consider all factors for your retirement plan.

✔ **MAKE IT FUN!**

When you review your retirement savings, express how well you're doing with a certain symbol that can vary in size, such as a car or dog: the more savings you have, the bigger the picture you put up. For example, when you reach $10,000 in savings, find a picture of a Smart car or chihuahua. Then when you reach your next milestone, find a slightly bigger version car or dog until you reach your target amount (let's say that's $1,000,000 for now) when you put up a picture of a Lamborghini or Saint Bernard.

☑ STEP 65 ACTION PLAN

☐ Your current retirement account might tell you your projected annual income by the time you retire, so pull out your latest statement for any retirement accounts you have.

☐ Total your projected monthly income from your personal account, workplace account, and Social Security or state pensions you might be entitled to.

☐ Decide how much you think you might need as an annual income once you're retired. Start with your current annual income and predict how much more or less you'll need. Remember that even if regular expenses such as a mortgage and work-related travel costs no longer exist, you likely will have other expenses replacing these, so it's wise to use a figure close to your current annual needs to start with. With time, you can modify this once you understand how your expenses might develop.

☐ Let's say you think you need $2,500 a month to live comfortably, which corresponds to $30,000 a year. Bear in mind that inflation would take the value of this $30,000 down. If you are thirty now and you work off a 3% inflation rate a year, those $30,000 will really need to be $92,600 when you are sixty-seven to have the same buying power as $30,000 these days.

☐ Compare this amount to your current projected monthly retirement payment.

☐ Find out whether you're on track to achieve your target retirement amount and how much extra you should put away yearly to get there. Remember that even if you can only set aside a small amount now, this will still be better than big amounts later on. Time is the biggest wealth accelerator, because compounding does the work for you.

☐ If you consider taking out your retirement savings as a lump sum instead of a set monthly income when you retire, find out the current regulations in terms of taxes and how much you might be allowed to take out free of tax charges. If you take out the full amount, you're likely to be in a much higher tax bracket than if you take out a monthly income, as your taxes are calculated on a yearly income.

☐ Based on how far away your current projected retirement account is from your target amount, consider whether you need to invest more in your workplace retirement account, or whether you need to open an individual retirement account. How much extra would you need to pay into a plan to get on track?

☐ Now that you know how much extra you want to start saving, compare the various retirement account options and decide on the best way to achieve this. Take the necessary steps: opening a new account, budgeting for the extra amount, talking to your significant other, or speaking to a financial advisor or your company's human resources department.

☐ Once you have a plan, get started and work toward a secure financial future now! Accept that you'll need to modify it along the way.

☐ Once a year, evaluate your plan and update it as needed.

Checklist Part 7

Use the following checklist to make sure you have done everything in Part 7 and are ready to continue with the next part.

☐ You understand the three different types of retirement accounts: Social Security or state pensions, workplace accounts, and private or individual retirement accounts. You also know which of these three you might be entitled to and what the projected payout would be at your national retirement age.

☐ You know the national retirement age, which is when you might be able to claim your retirement account. You know whether you can defer your retirement and the advantages of doing so, or whether you might face a retirement account gap.

☐ You know the maximum contribution you can make to your workplace retirement account, what type of match your employer offers, the tax advantages you might be eligible for, and the types of assets you have in your portfolio.

☐ You have compared various private retirement account funds on some key details to find out which one would be most applicable to your situation and needs.

☐ You understand the advantages and disadvantages of an annuity and have compared some options that might be available to you. You have made a decision as to whether an annuity is right for you at the moment.

☐ You have put together a retirement plan based on how much you think you will need, how much you would currently be entitled to from any Social Security or state pension, workplace accounts, and private retirement accounts, and how you will start working toward bridging this gap.

💬 PERSONAL STORY: ESTEBAN

My dad set up a wine distribution business about twenty years ago, and his plan was always to grow and build the business so that he could either live off that in his retirement, or sell it off. Unfortunately, when the financial crisis hit some of the worst things affected were luxury products like expensive wines. He was forced to close the business, and so at sixty-eight years old he found himself with no business, no savings, and just the bare minimum state pension to survive on. This barely pays off the bills and food, and so my parents survive in their old age with whatever my mum can make from doing freelance work as a translator.

My dad never set up a private retirement account, which is why they are currently struggling financially. If he had and had made contributions to it throughout his working years, they would have been a lot better off.

Seeing this firsthand in my own parents has made me more determined to make sure I set up a retirement account regardless of the fact that I feel I am not making enough money to contribute. I want to avoid finding myself in the same situation so even if I can only pay in €25 ($30) a month, I know long term it will still be worth it.

—Esteban Sanchez, Spain

PART 8

Investing

After starting to pay down your debt, saving more money, and looking at ways to increase your income, investing is a logical next step on the way to financial independence. If you're serious about money, sooner or later you will need at least a basic understanding of the stock market: what it is, how it works, and whether you want to put some money in it yourself. Investing is often a long-term decision, and depending on the risks you're willing to take, you might or might not feel that investing is the right thing for you. Bear in mind, however, that most retirement account funds are sustained by investing the money paid in, so if you're making any retirement account contributions to a workplace or private plan, you likely already have at least some of your money invested in the market.

Investing is very complex and billions of books and articles have been written about it, some of which you might want to consult if you're serious about investing. You can find a reading list at the back of this book with some recommended reading on this topic. But for the most basic information, Part 8 is the place to start. After reading this part, you can decide whether to incorporate investments into your long-term plan to financial independence.

You will learn about stocks, bonds, how to invest and discover different techniques to manage your investments in the best way possible. At the end of Part 8 you'll also know exactly how money much you'll need in order to be able to become financially independent.

To Invest or Not to Invest

How many millionaires do you know who have become wealthy by investing in savings accounts? I rest my case.

—ROBERT G. ALLEN

DIFFICULTY LEVEL: Difficult

OBJECTIVE: Decide whether to start investing to generate another income

REVIEW TIMES: Yearly

Ask anybody whether you should start investing and you're likely to get very different answers, some saying they highly recommend putting in a little extra cash, others saying only the really wealthy or really dumb invest in the market, while still others see it as their main way to (early) retirement and put in as much money as they can possibly get together on a regular basis.

The truth is, whether or not to invest depends entirely on you, your personal (and financial) situation, and the reasons you might want to invest in the first place. In this step, I'll give you some pointers to help you determine whether investing is something for you at this stage in your life. Many of these points will be discussed in further detail in the next steps.

Why should you invest?

Let's start with some of the main reasons investing seems worthwhile to many.

- Investing is an alternative to saving: by setting money aside, people hope to grow their funds and with time build up some capital. The difference is that instead of your money being in a savings account, it is put in stocks and bonds.
- Over long periods, the stock market generally goes up. There is the occasional crash when prices go down, sometimes by huge amounts, and many people might lose a lot or even all of their money. But if you have the time and the patience to sit it out and wait for the market to recover, your investments will in all likelihood get back up again.
- On average, the markets go up by 7–10% yearly. That's more than most inflation rates, meaning your money grows in these scenarios, whereas if you left it tucked away under your mattress, it would lose value due to inflation.
- The market average is normally higher than interest rates offered on saving accounts, so if you left the money in a savings account it would grow less than if you invested it in the market.

Of course, none of this is a guarantee that you'll end up making money on the market. Nobody can predict what the market will do in the next five, ten, or twenty years.

Are you ready to invest?

Not everybody who has decided they want to try their luck in the stock market is always ready to start investing immediately. Below are some important

A fun feature of investing: many people like to track their investments and see how they're doing; it's a bit like betting at the horse races. The most fun part is watching the race and tracking your progress over time. Most investment companies give you the option to follow the development of your investments by logging into your account or installing their app on your tablet or phone. You can create a spreadsheet or use a notebook to note down the value of your investments at the end of each week or month and see how they change over time.

questions that can help you determine whether this is the right moment for you to start investing or whether you should wait and resolve some other financial areas first:

- **Do you have any high-interest debts?** Although people have different opinions as to whether you should pay off all your debts completely before investing, if you have debts with a high interest rate (above 5%), it might be wise to pay these off first. The returns you get on the market are unlikely to beat the compounding interest you're paying on these debts.

- **Have you got money available to start investing?** It's generally possible to invest with relatively low monthly or one-off amounts, sometimes as low as $50–100 depending on the brokerage firm and type of investments. But do you have that money available?

- **Can you and your family actually miss the money?** Investing often means that you tie away your money for prolonged periods, especially if you want compounding interest to do its magic. Have you got access to an emergency fund or other types of cash in case of an emergency? Or should you first continue to build some of your savings funds?

- **How much risk can you handle?** If it scares you that you might lose a lot of money on the market, then investing might not be a good idea, or maybe you just want to go for very safe bonds. Similarly, if you love a bit of a thrill, you might end up taking too much risk and thereby losing significant amounts of money. Would you be able to handle that? Can you find the right risk balance for you?

- **Why do you want to invest?** What would you want to use the money for? Typically the best results one can get on the stock market come about after a prolonged period. If you're looking to make a lot of money in a short amount of time, you should probably turn to other options.

- Lastly but not unimportantly: **Are you willing to read or have you read enough about investing?** If you don't know much about investing apart from the information in this book, don't jump in until you have learned some more. Pick up books from the local library, search the Internet, look for podcasts on the topic, and ask a trusted and experienced friend for tips. Most of all, make sure you know what you're talking about, how it all works, and what the fine print and conditions of the various brokers are. (My steps are an introduction and definitely not enough for you to say you understand investing inside-out!)

The above are just some factors to think about, but truth be told, investing is not something you should start doing overnight. It requires a fair bit of planning in order to figure out where in your budget you might be able to free up the money as well as to make sure you can deal with the financial and emotional risks. Regardless of how you invest (I describe the three different ways to invest in Steps 70–72), you need a broker to buy and sell investments for you, and you need to ensure you use a reliable and financially stable broker—you don't want to open an account with the first one you come across. Investing should not be taken lightly as your money gets tied up for long periods and is not readily available should you need it the way that money in a savings account generally is.

There's no need to rush making a decision straight away! As you progress through the rest of this part and learn more about investing, you'll also be able to feel more comfortable deciding whether or not investing might be right for you at this moment in time.

☑ STEP 66 ACTION PLAN

- [ ] Grab your pen and notebook or open your digital file.

- [ ] Go through the list of questions above to determine whether you're ready to invest. Write down as much detail as you want. Regard the money you would invest as "gone," and analyze the size of your emergency fund as well as your other funds in case you need to deal with an unexpected expense.

- [ ] Are there any other questions or reasons you can think of that would stop you from investing? They might be specific to you or your situation. Write them down and analyze why that might be important.

- [ ] If after answering these points you feel you are now ready to start investing, discuss the details and any plans with your partner (and revisit Step 23).

- [ ] As you go through the steps in this part, note down what else you need to know about investing and read up on this—either online or in books—or find a podcast on the topic.

- [ ] If you do not (yet) feel ready to invest or if you don't think investing is your thing, you can skip this part of the book and come back in a few months' time. Or you could continue reading the rest of Part 8 anyway, as you're guaranteed to pick up some more tips and knowledge that might help you when you revisit the question of whether to invest.

Understanding Shares

When buying shares, ask yourself, would you buy the whole company?

—RENE RIVKIN

DIFFICULTY LEVEL: Medium

OBJECTIVE: Understand what stocks are and how they can generate money

REVIEW TIMES: N/a

Stocks (also known as shares) are one of the key components of the stock market. In this step, we will find out what they are, why they exist, and how they can make or lose money.

Shares

Any company is made up of shares, whether they are public and trade on the stock market or are private and owned by just one or a few people. A share is essentially a very small part of a company. If you have a share, it means you own part of that very business. The more shares you have, the bigger the part of the company you own. Some companies might be made up by as little as a hundred shares, whereas others can have millions of shares.

Why companies issue shares

Why would businesses that trade on the market sell a part of their company to people like you and me who might know nothing about the enterprise or its industry? They do so because when they sell shares or stocks, they raise money for the company. If shares of a company are released at $50, that gives the company

$50 for every share sold. If they do this twenty thousand times, the company will raise $1,000,000. That money might be needed in order to expand, start up a new branch, or launch a new product.

But why would they not just borrow money from the bank instead of selling small parts of the company? The biggest advantage selling shares has for a business is that they never need to repay the money they raise. The $1,000,000 they collected is theirs; unlike a regular loan or bonds, it's not a loan, and there's no interest to be paid back on the money.

Why investors buy stocks

Now that we know why companies might issue shares, let's look at what makes it interesting for investors to buy them. There are generally three advantages of owning stocks.

- **Voting rights.** First, though probably least interesting for the average person, owning stocks and therefore part of a company gives you the right to vote at the annual meeting and sometimes at additional meetings, giving you a say in the company. Since this is a right but not an obligation, the vast majority of a company's shareholders do not attend as they do not have much interest in voting. In fact, unless you own a lot of a company's shares your vote will be quite small and your influence minimal.
- **Dividend payments.** A second advantage of owning stocks are the dividend payments that

most companies pay out on a yearly, biannual, or quarterly basis. Dividends are part of the company's net profit that is shared among the shareholders. The more stocks you have, the bigger the dividend payment you receive. Not all companies pay out dividends, however, and for the ones that do, the amount depends on the profit made minus any necessary loan repayments and investments, so these dividend payments can vary substantially from one year to the next. Similarly, when there are no net profits, there most likely will not be any dividend payments to pay out.

- **Capital gains.** Third, the price of stocks fluctuates over time, which is the essence of the stock market. If you buy a share of a company for $50 today, that same share in a year's time might be worth as much as $100. When a company does well, more investors want to buy their shares, driving the price up. The opposite can be the case if the company reports losses, internal strife, an incompetent CEO, and/or during a recession, in which case after a year that same share you bought for $50 might be worth no more than $15 or even less. Once a company has issued shares to raise their capital, the prices they are traded for are determined not by the company but by the market, i.e., what people are willing to pay for these stocks. When people buy stocks, they're hoping that the prices of those stocks will go up in the future so they can sell them at a profit, thereby generating a capital gain. If, on the contrary, the company and therefore its shares do not do very well, share prices might drop, leading to a possible capital loss for the investor if the shares are sold below the original purchase price.

Buying stocks can be very profitable with lots of possible financial gains, but as mentioned several times before, investing is not without risk. There are many reasons why share prices can go up or down. Prices are affected not only by the company's performance, profits, and expectations for the future, but also by global economics and even shifts in climate. Indeed, a political event anywhere on the globe can have massive effects on stocks all around the world.

- -

Although many people have made big fortunes on the stock market, others have also lost a lot of money or even gone into debt because of it. Whatever you do after finishing all of the investing steps of this book, make sure you take a calculated risk that will never put yourself or your life savings in danger. As a rule of thumb, only invest what you can spare.

☑ STEP 67 ACTION PLAN

With that very quick introduction to the basics of stocks, let's proceed to our action plan for this step. There will be several more steps on investing, so we'll keep it simple for now:

☐ Have a look at some of the financial news and in particular news items on the stock market. Don't worry about all the details, but look for some articles on stock prices and how they go up and down.

☐ The market is extremely volatile, so find some articles on how various events in the past year have affected the prices globally, both positively and negatively.

☐ Look on the Internet at some of the share prices of some big companies and see how they fluctuate over time. Just type in "prices stocks + [the company]" in your search engine and you will get a nice little graph with the evolution of the prices over time. Don't get carried away too much with the actual numbers and prices. You just want to get an idea of how the prices can go up and down over time.

Understanding Bonds

I never attempt to make money on the stock market. I buy on the assumption that they could close the market the next day and not reopen it for five years.

—WARREN BUFFETT

DIFFICULTY LEVEL: Medium

OBJECTIVE: Understand what bonds are and how they can generate money

REVIEW TIMES: N/a

Shares are only part of the market. The other major player involved in the stock exchange are bonds. In this step we will look at bonds in greater detail and find out why they can be interesting to invest in.

Bonds

A bond is in essence nothing more than an IOU that a government or company issues when they borrow money. In the case of a bond, the debtor (i.e., the government or company that issues the bond) agrees to pay back the full amount of the original loan to the lender, with interest.

A bond is traditionally an official paper with the following information:

- Value of the original loan, i.e., how much money the bond was bought for.
- Interest rate that the company or government will pay back yearly.
- Redemption date: the date when the issuer of the bond will pay back the original loan. This is usually anything between five and thirty years.

Like with stocks, companies and governments often issue many bonds at a time to raise capital they need for a new investment or expansion. Unlike most other loans, however, bonds are not paid back through monthly payments, but all in one go at the end of their life span. The only monthly payment is the interest on the capital.

Why companies issue bonds

Why do companies issues bonds to borrow money instead of borrowing it from the bank? The main reason is that companies can often get lower interest rates with investors than they can with banks. It also means they don't need to adhere to the restrictions that many banks impose on entities when they borrow money. Issuing bonds guarantees that companies have more flexibility and freedom when it comes to choosing between reinvesting and loan repayments when profits are made, whereas loans from banks are often tied to strict repayment conditions.

But why would a company not issue stocks instead of bonds? A drawback of stocks is that a company cannot just continue issuing more and more of them without annoying their investors. The more stocks are brought out, the more owners of the company there are, and the more reduced the earnings per share (EPS), because the same profit has to be divided among more investors. With bonds, companies don't have this problem as for each new loan needed, a new batch of bonds can be issued, without it affecting the other bonds. They can issue more as long as they can find new investors willing to lend them money.

Of course, the major disadvantage for companies of bonds over stocks is that the full amount needs to be paid back, unlike the capital raised through stocks, which doesn't need to be repaid.

Why investors buy bonds

Bonds give investors the possibility of making money in the following two ways:

- **Interest payment.** As with any loan, a debtor issuing a bond agrees to pay interest on an outstanding loan, so if you buy a bond of $100 at an interest rate of 5%, you can expect to get $5 every year until the redemption date, when the bond will be paid back in full.
- **Capital gains.** Similar to stocks, an investor can decide to sell their bonds to somebody else, meaning the new investor takes over the loan. Since bonds are traded on the market, their prices can go up or down. Bonds can be sold for more or less money than what the original investor paid and also for more or less money than was originally lent to the company, which will be especially important closer to the redemption date.

Two last notes on bonds

- Imagine you buy a bond worth $100 for $110 on the market (thinking you will either get enough interest on it to compensate for the $10 difference, or that you will be able to resell it again at an even higher price). Since the bond was originally issued for $100, when it gets to the redemption date, you'll only be given $100 by the issuer (in addition to any interest you collected periodically from the moment you purchased the bond)! If you don't resell it for a higher price or if you don't make $10 interest on it by the time the bond reaches its maturity date (not taking into account inflation), you've essentially lost money on the bond. If, on the other hand, you purchased that same $100 bond for $90, you will make $10 on the bond by its expiration date in addition to any interest earned on it in the meantime.
- If a company has issued both bonds and stocks, their bondholders must be paid interest on bonds before any profit can be given to the shareholders in the form of dividends. An investor is therefore more likely to get interest than dividends as there might not be any profit left over after interest has been paid.

- -

While bonds are not a guaranteed safe investment, they tend to be less volatile than stocks, which is why many beginning investors in particular start investing in bonds. This allows them to learn more about the market at the start of their investing experience without taking a big risk early on.

☑ STEP 68 ACTION PLAN

Like in the previous step, we are, for now, simply finding out about bonds and how they behave on the market.

☐ In Google or your preferred search engine, enter "bond prices + [a company]" to find out more about the characteristics of bonds, such as their interest rates, maturity date/redemption date, and current prices. See how this evolves over time. You don't need to focus too much on the actual details or numbers; just get an idea of how bonds trade on the market.

☐ It's harder to find information on bonds in the news, as news items tend to focus more on stocks because they sound more exciting due to their price fluctuations. Try to find some information on bond prices and anything else related to bonds so you can get a better picture of how bonds play an important role in the market.

The Difference Between Stocks and Bonds

The stock market is a device for transferring money from the impatient to the patient.

—WARREN BUFFETT

DIFFICULTY LEVEL: Medium

OBJECTIVE: Understand the key differences between stocks and bonds

REVIEW TIMES: N/a

Stocks and bonds can be a little confusing at first, and understanding the main differences between them is helpful if you're considering investing in the stock market at some point. As an investor, you can decide whether you want to invest in just stocks or just bonds, or whether to create your own mix of them. You might even want to change this mix with time and have more or less stocks at certain moments. So even if you start with a certain percentage of stocks versus bonds, this need not stay as such for the rest of your investment life.

This step will look at the main differences between stocks and bonds from an investor's point of view by comparing them on specific characteristics in order to better understand their advantages and disadvantages. Bear in mind that all of the points below are general and true most of the time, but some exceptions always exist.

Volatility

- Share prices are much more volatile, meaning they vary more day to day as well as over long periods: their value can increase or decrease faster.
- Bonds are generally more price solid and fluctuate less over time and at a much slower pace than stocks.

Long-term strategy

- Shares are generally more "offensive" and are seen as vehicles to build wealth. Stocks have— far more than bonds—the potential to increase an investor's capital due to their bigger price fluctuations. The downside of this is that stocks also have an increased risk of losing a lot of their value, which means the investor risks losing more money than with bonds.
- Bonds are more "defensive" since their prices do not fluctuate as much as stocks and are therefore regarded as vehicles that maintain wealth. Bonds will not normally make the investor big bucks. When looked at over long periods of time, they do, on average, increase an investor's capital and beat inflation rates, but they do this at a slower pace than stocks. Since they are less likely to lose as much of their value as quickly as stocks, the risk investors take with bonds is lower than with

stocks. Investing in bonds is still no guarantee to not lose money, however: they can still drop in price significantly over time during a recession.

Average returns

- Over very long periods (more than thirty years), the average annual return on stocks is around 7–8%.
- For bonds, the average return over several decades is around 3–4%, so about half that of stocks.

For both bonds and stocks, these returns can vary hugely per year, however. These percentages above are very rough guidelines to give you an idea of possible returns.

Life span

- Shares have no life span and continue to exist unless the company goes bust or is taken over and absorbed by another company. Dividends continue to be paid out as long as the company makes profits.
- Bonds in contrast, have a set life span, and you will know the end date of its existence when you purchase a bond, which is the moment you will be getting the original face value of the bond (the original loan) back. After that, your bond ceases to exist (though, of course, you could buy new bonds with the money you just got from the old bond).

Payments

- Owners of stocks are paid out dividends, i.e., profits shared among the owners of a business. Dividend payments go up and down depending on the profits of the company as well as the company's investments, expansion plans, loan repayments (including bonds), and other allocations for the money they make. As an investor, you don't know the amount of dividend to be paid out until the end of a period of time when companies present their profit numbers. However, companies can release a profit warning to let investors know that profits might be less than expected.

- In contrast, bonds pay out interest, which is a set rate for the duration of the bonds' existence. Interest can be paid annually or more frequently such as biannually or quarterly. The amount of interest paid out does not directly depend on the profit made that year.
- Both interest and dividend payments can often be reinvested again automatically, either in the same or a different company. This means that both bonds and stocks can benefit from the effects of compound interest. Alternatively, both interest and dividend payments could also be withdrawn and function as a side income, as we saw in Steps 54 and 56 on interest and dividend income, but that means the compounding interest effect cannot work its magic on the investment portfolio.
- Most states and countries will tax any revenue from both bonds and stocks.

Ownership

- Shares give you part of the company and allow you to have a say in the company by being able to attend and vote at the annual company meeting.
- Bonds do not give you any ownership of the company; they're nothing more than a loan. This means you have no voting rights in the company.

The stock market is complex and these are only some of the differences that exist between stocks and bonds. Additionally, these are guidelines only; there are some exceptions these days (there are some bonds with no fixed end date, for example, or stocks that do not pay out dividends). But this list does give you the most important differences for most stocks and bonds out there.

- -

Once you know the basics of stocks and bonds, the next three steps will explain more about investing from a practical sense by discussing the three most common ways to invest money in the stock market.

☑ STEP 69 ACTION PLAN

As an investor you can decide on your own mix of stocks and bonds, depending on your preferences, reasons for investing, and even age. In this action plan, we're going to look at how different mixes affect performance (returns) as well as risks (possible losses).

☐ Type in "example investment portfolios" into your search engine, and you'll likely get different example portfolios of stocks and bonds. Compare various graphs on the following factors:

- Assets allocation (bonds and stocks): What percentage of the portfolio is made up by stocks and bonds respectively?
- Performance: This is the return on investment, often indicated by a percentage. Look at this over longer periods of time, for example over five years, ten years, and more. Generally speaking, an average annual return of 7% over a long period is seen as a solid market performance.
- Risk: The potential losses over time. Stocks can lose a lot of money in a short time, so the short-term losses can be substantial, though in most cases if you hold stocks for a long time, the risks level out.

☐ Many investing firms offer example portfolios that they recommend based on two factors: the investor's age (the older you are, the less risk you generally want to run—more on this below) and the investor's risk tolerance, or how comfortable you are with the level of risk taken. Type "investing risk tolerance" into a search engine and you'll likely get several options for questionnaires that determine how much risk you're comfortable with. Complete a few just to get a rough idea of how much risk you would be comfortable with when it comes to investing. Don't see these results as set in stone. If you have no experience in investing, you will likely be a lot more cautious at first, though with time you might be willing to take slightly more risk.

Investing by Handpicking Stocks

> *If you have trouble imagining a 20% loss in the stock market, you shouldn't be in stocks.*
> —JOHN BOGLE

DIFFICULTY LEVEL: Medium

OBJECTIVE: Discover the advantages and disadvantages of handpicking stocks

REVIEW TIMES: Weekly at first, then yearly

Now that you know the *what* of investing (stocks, bonds, and the main differences between the two), it's time to learn about the *how* of investing—in particular, how one can enter the stock market.

Generally speaking, there are three different ways to invest in a stock market:

1. Handpicking stocks and bonds of individual companies
2. Getting a balanced mix of stocks and bonds through collective or mutual funds
3. Passive investing through index tracking or through exchange-traded funds (ETFs)

We'll look at each option to find out about each way of investing in detail in the current and next two steps. Here we start by looking at handpicking stocks and bonds of individual companies. Although I term it as "handpicking stocks," this refers to handpicking both stocks and bonds.

Handpicking stocks: an overview

Investing through handpicking stocks might sound like a very easy option, and in a way it is, as all you need to do is decide in which company to invest and buy some stocks. After a while, you might decide to sell those stocks, or maybe even buy some more. You don't need anybody to manage your portfolio; you just need a broker to buy those stocks for you and maybe sell them again at a later stage. Your only costs will be what you pay to the broker when they buy and sell the stocks for you and taxes when you sell your stocks.

This type of investing is a form of active investing in which you try to predict which stocks are most likely to make you money. A commonly known example of this are so-called day traders, who aim to make immediate profit on a daily basis by selling and buying investments as soon as they see prices move.

Deciding which stocks to buy

But here is the big question when investing this way: Which stocks are you going to buy? Let's imagine for a moment that you put all your money into one company that somebody told you was going to be *the* investment of the year. If the company is indeed successful and increases its yearly profit, you've got it made: not only do you get regular dividends, but the value of your stocks likely goes up, so if you decide to sell your stocks you'll have made money (capital gain) on your investment.

But what if the company does not do so well? What if profits go down, then become losses, and soon your dividend payments cease to exist? When you finally decide to sell your stocks, the prices may have dropped tremendously if people no longer have faith in the company. You might sell at 60% of the price you paid and have thus lost 40% on the original investment.

So how do you know which company to invest in and which one to avoid? This is exactly the problem that investors face. The truth is, unless you track the financial news meticulously, read company reports, and follow the market day in and day out, you probably don't know. And even if you know a fair bit about the financial markets, a company doing well at the moment might be on the verge of bankruptcy in just a few years' time.

Handpicking stocks means that when you choose your stocks well, you can make a lot of money, but if you don't choose well, you are likely to lose a lot of money.

Advantages of handpicking stocks

To simplify things, below are the key advantages of handpicking your own stocks:

* You are in complete control of what to invest in.
* There are no costs between the day you buy and the day you sell, as you don't have anybody managing your investments. (You will need to pay a broker in order to both buy and sell your investments, however.)
* You might beat the market and do extremely well.
* You can buy stocks that are still very cheap when they're not yet in the S&P 500 list[20], for example, if you foresee great success for that company.

* You decide which types of companies to invest in. Maybe you don't want to invest in the tobacco or arms industries or only go for tech or midsized enterprises, to name just a few options.

Disadvantages

The disadvantages of handpicking include:

* You need to know a lot about the individual companies on the stock market in order to make informed decisions.
* As a small investor, you will likely be able to only invest in a small number of companies, meaning your portfolio will not be very diversified. Less diversification means less risk spreading and therefore more volatility.
* You are on average and over time unlikely to beat the market (i.e., get better results than the market average).
* You might lose a lot of money.
* Investing can become very stressful as you will likely be anxiously trying to keep up with prices and end up buying and selling continuously based on press releases, profit warnings, and other financial news.

- -

The aim of the action plan below is twofold: to give you a better idea of how prices of stocks can fluctuate, but most importantly, how difficult or arbitrary it might seem to pick stocks if you have no idea where to start. Maybe you're in luck and manage to choose the right stocks and make a decent amount of (imaginary) money. But how long are you going to be lucky? Or you might lose 50% of your money within the next forty-eight hours. As I said, think very hard before you decide to handpick stocks as an investment strategy.

☑ STEP 70 ACTION PLAN

To find out more about handpicking stocks, let's do the following mental exercise. Imagine you are given $1,000 to invest. You can invest in as many or few companies as you'd like, as long as you stick to the $1,000.

☐ Open a spreadsheet in Excel or in another digital program or just use a piece of paper.

☐ Write $1,000 as your starting balance.

☐ Decide which stocks you want to buy. (You might want to decide which market to choose first, such as NASDAQ, Dow Jones, etc. If you have no idea, go for the S&P 500. Type "S&P 500 companies" in your browser or search engine and you'll find various websites with a list of the 500 companies. With this information, you can find the current stock prices for the various companies.)

☐ How are you going to decide on the companies? Do you want to read their yearly reports, projected profits, history of their stock prices in the last three months or three years? It's completely up to you how you make the decision. (Of course, if you ended up doing this with real as opposed to imagined money, you might need to pay for professional advice or read more articles, etc. But the point here is that when you handpick, these are all decisions *you* need to make.)

☐ Ignoring costs for a second (again, real life doesn't work like this, but since this is a mental exercise, let's pretend there are no costs), put down in your document which stocks you are buying and how many, as well as the total price based on the current actual prices. (Type in "stock price + [S&P 500 company]" and you'll find the current price.) For example:

- 10 stocks company A, $37.19 each = $371.90
- 2 stocks company B, $110.18 each = $220.36
- 20 stocks company C, $17.15 each = $343.00
- 1 share company D, 60.53 each = $60.53
- Total: $995.79 and $4.21 left

☐ Now start keeping track of your stocks over the next few days and weeks. You might want to do this daily or weekly. The more often you check in with your stocks, the more fluctuation you'll see, and the more interesting this exercise becomes.

☐ Once you've done this for a few days, let's say you can now also determine to sell your stocks. (We'll ignore selling costs for now.) For each transaction, put down how much they are sold for by checking today's prices of those stocks, then reinvest that money into another company—or decide to keep it.

☐ Keep this up for a few weeks and see how much money you manage to make or lose.

☐ Once a year come back to this step to reevaluate your investing strategy through picking your own stocks.

Investing in Mutual Funds

Mutual funds were created to make investing easy, so consumers wouldn't have to be burdened with picking individual stocks.
—SCOTT COOK

DIFFICULTY LEVEL: Medium

OBJECTIVE: Discover the advantages and disadvantages of investing in mutual funds

REVIEW TIMES: Yearly

An alternative to choosing which stocks and bonds to invest in yourself is relying on the opinion and expertise of somebody else, something you do if you invest through mutual funds (also called collective funds). Just like handpicking your own stocks, this type of investing has both positives and drawbacks.

Mutual funds: an overview

In the case of collective or mutual funds, the money of small investors is pooled together to raise capital to invest. A fund manager is appointed to manage the money and he or she decides which stocks and bonds to add to the portfolio, based on the latest market developments, company profits, and the fund manager's expectations of how well the company will perform. Fund managers need to follow the market continuously and buy and sell on a very frequent basis: as soon as they see prices of a particular stock drop, they try to offload as many of those stocks as quickly as possible, to avoid losing any more money. Similarly, if they see a share going up in price, they quickly buy some more to ride the lift as much as possible.

Beating the market?

Many mutual fund managers claim they can beat the market and get their clients better returns than the market average. Although this for sure sounds like a great promise, unfortunately many research and case studies suggest that mutual funds are unlikely to get better returns than the average of the market over long periods. Although every year there are indeed funds that outperform the market, there are even more funds that perform worse than the average. Even those fund managers who get better-than-average results are unlikely to maintain their success for long periods. A fund doing well now might perform far below average in a few years' time.

Fees

A second major problem with mutual funds is the high amounts of fees investors end up paying along the line, making this a very expensive way to invest. The fees paid for different mutual funds all vary from one fund to the next, but typically they include:

- **Management fees.** These fees are to cover the fund manager's salary as well as the costs for the company of running and managing the fund.
- **Trading costs.** Every time you buy or sell on the stock market, you're charged a small trading cost or stamp duty.
- **Load fees.** These costs are the sales commissions for the fund manager every time they buy or sell

a share. Not all mutual funds have load fees, but many do, and they can be as high as 5–6%.

- **Research fees.** Mutual fund companies spend a significant amount of time doing research on various corporations to be able to predict which ones will be worth investing in and which ones should be left alone.
- **Taxes.** Every time you sell an asset (in this case stocks), your virtual capital becomes actual money, which means you have to pay taxes. Since mutual fund managers buy and sell stocks continuously in order to stay ahead of the market, you also pay taxes every time your stocks are sold and liquidized. The more often you sell, the more taxes you pay.

The more frequent stocks are traded, the higher the total cost for the investor in expenses made up by load fees, trading costs, and taxes, which therefore eat away your profits. In the case of mutual funds, hardly any portfolio ends a year with the same stocks as the ones they started off with at the beginning of the year. According to the fund managers, this continuous trading is vitally important as it's their key to beating the market. But the question is whether this is vitally important to maximize their clients' profits or to make sure they get their commissions.

An additional problem in the case of these fees is that many of the above costs are not stipulated anywhere and are often hidden behind layers of complexities and jargon used by the mutual fund companies, so that investors are unlikely to even notice the various fees and costs they will incur.

Advantages

The advantages of mutual funds can be summarized as follows:

- Over the short term (one to five years), mutual funds can significantly outperform the market.
- Investors do not have to make (many) investment decisions.

Disadvantages

The disadvantages of mutual funds include the following:

- Mutual funds have many costs and fees, some hidden and some not, that can eat away any returns.
- Over long periods, a mutual fund is unlikely to outperform the market.
- Many mutual funds often specialize in a segment of the market, meaning portfolios are often not very diversified.

Many books have been written about this topic with far more detailed reviews of mutual funds. I strongly recommend that you read a few to inform yourself well of all the advantages and disadvantages in greater detail. The information above is merely a very basic introduction to the concept of mutual funds. Many podcasts on investing are also available and can provide you with invaluable extra information on this topic. Subscribe to the ones you like so you get notified when a new episode is released. (See Appendix D for a list of podcasts.)

- -

Investing in mutual funds is often seen as the default investment strategy for most. It's likely the one that you'll find easiest to get other people's opinion on.

☑ STEP 71 ACTION PLAN

Depending on where you live, the costs and funds available for mutual fund investing can vary significantly, so it's worthwhile finding out what your options are.

☐ Look for various (at least three or four so you can compare them well) mutual funds in your country or state.

☐ Find out as much as possible about the following details and make an overview per fund so you can compare them quickly:

- Minimum amount when paying a lump sum.
- Minimum monthly amount if making monthly contributions.
- Annual management and maintenance fees.
- Trading fees, commissions, advertising fees, and load fees. (You're unlikely to find much information on these, though, as most mutual funds do not stipulate these costs anywhere, or at least not clearly. They simply charge for them without notifying you.)
- Tax advantages offered.
- Types of funds available, i.e., small-companies funds, aggressive funds (less bonds), global funds, etc.
- Performance history of the fund. (Remember that any past results are no guarantee for future results, though.)
- General information on the company offering the fund as well as the fund manager(s) and their investment style or strategy.

☐ Remember that even if the fees sound small to you, 1.5% can quickly add up to several thousands of dollars over long periods that you end up paying for. For example, if you invest $10,000 now and leave it in an investment account with an average return of 7%, that money will have grown to $76,000 after thirty years. If, on the contrary, you pay out 1.5% of your returns in fees, leaving you with a net return of 5.5%, your portfolio will be worth less than $50,000, a difference of $26,000!

☐ Once a year, come back to this step to reevaluate your mutual funds investing strategy.

STEP 72

Investing in Index Funds / ETFs

Index investing outperforms active management year after year.

—JIM ROGERS

DIFFICULTY LEVEL: Medium

OBJECTIVE: Discover the advantages and disadvantages of investing through index funds

REVIEW TIMES: Yearly

As you were able to appreciate in Step 70 on hand-picking stocks and Step 71 on mutual/collective funds, both ways of investing have some distinct advantages, most notably the possibility of making a fair bit of money on the stock market. Yet the opposite is unfortunately also the case: investors can also lose big amounts of money by investing in these ways. As we'll see in this step, index investing, a third way of investing, aims to find a middle ground between making money on the market while avoiding big risks.

Index investing: an overview

An index is essentially a group of publicly traded companies in which investors can decide to invest. There are many different indexes throughout the world, but some of the most well known include the S&P 500 (five hundred large-cap companies), the Dow Jones (thirty large companies), or the NASDAQ (three thousand companies, many of them in information technology).

In index investing, you choose one index, and instead of deciding which stocks to buy within that index (as is the case in handpicking stocks or mutual funds), you simply buy shares of every single company in that index in the same proportion as they make up the index. Let's say the index is made up of 100 shares: 40 shares are from company A, 25 shares from company B, 20 shares from company C, and 15 from company D. If you invest $100, you buy the shares of these four companies in exactly the same proportion: 40% of your money will be used to buy shares from company A, 25% to buy company B shares, and so on. You basically copy the exact market and will therefore get almost exactly the same returns as the market average. (It will normally be just a fraction below due to the small fees you pay.) If the index goes up by 8%, your return will be a little below 8%.

Passive investing

In index investing, investors refrain from making predictions as to the companies' performance and which stocks you should therefore buy and sell. All stocks (and bonds) are simply bought or sold depending on the relative market value of the company in a particular index. If a company does not perform well and gets taken out of the index, then so will those shares, and they will be replaced by those of new companies entering the index.

Index investing is also known as "passive investing" as investors do not aim to beat the market by responding to market developments and changes on a daily basis. Instead, the aim is to replicate the market returns. Passive investing is therefore especially interesting for long-term investors who look to build up wealth in a relatively safe but efficient way.

Index fund characteristics

Of course, as a small investor, you are unlikely to have enough money to buy stocks of all the companies in the index, which is why index investing—like with mutual funds—pools money of different investors together to increase buying power. That said, with index investing there are no fund managers, making this route to investing a lot cheaper than mutual funds. The absence of continuous trading furthermore avoids load fees, excessive taxes, and other fees paid in many mutual funds. Portfolios are generally very diversified, which leads to risk being spread, so that even if one particular industry does not perform well one year, their lower results can be compensated by the returns of an industry that performed better. The more diversified your portfolio, the more spread out the risk of losing money.

Replicating instead of beating the market

The biggest disadvantage of index funds is that you will never beat the market. An investor will always get the average return, nothing more and nothing less. It is a relatively safe way to invest (though you can still lose a big chunk of your money if the market crashes!) and though you can never underperform, you can never outperform the market, either.

A note on ETFs

A special type of index investments are ETFs or exchange-traded funds. Whereas an index fund is a collection of stocks, an ETF is more like a stock in itself. ETFs can be traded almost the entire day when the markets are open, whereas index investing trading often only happens between once a week to a maximum of twice a day. The advantage of being able to trade pretty much all day means that you can play the market more, by reacting almost instantly when prices change. The potential danger with ETFs is

therefore that it can make investing semiactive again, with investors reacting to price drops or increases.

Since ETFs are not real stocks but artificial stocks created by investment banks, they can go bust. If you end up investing in ETFs, make sure they're backed up by real stocks, as otherwise you are left with nothing if this happens.

In short, the advantages and disadvantages of passive investing are:

Advantages

- The only decision you need to make is which market(s) to follow and how much of your portfolio you want to put into stocks and how much into bonds.
- Companies that do not perform very well and are dropped from the index just get replaced by new companies, so you never lose all of your money.
- Costs are very low (think 0.25% a year and maybe a small buying fee).
- You will always get about the market average return.
- If you follow a buy-and-hold strategy, you only pay taxes on dividend and/or interest payments received over the year, instead of paying taxes on the continuous gains made in mutual fund investing.
- Portfolios are often more diversified, ensuring a decent spreading of the risk.

Disadvantages

- You will never beat the market.
- You might end up with stocks you don't want.
- In the case of index investing, trading often only happens at set moments—although ETFs allow you to trade throughout the day.

When you know more about the three common ways of investing, there are quite a few more investing-related concepts worth knowing about before deciding on your own plan of action. Read on to find out what investing can look like on a more practical level.

☑ STEP 72 ACTION PLAN

☐ Investigate what's available to you if you were to open an index investing account. Search the Internet for "index investing broker + [your country]" and look for the following information on various brokers:

- Minimum amount when paying a lump sum
- Minimum monthly amount if making monthly contributions
- Yearly maintenance fees
- Trading fees
- Tax advantages offered
- Types of funds (both stocks and shares) available
- Average performance of funds over last few years (this should pretty much reflect the corresponding market averages)

☐ Compare various brokers to see what would be most suitable for your situation.

☐ Many financial bloggers share their experiences on brokers as well, so find some established bloggers in your country and read about their experience with various index fund brokers.

☐ Find a podcast, read a book, or start following a blog on index funds to learn more about this way of investing.

☐ Once a year, come back to this step to reevaluate your index investing strategy.

Bull and Bear Markets

Be fearful when others are greedy and greedy when others are fearful.

—WARREN BUFFETT

DIFFICULTY LEVEL: Difficult

OBJECTIVE: Learn how to take advantage of bull and bear markets

REVIEW TIMES: Yearly and whenever the market drops

Bull and bear markets are common terms used to refer to the performance of the stock market. In this step, we'll discover what bull and bear markets are and what to do when either of these take place.

Many on their way to financial independence see index investing as the safest and easiest way to invest. Though some regard it as boring, many investors recognize that it's a great way to get decent results. Of course, not everybody agrees, but in this step on bull and bear markets, I will mainly be referring to index investing when applying the market concepts. Therefore, not everything in this chapter is applicable to the other ways of investing.

Bull and bear markets

During a bull market, the stock exchange generally performs well: The economy is growing, consumers feel confident and spend money, and this leads to increases in prices and company profits. That in turn makes investors feel positive and leads to more investing. As demand starts to exceed supply, stock prices are pushed up further: every day more

people want to invest in the market and portfolios grow steadily in value.

The opposite of a bull market is a bear market: Prices drop, sometimes very quickly, and investors see the value of their portfolio go down and might try to quickly sell their stocks to avoid bigger losses. People lose confidence in the market and try to get out. If this happens too quickly or on a big scale, they might even end up selling below the original purchase price as they desperately try to offload their investments. Since there's more supply than demand, prices decrease even more.

I'm sure you can see which one of these markets is the one to hope for, right?

Profits and losses

Let's have a look at some key investing principles before we actually answer that question.

- When prices drop (a bear market), people often sell, hoping to at least cash in what they can before it's too late, worried stocks will not recover soon or fearing that a company will underperform or cease to exist altogether.
- Stocks and bonds have no actual value until you sell. On paper you might have $50,000 in stocks, but that money isn't yours unless you liquidate, and whatever their value is today might be completely different the moment you decide to sell.
- Taking the above point into consideration, you

don't actually take a loss until you sell. If you invest $10,000 today and see your stocks drop in value to $5,000 tomorrow, as long as you don't sell, you won't actually have lost anything.

- The same is true with any increases in the value of your assets: if your original $10,000 investment is worth $20,000 today, the value might go right down to $10,000 again tomorrow, and the $20,000 you had in between accounted for nothing.
- Until you sell, you don't pay income taxes on your assets (although you might be charged wealth tax on your assets depending on where you live—some countries in Europe especially have wealth tax—but this is usually lower than income tax). See also Part 9 for more on this.
- Once you sell, you pay taxes. If you invest $10,000 then sell a month later at $5,000, you will not only have lost $5,000, but you will also need to pay taxes on the $5,000 that you liquidated from selling your stocks.

Taking advantage of a bear market

With these basic investing principles in mind, let's see how to take advantage of a bear market.

- If you happen to invest a lot of money right before the start of a bear market, you'll likely see the value of your portfolio drop very quickly, as you would have bought stocks when they were at their most expensive right before their value started spiraling down.
- If on the contrary you invest at the bottom of a bear market right before the start of a bull market, you will likely make considerable gains as your stocks would have been very cheap when you bought them and then quickly increased in value right after that.
- During a bear market, most people panic and sell their portfolio at supercheap prices. What if instead of joining the crowds and liquidating your capital losses, you retained your investments? If you have the time and the

patience, follow this secret that's held up over the ages: prices will go up again (provided your portfolio is diversified and not made up of just a few companies that might go bust completely). It might take six months, a year, three years, or even longer. But remember that you won't lose money until you sell, so instead of counting your losses now, you could hold on to your investments and wait for the market to recover.

- The biggest challenge with the above strategy? Your emotions: fear resulting in panic. Fear that prices will drop even further, fear that the market will never recover, fear that you're the only one (or so you think!) holding on, while everybody else is at least cashing in what they can. Fear that you'll lose your entire savings or retirement account. But as long as you can overcome your fear, you can also overcome the financial loss. Consider the option to sit still and do nothing. Stop looking at your investments on a daily basis and just wait for better times.
- Another reason not to sell is that, unless the market experiences a real crash and the economy turns into a recession with companies no longer being able to share profits, normally even when stock prices fall, you are most likely still earning some dividends on your stocks even from just small amounts of profit some companies might be making or interest on bonds. If you automatically reinvest that money when share prices are low, you're buying stocks at a low cost.
- Now consider taking all of this another step further: What if you used a bear market to your advantage? Stocks and bonds are very cheap at this stage, so see it as one giant sale that you can use to your benefit. Buy now when your money can get you more stocks than ever, then patiently wait for the market to recover.

At the start of this step it maybe sounded like bull markets are the ultimate moment to invest, and that is indeed what most people do (thereby pushing up prices even further and helping the bull market to continue). But are they really, upon closer inspection? Bull markets drive the prices up, which is great if you want to sell now (or just for your own peace of mind). But from a long-term point of view, if you're interested in building wealth, a bear market is actually the better situation, because you can buy lots of stocks at low prices. However, you must have the patience and the time to let those stocks recover again. If you need the money soon, a bear market can have disastrous effects on the value of your portfolio.

Investing is all to do with emotions. Or, better said, controlling emotions. If you can resist fear, panic, and social pressure and instead use your logic to "sell when everybody is buying and buy when everybody is selling," you'll generally fare much better in the long term, especially when using a passive investing approach.

☑ **STEP 73 ACTION PLAN**

☐ Now that you've read about the characteristics of bull and bear markets, think about the following situations:

- Imagine you have investments and stock prices start to fall. What would you do? Do you think you could resist the temptation driven by fear or panic to sell?
- What if your friends, colleagues, family, or financial advisor all urge you to sell, saying you'll lose all of it if you don't liquidate right now? Could you resist the pressure?
- Taking it to the next level, would you be able to take advantage of the situation and actually increase your investments when stocks are on offer due to low prices? Or would you be too worried to put money in a tumbling market?

☐ After trying to answer those questions truthfully, go back to your virtual investing experiment from Step 70. Some of your stocks will have gone up in price while others will have dropped. What did you do instinctively when this happened? Did you buy more of the ones that were cheap? Or did you buy more of the ones going up in price?

☐ It's easy to think we can resist the temptation to join the masses and that we can be more intelligent and patient than the next person—but can we really? When push comes to shove, can you actually withstand the pressure to sell in a market experiencing a big drop? This step is rated as "difficult" not because it is a complex step to go through, but because of the difficulty most people experience when trying to implement it.

☐ Grab your file and write down a "contract" with yourself that if you own stocks at some point in the future and see prices drop, you will do the exact opposite of what the majority of people do: you'll hold on to what you have and not sell your stocks at discounted prices. Even better, you'll put in extra money, if possible, to buy more stocks during a bear market. Use the above questions to phrase your own "code of conduct" for the next bear market. Add in a note to reread this step if or when the time comes to remind yourself of the advantages of a bear market and take away (some of) your fears of investing when prices drop.

Dollar Cost Averaging

> *Risk comes from not knowing what you're doing.*
> —WARREN BUFFETT

DIFFICULTY LEVEL: Difficult

OBJECTIVE: Set up an investment account and learn how to deal with price fluctuations

REVIEW TIMES: Yearly

Going back to the more practical side of investing, there are a few more investment topics to look at. The first one is dollar cost averaging, which is a very powerful and clever investment strategy that turns market volatility to your advantage.

Dollar cost averaging introduced

Dollar cost averaging is the process by which the average cost of your investments (i.e., what you pay when you purchase them) goes down over time by taking advantage of price changes. This is achieved in two ways:

- When the market is up you buy fewer stocks, thereby avoiding buying too many when they're overpriced and expensive.
- When the market is down, you buy more stocks, thereby making the most of the stocks' cheaper price.

Let's look at how this works in detail by comparing the two most common investment strategies: investing a lump sum or investing a set monthly amount.

Lump sum investing

Imagine you've decided to invest $10,000 of your savings. Of course you never know what the market is going to do and whether today is the best day to invest, whether tomorrow will be better, or indeed if yesterday would have been the best day to pour that money into the market. If you invest it all in one go when it turns out the market was at a peak, prices are high, meaning you get less investments for your dollars, whereas the opposite is true when prices are low.

- Let's say the average price of stocks at the moment is $100, which, ignoring costs, means you would get a total of 100 stocks for your $10,000.
- Now imagine that prices drop to an average of $80 in the next two months. Not only does this mean your portfolio will lose $2,000 in value, what's more, if you had waited another two months to invest, you would have been able to buy 125 shares, i.e., 25% more!
- If after another two months prices climb back to their original value of $100, there are two interesting possible outcomes. If you entered the market when shares were $100 the first time, despite their drop halfway through, your portfolio will still be worth $10,000 in four months when prices bounce back to $100 a share. If, on the other hand, you held off investing and waited for prices to drop to $80

before you invested your $10,000, your portfolio would be worth $12,500 two months later.

- If the opposite happened in two months, i.e., prices going up to $120, then of course you'd be better off investing your money when they're $100/share rather than waiting until prices are 20% higher.

Disadvantages of lump sum investing

The problem with the above is that timing the market is almost impossible. Nobody—barring maybe a handful of exceptionally good (or lucky?) investors—can really predict what the market will do and when the highest or lowest point has arrived. Who knows whether prices will drop in the next two months or continue to go up? Who can tell whether the price of $80 will be the lowest point or whether to wait another few months for the price to go down even further?

Added to the unpredictability of the market is once again the psychological component of human behavior that comes into play when investing: fear often stops people from investing when markets are dropping. Throwing $10,000 at the market when prices go down every single day requires a strong stomach. And not stepping in when markets are on a high and prices are rising every day is equally difficult, especially when you hear many others boasting about their results and convincing you that now is the time to join, even if your logic tells you stocks are hugely overpriced.

But even if you can master those fears and decide you will only invest when the market is low, you have the extra problem that you never know how long to wait. If there's a bull market that lasts a whole three years, then all that time your $10,000 is sitting idly, losing value due to inflation. In that case, you might have done better investing it at $100/share after all.

How dollar cost averaging helps

Enter dollar cost averaging, a strategy in which you don't try to time the market but simply buy more stocks when prices are low and less stocks when prices are high. How do you do this without having to follow the market continuously? The answer might be easier than you think: by investing a set monthly amount.

- Instead of saving money every month to invest $10,000 in one go, let's say you instead decide to invest a set monthly amount of $300.
- When prices are $100 per share, you can afford three stocks a month.
- When prices go up, you keep investing the same amount of $300 a month. The higher the prices, the less stocks you can buy, so if stocks go up to $150, you end up only buying two stocks.
- When the opposite happens and prices drop to $75 a share, you keep calm as your steady investment strategy now buys you four stocks, thereby helping you profit from the cheap stock prices.
- In this way, you keep building up your portfolio in a way that maximizes profits from cheap stocks and minimizes the high costs when prices are close to a peak.
- With time, just like any portfolio, your assets will grow along with the market, but you know that you've used market drops to your advantage and avoided spending too much when prices were high. You therefore don't need to worry about timing the market and waiting for the best moment to step in.

That is the essence of dollar cost averaging—simple yet effective. The added beauty is that it takes away the human factors of greed and fear when prices are rising or dropping. It ensures you keep your cool and stick to your plan without getting distracted and without having to worry about when to invest.

- -

When following a dollar cost averaging strategy and a steady and continuous investment plan, you likely profit more from the volatility of the market than when using a one-off lump sum investment.

☑ STEP 74 ACTION PLAN

☐ Look at your budget and determine the monthly amount you would feel comfortable investing.

☐ If you already have a lump sum of money available that you might want to invest, consider dividing that up into smaller payments over several months in order to profit more if prices are yet to drop.

☐ Determine your ideal asset allocation between bonds and stocks. There are many different ways of determining how aggressive or offensive your portfolio should be, depending on your age, risk tolerance, and plan for your portfolio. Two common strategies are:

- Take your age and put that percentage in bonds, take the rest and buy stocks. Somebody who is 40 would in this way have 40% of their portfolio invested in bonds and 60% in stocks.
- If you have quite a bit of time still before you need the money, consider going for a very aggressive portfolio and keep 80% in stocks and 20% in bonds. Note that with this option, your portfolio is much more volatile and therefore more likely to make as well as lose money in the short term.
- If you're unsure what allocation matches your goals and the risks you feel comfortable with, ask a financial advisor to help you with this.

☐ Keep a set percentage of your wealth in your savings account as part of your asset distribution. In this way, you have money to fall back on in case the market crashes and you need money but don't want to sell your investments when they're worth much less.

☐ Determine how to allocate your money: How much do you want to invest in stocks and how much in bonds? Of course, these are only two possible examples; you can decide on your own mix however you want. Make sure to also refer to Steps 77 and 78, which cover other assets to include in your portfolio.

☐ If you've weighed all the pros and cons of investing and feel you're ready to invest, compare various brokers on their investment options, fees, and conditions. Open an investment account with the brokerage firm that meets your criteria.

☐ Set up an automatic monthly payment into your investment account.

☐ Know that when prices fall or rise, you will still be investing the same amount every single time. Do not deviate from this. Stick with your monthly amount and remember that greed or fear will not get you to your end goal, but a reasonable plan will.

☐ Track your investments and see how after each monthly investment you end up with more stocks every time the market drops and how you don't overspend on buying more when prices rise.

Rebalance Your Portfolio

It's not the situation, but whether we react (negative) or respond (positive) to the situation that's important.
—ZIG ZIGLAR

DIFFICULTY LEVEL: Medium

OBJECTIVE: Determine how to distribute your assets and set a yearly date to return your assets to this ideal allocation

REVIEW TIMES: Yearly

Any investment portfolio will require some long-term management to ensure it remains aligned with your goals. With time, some assets might grow faster than others, your financial goals might change, or you might want to adjust the risk level of your investments the closer you get to your goals or target dates. An easy way to ensure your investments adapt to these developments is to rebalance your portfolio and reallocate your assets. Similar to the investing principle of "buy when everybody else is selling," which we discussed in Step 73, the rebalancing of your portfolio is another investing concept that's easy to understand and execute logically, but can be difficult to implement from a psychological perspective.

Yearly rebalancing

A yearly rebalancing of your portfolio ensures that if one area of your portfolio does really well in a particular year, you don't deviate too much from the original asset allocation you had in mind for your portfolio. If one asset grows much more than another, it might make your portfolio too volatile or too defensive for your goals and risk tolerance.

To illustrate this point, assume that you want 70% stocks and 30% bonds in your portfolio. You have $10,000 in your investment portfolio. To make things easy, let's say that both bonds and stocks happen to be $100 per unit. Ignoring purchasing fees for the sake of this example, that means you would have $7,000 in stocks and $3,000 in bonds.

When you evaluate your investments a year later, your stocks have far outperformed the bonds. Both have gone up in value, but your bonds are now worth $3,150 (a 5% increase), whereas the total value of your stocks is now $8,050 (an increase of 15%). The stocks and bonds allocation as shown in Table 14 is now no longer 70/30 but 72/28. Not a huge difference, you might think—but if the stocks keep outperforming bonds by that much, you might end up with an 80/20 portfolio in just a few years' time.

With time, this might become too risky for you as you end up having more of your money in stocks, making your portfolio very volatile. (The opposite would of course happen if bonds outperform your stocks.) Presumably you started with a 70/30 allocation for a reason, as that was probably the optimal risk/return balance that you were looking for, so deviating too much from that balance means your portfolio is probably no longer in line with your long-term goal.

Table 14: Evolution of the relative size of assets in a portfolio

	Value stocks	% stocks	Value bonds	% bonds
Year 1	$7,000	70%	$3,000	30%
Year 2	$8,050	72%	$3,150	28%
Year 3	$9,258	74%	$3,308	26%

Note: Calculations based on an assumed 15% growth for stocks and 5% for bonds.

Rebalancing strategies

This is where the rebalancing of your portfolio comes in. When you rebalance, you return your portfolio to the original distribution of stocks vs. bonds that you had in mind, in this case 70/30. You can do this in two ways:

STRATEGY 1

Sell some of the assets that produced greater results in order to buy more of the ones that have fallen behind, so you get back to your original asset allocation. This has two advantages in itself:

- It allows you to liquidate the good returns for that year by selling some of those assets (remember you never know whether your $8,050 stocks might go down in a few months if share prices drop, so selling at a high lets you take advantage of the current high of these stocks).
- You're able to buy the lagging asset at a cheaper price (since bonds have gone up in price a lot less than stocks, they are much cheaper to purchase than stocks). You're essentially freeing up money to buy some cheaper assets—in this case, bonds.

STRATEGY 2

Alternatively, if you invest monthly, you can stop buying new stocks for a while and focus on buying bonds until the original allocation is back to 70/30.

This might take longer to achieve, but the advantages of this approach are:

- You don't need to pay taxes on the capital gains you would have gotten if you used strategy 1 to sell some of your stocks.
- Strategy 1 forces you to sell some of the stocks that have given you pretty decent returns. It might be psychologically difficult to sell investments after they just made you lots of money and are also paying out dividends.

Either strategy can prove to be difficult to implement as you are "sacrificing" your strong assets in favor of the weaker ones, which of course is a tough emotional decision to make. But if you want to make sure your portfolio is still aligned with your goals, you need to avoid letting it get out of balance. Rebalancing gives you the perfect way to get back to your original allocation.

How often you should rebalance

Generally speaking, rebalancing your portfolio once a year is a good interval to shoot for. It gives your assets some time to develop and profit from possible increases in the market while at the same time not letting your portfolio be too uncontrolled and get to an asset allocation that's way off what you had in mind. Of course, you can decide to rebalance more often or less frequently, depending on your own personal investment plan, but using the one-year mark as an initial guideline is a safe and effective way to start.

Rebalancing your portfolio is an efficient way to realign your investments with your goals and plans long term. There is, however, another way rebalancing your portfolio can prove to be an efficient strategy to employ to reach your goals, in particular when you get closer to retirement. The next step will look at that in more detail.

☑ STEP 75 ACTION PLAN

☐ Decide on a yearly rebalancing date to rebalance your portfolio. The end of the year or just before filing taxes can be good times to do this, although it can of course be any date that makes sense for your situation.

☐ If you already have an investment portfolio, look at its current balance and see how it compares to your ideal allocation. If you've just started investing or are not yet investing, you can ignore this for now.

☐ If you have different markets in your portfolio (for example, a U.S. stock index, a European index, and an upcoming markets index), you can apply the rebalancing to the different indexes, too. For instance, you can have a certain percentage in the international index, another in the U.S. index, and so on. In that way, if the upcoming markets do a lot better than your U.S. index, you can apply one of the two rebalancing techniques to get back to your ideal asset distribution among the various markets.

☐ If you expand your investing portfolio with other assets later on, such as real estate, gold, or commodities or through crowdfunding (see also Steps 77–79), update your asset allocation to incorporate all of your asset categories.

☐ Once a year, reevaluate not just whether you need to rebalance but also whether you're still happy with your asset allocation percentages. With time, you might want to keep more of your money in savings or bonds, for example.

Lifestyle Investment Strategy

Many people take no care of their money till they come nearly to the end of it, and others do just the same with their time.

—JOHANN WOLFGANG VON GOETHE

DIFFICULTY LEVEL: Medium

OBJECTIVE: Learn how to reduce the volatility of your long-term investments for retirement

REVIEW TIMES: Yearly

In the previous step, we looked at asset allocation and using a yearly rebalancing technique to keep the right balance between your various assets. In this step, we'll uncover how rebalancing your portfolio can also help to readjust your investments when you get closer to your financial goals.

In the examples below, I mainly use retirement as a goal, but it can of course be any other goal you might have in mind for your investments, such as a college fund for a (grand)child or a down payment on a house.

Lifestyle investment strategy

Assume that you have a 70/30 stocks/bonds allocation to start with in your portfolio and that the main goal for that portfolio is to use it as (an addition to) your retirement provision. As you near retirement, you might become a little nervous about the possible volatility of this portfolio. What if there were a sudden crash in the market and you lost a big chunk of the money right before or just

after you were planning to retire? Of course, when you're thirty or forty, having a portfolio with a bigger risk factor doesn't matter as much, because your portfolio still has time to recover. But when you're close to retirement age, you don't have the luxury of time, and you probably don't want as much volatility as when you were younger.

An often used strategy to combat this potential problem is the lifestyle investment strategy: a long-term gradual rebalancing of your portfolio in which you slowly move to a less volatile mix by increasing the percentage of bonds and decreasing the percentage of stocks. With a 70/30 portfolio, when you reach fifty, you might start rebalancing by 2% each year, meaning you would go to a 68/32 portfolio when you're 51, 66/34 the next year, and so on until you get to a 40/60 portfolio when you're sixty-five. If that's still too many stocks to your liking, you could start rebalancing with 2% and then increase it to 5% from 60 onward, which gets you to 25/75 by age sixty-five. Of course, you could also start adjusting earlier or later and with more or less yearly adjustments, depending on what you think is best for your situation.

Reducing risk

The lifestyle investment strategy is a very safe and secure way to make your portfolio less volatile while keeping the bulk of your money invested so you can still profit from market returns. You trade the possibility of higher returns (via more stocks in your portfolio) for more security by selling some stocks and purchasing bonds instead.

Rebalancing over several years instead of in one go means you don't take big risks as you only adjust by a small percentage each year. You're therefore unlikely to experience any radical changes in your portfolio and you follow a similar strategy to dollar cost averaging as you spread out the adjusting over a prolonged period.

Rebalancing your portfolio and the lifestyle option are excellent ways to keep your portfolio working for you in the right way instead of leaving it up to chance what will happen. It requires some planning and it might prove to be difficult, especially at times when you need to sell your high performing assets or stop purchasing those same assets in favor of the underperforming ones though, so you want to be sure to reread these steps when you are faced with a difficult decision like this.

☑ STEP 76 ACTION PLAN

☐ Regardless of how far away from your (retirement) goal you are, think about when you'd like to reach this goal and what you want your portfolio to look like by that time in terms of assets distribution.

☐ Plan when to start rebalancing to move toward this portfolio. Most investors do this anywhere from five to fifteen years before retirement to balance out any possible market oddities and volatility.

☐ Write down a plan detailing how much you want to rebalance each year by adjusting the percentages of your assets little by little. This can be anything you like; it just depends on your current asset distribution as well as your desired target allocation by the time you retire. For example, if your end goal is to retire with 30% stocks/70% bonds, your rebalancing will look different if you start with an 80/20 portfolio than a 60/40 portfolio. The first one will need more adjusting than the second.

☐ Take your asset allocation one step further and think of the percentage other assets should take up in your portfolio: retirement accounts, savings, real estate etc. Make a bigger asset allocation plan by having a clear percentage distribution for all of them, both at the moment as well as by the time you would like to retire. This means that a rebalancing might not only take place between stocks and bonds, but could also happen between stocks and cash or cash and retirement account funds if any of these grew substantially faster than the others.

☐ Every year when you rebalance your portfolio (as per Step 75) also review your lifestyle option investment plan to check whether any of your goals, end date or other circumstances have changed and therefore might need to be updated.

Investing in Gold and Commodities

> *Always keep your portfolio and your risk at your own individual comfortable sleeping point.*
>
> —MARIO GABELLI

DIFFICULTY LEVEL: Medium

OBJECTIVE: Find out about the advantages and disadvantages of investing in gold and commodities

REVIEW TIMES: Yearly

Whereas many investors have big chunks of their money (if not all) invested in a mix of bonds and stocks, there are other investment options to consider that offer additional diversification to your portfolio. Once you get a taste for investing, you'll likely want to find out more about these other options, whether it's to diversify your portfolio, increase returns, or simply learn more about other market areas.

The current and next few steps look at some of these alternative investments. Let's start with gold and commodities.

Investing in commodities

Commodities are a raw material or primary agricultural product. They are important assets for the stock market in two ways. First, they can be invested in directly, just like stocks and bonds, and they're traded on the market in a similar way.

Second, many companies rely on commodities.

If you have Coca-Cola shares, then sugar prices will at some point affect Coca-Cola's expenses, profits, and consequently dividend returns and share prices. For any shares you might have in big retail or fashion stores, wool prices will similarly affect their overheads and hence share prices. Many other companies rely on such commodities as oil, copper, grains, and aluminum.

Types of commodities

Commodities can generally be divided into two classes:

- **Soft commodities:** cocoa, wool, cotton, wheat, rice, coffee, etc. These prices can fluctuate a lot, especially when a shortage exists (think about how a bad harvest for grains, rice, potatoes, or coffee could drive up prices). Apart from the weather and shifts in climate, other factors such as a growing population, political relations, as well as people's eating patterns can affect these prices.

- **Metals:** zinc, aluminum, copper, etc. Prices for metals are less volatile than soft commodities as their production or cultivation time is much longer. Just consider how long it takes to find a new source of these metals, raise funds, and then finally build and operate a new mine. The development of new technologies such as microchips that use different metals can often affect the evolution of metal prices.

Commodity price fluctuations

Whereas stocks and bonds tend to move together (when stocks go up, bonds usually go up too, although much less dramatically), commodities often move in opposite directions from the rest of the market. They therefore make an interesting addition to many portfolios as they can provide some stability when the market moves a lot.

The reason for this opposite movement is actually quite simple: When the market goes down in an economic recession, people want to invest in security, which commodities provide—after all, we all need to eat! This drives commodity prices up. In reaction to this, more commodities are produced as more people see that farming or mining is becoming more lucrative. The increase in demand leads to a gradual increase in supply. Since this increase is often delayed, however (it takes a while to farm, mine, and otherwise produce the commodities), the reaction to the increase in demand is slow. Once supply finally starts to increase, prices go down again due to a surplus in resources, meaning that fewer people invest in commodities, and so fewer people farm or mine commodities because they generate less income, which leads to a reduction in the supply. The cycle is then repeated again. As you can see, price, supply, and demand are all factors that keep this process in balance.

Investing in gold

In addition to investing in commodities, many opt to invest in gold. One of the major advantages of gold is that it does well when the market doesn't do well. Just have a look online at "historic gold price chart" and see how much the price for gold soared following the 2008 crash. Investors see gold as a very safe investment which—unlike most companies' stocks and bonds—has been around for thousands of years and will be around for many more. When people are fearful about the market, they invest in gold as a "stable" investment.

Gold itself, unlike bonds (via interest), stocks (via dividends), and real estate (via rental income—see Steps 58 and 78), does not produce an income. The price simply goes up or down. There are times when gold prices have done well and have gone up significantly, but there have also been long periods (such as for about twenty years between 1984 and 2004) when prices were pretty much flat or even went down consistently. So whereas gold can be a good investment and a way to diversify, it doesn't always have the same wealth-generating potential as stocks and bonds.

Although often referred to as "investing in gold" because that's the most common variant, gold is part of a bigger investment category of precious metals, which also includes silver and platinum, both of which tend to be slightly more volatile than gold.

- -

If you decide to invest in gold or commodities, you'll probably end up holding just a very small percentage of your portfolio in these assets. But they can both provide extra stability, especially if you fear another recession and would like to have some stable assets in case you need to liquidate part of your portfolio.

☑ STEP 77 ACTION PLAN

☐ Find out more about commodity categories and how their prices have evolved over the last years and decades.

☐ The above is only an introduction to investing in commodities and gold. Before taking it to the next level, make sure to educate yourself on the options, risks, and costs by reading books, articles, and trustworthy websites, or by consulting a financial advisor.

☐ Investigate available options for investing in commodities and/or gold and compare the fees, conditions, and small print among different brokers.

☐ Decide whether to take gold and/or commodities up in your investment portfolio and if you do, set up an investment account and make your first contribution.

☐ Once a year, reevaluate your investment strategy and decide whether to change your gold and commodity investments.

Investing in Real Estate

Real estate investing, even on a very small scale, remains a tried and true means of building an individual's cash flow and wealth.

—ROBERT KIYOSAKI

DIFFICULTY LEVEL: Medium

OBJECTIVE: Learn about three ways to invest in real estate

REVIEW TIMES: Yearly

As we saw in the previous step, investing in gold and commodities can be an interesting addition to your portfolio that spreads out your risk. In this step, we'll look at yet another way to diversify your investment portfolio: investing in real estate. Even if at the moment this doesn't sound like something you would want to pursue (soon), it's worth exploring to at least consider all the options for your long-term financial plan.

Investing in real estate

In Steps 55 and 58, we discussed various ways real estate can provide an extra income, such as through renting out a property for a regular monthly income stream, as well as the possibility of a capital gain when the property is sold. These are two ways to invest in real estate, but here are other options for investing in real estate via the market:

- **REITs, or real estate investment trusts:** REITs are funds for which a trust pools together investors' money in order to purchase real estate

and then rent it out to generate income. In the case of REITs, you don't own any property yourself, but instead own a part of the trust's property portfolio, similar to how a share gives you part of a public company. Like stocks and bonds, REITs trade on the market and can therefore go up and down in price like any other publicly traded asset. The advantage of REITs is that they must pay out a big chunk of their profits as dividends in order to keep their status as a REIT, meaning that returns can be higher than dividends or interest payments.

- **Real estate investment groups:** This option is ideal if you want to actually own a property to rent out but don't want to deal with the hassle that comes with it: finding tenants, collecting rent, dealing with maintenance issues, etc. As an investor in a real estate investment group, you buy one or more units or apartments of a bigger apartment complex owned by an investing company. By buying a unit, you become part of the real estate investment group and the owner of an apartment, but the investing company deals with the day-to-day issues and operations of the units on a collective basis so you don't need to. The investment group will take part of the rent you generate to cover their services. In this way, you create an income stream by renting out your property without having to take care of the daily operating.

- **Real estate trading:** Also known as flipping, this is a practice in which somebody buys a property, holds it for normally just a few months, and then sells it again at a higher price. This is especially effective if one is able to buy a property that's highly undervalued, with the possibility of selling again at a much higher price. Contrary to capital gains over a long period, real estate trading is focused on capital gains made in just a few months. Bear in mind that taxes on short-term capital gains can be significantly higher compared to capital gains made on assets that were held for long periods, though.

For investing purposes, real estate can be residential housing, but it can also include other types of real estate such as commercial property (think about offices and factories). Housing options for seniors, for which demands are increasing due to aging populations, are another investment possibility in the real estate market.

- - - - - - - - - - - - - - - - - - - -

If you would like to add real estate to your investment portfolio, you can either do so on a small scale by investing in REITs, or on a much bigger scale by buying your own investment property. The flexibility real estate gives makes it a good candidate for a widely diversified portfolio.

☑ STEP 78 ACTION PLAN

- ☐ Remember the above is only an introduction to investing in real estate. If you're considering this option, make sure you understand the risks, responsibilities, and possible returns this option might give you.

- ☐ Investigate your options for investing in real estate and commit to reading more about it online and by listening to podcasts. If after the extra research you feel that investing in real estate might be right for you, buy a book that is specifically about investing in real estate in your country and includes information on legal and tax consequences.

- ☐ Investigate brokers or investment companies that offer real estate in their portfolio. Read up on their terms and conditions, fees, transaction costs, and any other small print to see which best suits your needs.

- ☐ Make sure you fully understand the rules and regulations when it comes to investing in real estate, especially the legal side such as tax laws and licenses needed if you want to rent out your property, as there can be a substantial amount of money involved in real estate investing.

- ☐ Determine whether to take up real estate in your investments and if you decide to do so, take any necessary next steps to get started.

- ☐ Once a year, reevaluate your investment strategy and decide whether to adjust your investments in real estate.

Investing through Crowdfunding

When something is important enough, you do it even if the odds are not in your favor.

—ELON MUSK

DIFFICULTY LEVEL: Medium

OBJECTIVE: Discover how crowdfunding works and decide whether to participate to generate some money

REVIEW TIMES: Monthly tracking, yearly evaluation

A type of investing that's become hugely popular in recent years is crowdfunding. Crowdfunding is a way for companies, entrepreneurs, and start-ups to get together a sum of money to set up a business, launch a new product, or expand and open a new project or department. Many new platforms on the Internet have jumped into this emerging market and have made crowdfunding available to the wider public.

Types of crowdfunding

Raising money through crowdfunding can be done in three different ways:

- In **P2P** (peer-to-peer) lending, capital is raised by getting many different loans of small amounts together from many different people. Traditionally a company or start-up needing money would have had to get a loan from a bank or private investors, but with crowdfunding, they might get as many as two hundred different people lending them

amounts between $50 and $1,000. As with a traditional bank loan, a company who secures capital through crowdfunding commits to paying their investors these loans back over a set amount of time, with interest.

- **Presales** is a type of crowdfunding in which people can preorder a new product or service even before it's been produced or developed. In return, initial investors get a first release or even a small present once or several times a year (for example, a new exclusive wine). The money collected through presales is used to then produce or deliver the product or service.
- Lastly, **selling shares** and having people invest in your company in return for a small ownership can be another way to get together capital for a new project, product release, or expansion. Like we saw before, this means the investor(s) will be entitled to part of the profit—i.e., dividends— and will have a say in the company. As these are shares and not a loan, they will not be paid back the original amount of money that they invested and investors should be aware that these shares are often not straightforward to resell as they are not traded on the public market.

Why raise capital through crowdfunding?

For anybody looking to grow their money through crowdfunding, the first option of P2P lending is the most common type to pursue. But why would start-ups want to raise money through P2P lending? There are several advantages with raising capital through crowdfunding as opposed to getting a loan at the bank:

- It can be very difficult to get a loan from a bank these days. Banks are more cautious when it comes to accepting new applications, especially for start-ups, as they on average have a high failure rate. Therefore, for new companies, it's often a lot easier to get the money together through crowdfunding.
- Interest fees charged by banks are high and can be kept lower through crowdfunding.
- A start-up successfully raising capital through crowdfunding will automatically create a network of people who will likely provide support in many other ways to help the company become successful. In other words, crowdfunding builds a small group of people to help launch, promote, and recommend the company, thereby increasing sales through the company's investors or "ambassadors".

✔ **MAKE IT FUN!**

Crowdfunding can be even more satisfying if you connect with the start-up on a personal level. Follow them on social media; use their services; if you invested in a restaurant, have dinner there and then post about your (hopefully) great experience, or recommend it to friends. In this way, you become more involved in the project which can make the success of the company about more than simply earning a little extra money.

- There is no limit on the amount that can be raised through P2P lending, whereas banks often have a maximum they're willing to lend.
- To secure a bank loan, you often need a good amount of start-up capital to begin with or backing by investors. Start-ups and product launches that don't yet have the means to get this together often find this difficult. Crowdfunding often works better for them.

Advantages of investing through crowdfunding

For investors, investing through crowdfunding can be profitable for the following reasons:

- Returns can be higher than average returns on the stock market.
- You can decide how much to invest. There is often no compulsory monthly contribution or minimum amount. Many platforms let you invest with as little as $100 or even $50, and you can decide how often and how much you want to put into these new projects, even if that's just once or twice a year.
- You can be very specific about what you want to invest in; you choose your own projects. This means you can support just those start-ups that you identify with, whether they offer new gadgets, have a humanitarian focus, or promote wildlife conservation—you select exactly those that meet your standards.
- It can be more fun and rewarding knowing that you helped create or support a new product or start-up. Buying stocks or shares from big companies that already have a revenue of many billions of dollars per year is not the same as giving a new entrepreneur the possibility to realize their dream with some start-up capital.

Disadvantages of investing through crowdfunding

There are also possible risks or disadvantages of investing through crowdfunding:

- You need to inform yourself very well and investigate much more than if you were to invest in a big company on the international market. Is there a decent business plan? What is the project like? When do they expect to make a profit, and how likely are they to succeed?
- There is a higher risk of companies not surviving. Start-ups have a bigger chance of failure than existing companies, and if they go bust before paying back their loans, the company will be gone and so will your money. Therefore, with crowdfunding, you run a bigger risk of not getting (some of) your money back. This of course is offset by the bigger returns on investment.
- New projects open to funding can fill up quickly, sometimes in just a day, so it can be difficult to actually invest in a project you're looking for unless you're monitoring the platform regularly.

Crowdfunding can make investing more tangible as it's on a much smaller scale and it's easier to track individual projects on a regular basis compared to investments made in the big, anonymous market. Part of the fun with crowdfunding can also come from tracking the returns on a regular basis and reinvesting the money regularly to keep your capital growing.

☑ STEP 79 ACTION PLAN

☐ There are different websites and platforms on which projects can be found, such as Kickstarter, Crowdfunder, and GoFundMe. Start investigating some of these platforms and read their specifics. Like with investing accounts, make sure you check the following details:

- Minimum amount to invest
- Costs
- Success rates and how many of their projects default on their payments
- Client feedback: how content they are with the services, the level of customer service, etc.

☐ Read up on some of the projects advertised. Often the websites will divide projects based on risk, return, length of loan, and so on. See which types of projects you might consider sponsoring.

☐ Determine whether you want to start investing through crowdfunding. You might not want to put all of your money in this type of investing, but you could of course allocate a small portion of your investment money to crowdfunding or even just try one and see how it goes. You can also decide to start with two or three projects and only take on any new projects once you've been paid back enough from these first few.

☐ If you decide to sponsor any crowdfunding projects, keep track of the project on a spreadsheet or in your notebook. Indicate how much you have invested per project and update monthly how much you've received, whether any projects are defaulting (i.e., not able to pay back their investors), and the interest you're receiving.

☐ Once a year, reevaluate your crowdfunding investments to determine whether to increase or decrease your contributions.

The 4% Rule

> *Every day is a bank account, and time is our currency. No one is rich, no one is poor, we've got twenty-four hours each.*
>
> —CHRISTOPHER RICE

DIFFICULTY LEVEL: Difficult

OBJECTIVE: Calculate how much money you need to become financially independent

REVIEW TIMES: Yearly

Now that we're advancing through the 100 steps and financial independence is becoming more and more tangible, I can almost hear you think, "How much money do I actually need to retire or to achieve financial independence?" It's about time we started putting together a lifetime plan for your financial journey, one that will provide a blueprint to achieve your goals.

The Trinity Study

In the late nineties and then again in 2009, three professors from Trinity University conducted a now famous study[21] on how well investment portfolios would have done in funding retirement by selling off part of the investments each year to generate an income. They wanted to know how different withdrawal percentages affected various portfolios over long periods.

They were interested in how the portfolios stood up against various withdrawal rates, i.e., whether the portfolios would stand the test of time and outlive those regular outtakes. If a particular

rate succeeded, it meant there was still money left over in the portfolio after the withdrawals ended. Since they looked at long periods of time, inflation was an important factor to bear in mind, so they not only looked at the effect of specific withdrawal rates, but also the effect of adjusting withdrawals to inflation. So if a portfolio had a value of $1 million and the starting withdrawal rate was 4%, they took out $40,000 in the first year. For the second year, this amount would be adjusted for inflation: say it had been 3% that year, so they would withdraw $41,200 in the second year, 3% more than the year before.

The results

The Trinity Study was a huge study and the most important or interesting findings included the following:

- Even if you keep up with inflation and adjust withdrawals accordingly, starting withdrawals at 4% per year is a safe bet. With that approach, portfolios had the following success rates (i.e., chance of having funds left over at the end of the payout period):

  a. 100% stocks/0% bonds: 100% success rates for payout periods of fifteen, twenty, and twenty-five years. For thirty years, the success rate was 98%.

Table 15: Survival changes of portfolios with different asset allocations with a 4% inflation-adjusted withdrawal rate

	100% stocks/ 0% bonds	75% stocks/ 25% bonds	50% stocks/ 50% bonds	25% stocks/ 75% bonds	0% stocks/ 100% bonds
15 year withdrawal period	100%	100%	100%	100%	100%
20 year withdrawal period	100%	100%	100%	100%	97%
25 year withdrawal period	100%	100%	100%	95%	62%
30 year withdrawal period	98%	100%	96%	80%	35%

b. 75% stocks/25% bonds: 100% success rates for all payout periods.

c. 50% stocks/50% bonds: 100% rates for payout periods of fifteen, twenty, and twenty-five years. For thirty years, the success rate was 96%.

d. 25% stocks/75% bonds: 100% success rates for payout periods of fifteen and twenty years. For twenty-five years, the success rate was 95%, and for thirty years, it was 80%.

e. For a 100% bonds portfolio, the rates quickly decrease from 100% (fifteen years) and 97% (twenty years) to 62% (twenty-five years) and 35% (thirty years).

- For higher withdrawal rates (5% and more), there are significant chances that the portfolio will not last until the end of the withdrawal period, i.e., that it runs out of money before the end of the envisioned retirement period.
- When you stick to a 3% withdrawal rate, even after adjusting for inflation, you have a 100% success rate in pretty much all scenarios. The only exception is a thirty-year withdrawal period for a 100% bond portfolio, when the success rate dropped to 84%.

The 4% rule

Based on the results of this study, the researchers concluded that if you stuck to a 4% withdrawal rate and you had anywhere from 50% to 100% of your portfolio in stocks, there was at least a 96% chance that your portfolio survived a thirty-year payout period in the years between 1926 and 2009. Stick to 3% and your portfolio would be almost guaranteed to outlive you.

Note how it says *almost* guaranteed! Nothing is certain, especially not on the stock market. Past results are definitely no guarantee for future results, and the 2007–2009 market downturn will have had significant effects on the survival rate of portfolios of anybody who withdrew from their portfolio during that time. Step 81 on sequence of return risk looks at this in more detail.

How to guarantee the success of a 4% withdrawal rate

Because of these findings, 4% is commonly referred to as the safe withdrawal rate. It means that if inflation is 2–3% and the market goes up by an average of 7% (the average expected annual return), you can spend the remaining 4% freely without your investments losing value. Does this always hold up? No; every situation is different depending on market developments and your personal situation. Do you expect to have some big lump sum expense coming up, such as a child going to college, a new car, or buying a second house? If you're planning to pull this money from your investments, then the 4%

rule likely won't serve. Also, if you live in a country or state where your wealth or your withdrawals are taxed, you have to take this into consideration as it means your costs are higher. Lastly, if the market experiences a particularly big downturn, the 4% rule might not hold up (the next step covers what to do in those situations). But other than that, the 4% rule is a pretty safe bet.

- -

The more familiar with the 4% rule you'll get, the more you'll be able to appreciate its popularity and simplicity when it gets to planning your financial independence.

☑ STEP 80 ACTION PLAN

☐ Let's go back to our original question at the start of this step on how much money you need to become financially independent. To calculate your portfolio needs, first decide what percentage withdrawal rate you feel comfortable with. Do you want to stick to the 4% rule, or would you rather play it even safer and use 3% or 3.5%? Do you have enough other sources of income or retirement funds or another type of safety net to chance withdrawing 5% or 6%? Decide on what you feel comfortable with and the risk you want to take.

☐ Calculate the annual expenses you expect to have by the time you want to be financially independent or retire.

☐ Estimate how much of those expenses can be covered by other sources of income, such as retirement accounts, passive income and savings.

☐ Determine how much of your annual expenses are still left to pay for with your investments.

☐ If you decide on a 4% withdrawal rate, divide those remaining annual expenses by 0.04. This gives you the total amount you need in your portfolio to live off yearly and cover your expenses. If you want to go for a safe 3%, divide your annual expenses by 0.03.

  - For example, if you need $45,000 a year and have no other sources of income, then you need to have a $1,125,000 portfolio with a 4% withdrawal rate. At a 3% withdrawal rate, you'd need $45,000 / 0.03, which is $1,500,000.

☐ If you expect your annual expenses to go up or down significantly once you retire, adjust your projected annual expenses accordingly.

☐ Remember the above calculation does not take inflation into account. If you're thirty years away from retirement, then an annual expense of $45,000 today will be more than $96,000 in thirty years at an inflation rate of 2.5%. In this scenario, you wouldn't need $1,000,000 but $2,400,000 to retire, assuming you also withdrew 4% and lived the same lifestyle. To adjust the amount for inflation, look back at Step 47 and / or use an online calculator.

☐ Once a year, review your calculations and adjust them for changes in expenses, investments, or inflation.

Sequence of Return Risk

The four most dangerous words in investing are: This time it's different.

—SIR JOHN TEMPLETON

DIFFICULTY LEVEL: Difficult

OBJECTIVE: Protect your retirement account against poor market returns by understanding sequence of return risk and building in safety nets

REVIEW TIMES: Yearly

To finish off the part on investing and portfolio projections, we'll look at one last factor to take into account when planning your financial independence. Sequence of return risk—or sequence risk—can pose a serious threat to your portfolio, and as such it's important to take measures against it when planning your retirement. Sequence of return can hamper a secure retirement, whether you plan to retire when you're forty, sixty-five, or eighty. It can seriously increase your chances of outliving your portfolio, meaning you might be left with no funds at some point during your retirement.

What is sequence of return risk?

Sequence of return risk is the risk of your portfolio being hit by bad market returns early on in retirement when you start making withdrawals from your portfolio. Whereas you have time to recover from a few bad years if you're still building up your portfolio, once you start withdrawing from it, you

no longer have this time to recover. The value of a portfolio can be affected by sequence of return so much that it threatens its own chances of survival. If you withdraw when the markets grow, there's no real danger, as long as you stick to a safe withdrawal rate and monitor things carefully. But if you withdraw *and* there's a market drop, your portfolio is doubly hit.

The effects of sequence of return

To highlight the devastating effect sequence of return risk can have, we're going to look at an example retiree's portfolio. Let's say she has $1,000,000, and the market returns an average of 8% over the first twenty years of her retirement, but these twenty years are characterized by some very good and some incredibly bad years. This retiree takes out $40,000 (4%) in her first year and then adjusts for 3% inflation each year. Table 16 shows how her portfolio does in those twenty years.

Despite the average 8% yearly return, as you can see, this portfolio takes a big hit at the start of retirement with big negative returns and therefore a huge decrease in value early on. Unfortunately, after seventeen years, the portfolio is completely depleted and this person is no longer able to draw anything out of it. Of the $1,000,000 she started with, she was only able to take out just under $835,000. The rest of the value of the portfolio evaporated when the market entered a recession.

Table 16: An example of how sequence of return can devastate a portfolio

Year	Value portfolio start of year	Money withdrawn	Market return	Total left over
1	1,000,000	$40,000	-10%	$864,000
2	$864,000	$41,200	-15%	$699,380
3	$699,380	$42,436	-25%	$492,708
4	$492,708	$43,709	5%	$471,449
5	$471,449	$45,020	0%	$426,429
6	$426,429	$46,371	-15%	$323,049
7	$323,049	$47,762	5%	$289,051
8	$289,051	$49,195	20%	$287,827
9	$287,827	$50,671	10%	$260,872
10	$260,872	$52,191	25%	$260,852
11	$260,852	$53,757	30%	$269,224
12	$269,224	$55,369	15%	$245,932
13	$245,932	$57,030	-10%	$170,012
14	$170,012	$58,741	15%	$127,961
15	$127,961	$60,504	25%	$84,322
16	$84,322	$62,319	30%	$28,604
17	$28,604	$28,604	-15%	$0
18	$0	$0	15%	$0
19	$0	$0	30%	$0
20	$0	$0	25%	$0

Let's look at a second example in Table 17. This person also starts with $1,000,000, takes out 4% in their first year, and readjusts for a 3% inflation each year. Although she experiences the same average of 8% market return over twenty years, the order of these market returns is completely reversed: she experiences great returns early on in retirement and big negative returns later on.

This person's portfolio far outlives the twenty-year withdrawal period. Although it starts to take hits toward the end, her portfolio is still more than double from what she started with. In addition, she's been able to take out close to $1,075,000!

Strategies to combat sequence of return

How well your portfolio performs and indeed survives from the moment you retire is partially luck—there isn't much you can do about these market returns. What you *can* do, however, is change your investment and retirement strategy to ensure you don't outlive your portfolio, as is the case in the first example. Below are five ways to do this.

1. RETIRE LATER

If you can delay your retirement age and start withdrawing from your portfolio just a few years after the initial market crash, this could have a huge impact. In the example of the first retiree, if she had held off withdrawing from her portfolio for just three years (and without even continuing to make any extra contributions), her assets would have fared a lot better. If withdrawing nothing during the first three years, then from year four on, taking out the same amounts as in the original plan ($43,709 in year four), she would have ended up with over $122,000 twenty years later, seventeen years after she started withdrawing.

2. ADJUST YOUR WITHDRAWAL AMOUNT

Adjusting the withdrawal amount depending on the value of your portfolio can have incredible impacts. If the person from the first example had adjusted

her withdrawal rate to 4% of the actual value of the portfolio each year, she would have ended up with more than 1.5 million left over after twenty years. So instead of sticking to the amount based on 4% of the value of the portfolio at the start of retirement and then simply adjusting for inflation, each year you reevaluate how much 4% of the current value of your portfolio would be. In year two, when her portfolio had dropped to $864,000 she would have only withdrawn $34,560 that year.

Although this strategy means there are certain years she could only have withdrawn a meager amount, this portfolio at least provides some income all along. And after twenty years, it would have experienced a significant increase in value.

3. RELY ON CASH DURING LOW RETURNS

Avoid withdrawing from your portfolio during low market returns, for example by relying on cash reserves during tougher times. Having some of your funds tucked away in a savings account instead of investments means you have an alternative to draw from during market crashes. This can be a safe way to avoid depleting your portfolio faster than you want. This strategy can easily be used alongside the previous strategy (adjusting the withdrawal rate) so you need not even rely on cash completely. Of course, any money sitting in a savings account will not make you any money if it's not receiving much interest. It probably even loses value over time due to inflation, so you shouldn't keep too much money sitting in a savings account idly.

4. HAVE OTHER INCOME STREAMS

Supplement your withdrawal from your portfolio by other income streams such as a state-sponsored retirement plan, annuity, or rental or profit income. Depending on when you plan to retire, your retirement funds might kick in at exactly the right moment anyway—but if you retire before the official retirement age, you might not receive any funds for another couple of years. If you can rely on an annuity in the meantime, this might give

Table 17: A portfolio with the same market returns as Table 16 but in reverse order

Year	Value portfolio start of year	Money withdrawn	Market return	Total left over
1	$1,000,000	$40,000	25%	$1,200,000
2	$1,200,000	$41,200	30%	$1,506,440
3	$1,506,440	$42,436	15%	$1,683,605
4	$1,683,605	$43,709	-15%	$1,393,911
5	$1,393,911	$45,020	30%	$1,753,558
6	$1,753,558	$46,371	25%	$2,133,984
7	$2,133,984	$47,762	15%	$2,399,155
8	$2,399,155	$49,195	-10%	$2,114,964
9	$2,114,964	$50,671	15%	$2,373,937
10	$2,373,937	$52,191	30%	$3,018,270
11	$3,018,270	$53,757	25%	$3,705,642
12	$3,705,642	$55,369	10%	$4,015,300
13	$4,015,300	$57,030	20%	$4,749,923
14	$4,749,923	$58,741	5%	$4,925,741
15	$4,925,741	$60,504	-15%	$4,135,452
16	$4,135,452	$62,319	0%	$4,073,133
17	$4,073,133	$64,188	5%	$4,209,392
18	$4,209,392	$66,114	-25%	$3,107,459
19	$3,107,459	$68,097	-15%	$2,583,457
20	$2,583,457	$70,140	-10%	$2,261,985

you the option to ride out the low returns until you can start withdrawing more from your portfolio again. Of course, having other sources of income such as rental income or profit income can also provide an excellent alternative to withdrawing from your portfolio.

5. DIVERSIFY

As we've discussed many times, if you diversify your portfolio, you don't get affected by lows as much as when you only have one asset class. You're not relying on just stocks (or real estate or commodities) but on other asset classes as well. So even if your stocks portfolio drops by 20%, your bonds might still be holding up, or maybe you can start withdrawing a little more from your gold supply. Depending on which assets have performed better (or less bad), you can adjust the part of your portfolio you're withdrawing from, thereby avoiding liquidating your losses.

- -

Will sequence of return affect your portfolio when you retire, or will you be lucky and experience good returns at the start of your retirement? There's just no way to predict. But if you start out prepared, you avoid running out of money later on.

☑ STEP 81 ACTION PLAN

☐ Plan for the possible risk of sequence of return on your portfolio during your early retirement years by implementing several of the options described earlier into your long-term financial plan.

☐ Be flexible with your retirement age. Of course, you can have a goal to retire at a certain age or date, but remember it might be worth considering retiring one or two years later if it means your portfolio stays healthy and your retirement secure.

☐ Prepare for a flexible income. Pay off as many of your debts as soon as possible so you don't need to pay off anything when retired, including your mortgage. Design a lifestyle in which you can easily cut costs. In that way, it will be a lot easier to aim for a 4% withdrawal rate even if that means a significant reduction in your income from one year to the next.

☐ Decide how much cash reserves you want to have and might need and how and when to start building them up.

☐ Build up other income sources:
- Start funding your retirement accounts as early as possible (see Part 7).
- Develop other income streams aside from your income that might give you an income by the time you retire (see Part 6).

☐ Diversify your portfolio and invest in various asset classes: stocks, bonds, real estate, gold, and commodities, as well as across markets: national, international, emerging markets, small cap and large cap, etc.

☐ Start de-risking your portfolio closer to retirement age (lifestyle investment strategy) by increasing your percentage of bonds and decreasing your value of stocks (see Step 76).

☐ At the end of each year, analyze your long-term plan to financial independence designed in this step and make any necessary changes.

☐ Once you retire, keep a close eye on the value of your portfolio and adjust your strategy on a yearly basis. At the end of each year, determine how much you can safely take out of your portfolio based on last year's returns and the total value of your portfolio by then.

Checklist Part 8

Use the following checklist to make sure you have done everything in Part 8 and are ready to continue with the next part:

- [ ] You have analyzed whether now is the right time to start investing, and if it is, you've opened an investment account, after comparing various brokerage firms, and have made your first contribution.

- [ ] You understand what stocks and bonds are, some of the key differences between them, and how they can make you money.

- [ ] You understand the advantages and disadvantages of handpicking stocks and have simulated a few weeks of selecting stocks while keeping track of the returns.

- [ ] You know the advantages and disadvantages of investing in mutual funds as well as of index fund investing. You've done research on the types of funds available along with the various fees they might charge.

- [ ] You know what bull and bear markets are and have learned how to take advantage of both these markets through dollar cost averaging. You have written a contract or reminder to yourself about what to do when market prices drop.

- [ ] You have decided on your ideal asset allocation and have set a yearly date to rebalance your portfolio to return your assets to this ideal allocation.

- [ ] You know your long-term retirement portfolio allocation and have a gradual de-risking strategy the closer you get to your planned retirement age (lifestyle investment strategy).

- [ ] You understand the advantages and disadvantages of investing in gold and commodities and have decided what percentage of your investments to keep in these assets.

- [ ] You know the three ways you can invest in real estate and have analyzed whether this investment option is something for you to pursue at this time.

- [ ] You have learned how crowdfunding works and have decided whether to invest in any projects.

- [ ] You know what the safe withdrawal rate is and have calculated how much you need in your investment portfolio to become financially independent.

- [ ] You have built some safety strategies into your retirement plan to protect your portfolio from sequence of return risk and it being depleted quickly early on in retirement in the case of poor market returns.

Investing is not something I ever had any interest in. I didn't know much about stocks and bonds and to be honest I probably felt like it was something you needed a lot of money for to start with in the first place.

We've recently started building up a portfolio, however. My partner and I spoke about it for a long time and we are sticking to relatively safe investments via index investing. Of course we are aware that nothing is really 100% safe, but we are only using money that we don't need right now and since we are investing for the long term, we feel index investments are giving us the best balance between security and returns.

Our goal is to build a small portfolio that will at some point hopefully allow us to use as a supplement to our normal income for things like holidays and days out. We live in the south of Spain where wages are very low, so it's hard to set aside a lot of money, but we're hopeful that with time we'll be able to build up a nice fund.

—Carolina Rodríguez, Spain

PART 9

Your Financial Protection, Taxes, and Paperwork

Now that your major financial plans are put together, we're moving on to another area of your financial life: financial protection, taxes, and paperwork. Risk management and insurance is an important part of financial planning, although surprisingly often overlooked. Many feel insurance is dull or unnecessary—but the truth is that years of careful financial planning amount to nothing if a small oversight leads to a financial disaster for you or your family. Choosing which types of insurance you need and making sure the ones you have are still up to date and applicable to your current situation can be a bit of challenge, so this part talks you through everything you need.

Two other topics related to financial protection and security are estate planning and protecting your money online. They will be covered in this part as well. We then move on to finding out more about taxes. After all, the more you grow your wealth, the more liable to paying taxes you probably become, so a basic knowledge of taxes is essential in further building your wealth.

Lastly, we discuss the option of digitizing your paperwork if you prefer to work with a digital copy of your filing system instead of, or in addition to, your paper files that you organized in Part 1.

Life Insurance

> *If there is anyone dependent on your income—parents,*
> *children, relatives—you need life insurance.*
> **—SUZE ORMAN**

DIFFICULTY LEVEL: Medium

OBJECTIVE: Get the life insurance you need to financially protect your family

REVIEW TIMES: Yearly

Insurance is essentially financial protection you buy against the risks of a possible loss. You might never need some of the options I'm going to cover (in fact, I hope you won't!), but for those situations when you do, without insurance, you or others around you might not be able to deal with the financial consequences when confronted with a crisis.

In the next few steps, we'll go through the most common types of insurance you might need, starting with life insurance.

Why life insurance?

Life insurance covers others, who might financially rely on you for certain economic support, if you passed away. With life insurance, you're insuring not yourself, but the people around you who would be affected financially if you died. There are different situations in which people might depend on you financially:

- Your children who would not otherwise be able to provide for themselves.

- Your partner if you have a mortgage or other big debt together. If you died, your partner would potentially be unable to pay the debt themselves.
- Your partner if they rely on your income, for example, if they do not or cannot work.
- Your partner if they are the one working and you are a stay-at-home parent. If you were to pass away, your partner would need to pay somebody to take over your responsibilities at home.
- If you have a debt with a cosigner (i.e., somebody who guaranteed they would pay the debt for you if you no longer can).
- If you have family members with special needs who require ongoing care.
- If you have a business partner: so they can buy your part of the business if you died.

Types of life insurance

There are different types of life insurance. Which one you choose depends on your personal and financial situation and could potentially change over time, which is why it's important to reevaluate your life insurance every so often to make sure you still have the best policy for your situation.

- **Term life insurance:** With term insurance, you pay a set monthly or yearly premium in return for a lump sum of money that would be paid out if you died during a specific time frame, for example, twenty years. After that time, your insurance ends: you no longer pay for it and you are no longer insured. Term insurance is common when you take out a mortgage with your partner or if you have children who are underage. This type is usually relatively cheap, especially when you're young, although it can become more expensive as you get older.

- **Permanent life insurance:** With permanent insurance, you pay for a lasting lifetime insurance, making it a lot more expensive, as at one point the insurance company will need to pay. This is contrary to term insurance in which you get nothing at the end of the insurance term. In the case of permanent life insurance, the money you pay is usually invested. You pay a premium for a certain amount of time, at the end of which you can either leave the money as it is for it to continue to serve as insurance when you pass away, or you can opt to take out the money or even borrow parts of it, depending on the conditions originally agreed to. There are generally several variations of permanent life insurance available, such as whole life and universal, among others, with the main differences being the flexibility to change the payments you make as well as the payout conditions.

The right option for you depends on your situation and what you feel you need now as well as possibly in the future. For most people, term insurance works just fine for what they need and is considerably more affordable than permanent insurance.

- -

Having life insurance, along with your estate plan (see Step 88), is one of the best ways to protect your family from the possible legal and financial consequences they might be faced with when you pass away, and is always worth the effort to pursue as soon as you can.

☑ STEP 82 ACTION PLAN

☐ If you don't have life insurance, consider whether you should take out a policy. Refer to the list above for some common reasons to contract life insurance. You might not need it if nobody is financially dependent of you, but if you do have somebody who might get into trouble financially if you passed away, you should probably take one out as soon as possible.

☐ If you already have life insurance, pull out your policy with its details and payments, including cancelation conditions.

☐ Determine whether term or permanent life insurance is (still) the best option for you and your situation.

☐ Get quotes from several different insurance companies to compare, even if you already have life insurance, to make sure you're getting the best conditions possible. If you haven't yet decided whether term or permanent is your best option, get quotes for both.

☐ Compare the quotes on several key factors:
- Yearly contributions.
- Whether yearly payments stay the same or go up or down.
- Conditions for canceling the insurance.
- Lump sum payment conditions.
- Special conditions for earlier payout—for example, in case of a terminal illness.
- What is excluded? Think about death due to suicide, dangerous sports, or crimes.

☐ If you already have an insurance policy and would like to change your conditions after comparing the various options, call your current insurance company and see what they can offer you. It might be cheaper to stay with the same company but make some small changes. Don't shy away from saying that you have other offers from other companies that are a lot cheaper.

☐ If you've decided to buy or change a life insurance policy, schedule a day in your calendar to complete all the paperwork and cancel your current insurance, if applicable.

☐ Life insurance can be very complicated; especially in the case of permanent life insurance, the complexity increases and conditions can be difficult to decipher. Consider getting the help of an independent financial advisor to make sure you have the best insurance for your situation.

☐ Make it a habit to check the conditions of your life insurance once a year and mark the date in your calendar.

Health Insurance

Without health insurance, getting sick or injured could mean going bankrupt, going without needed care, or even dying needlessly.
—JAN SCHAKOWSKY

DIFFICULTY LEVEL: Medium

OBJECTIVE: Get the health insurance you need to cover your medical bills

REVIEW TIMES: Yearly

Depending on where you live, health care can be very if not extremely expensive. In some countries, it's compulsory to have health insurance, but there are other countries where this is not the case, meaning that if you don't have health insurance, you might not be able to pay for even basic or emergency treatment (at least not without going into debt). A health insurance policy ensures you have access to the medical care you and your family may need without afterward being presented with excessive bills. Even with health insurance, your monthly health care costs might take up a substantial amount of your monthly budget, such as in the US, which is notorious for its expensive health care.

Types of health insurance

The types of health insurance you generally have access to can vary significantly from one country to the next, but there are three common routes to health insurance:

STATE HEALTH CARE

If you live and work in a country that offers state health care, you likely pay social security contributions, of which part is assigned to health care provisions. This means you usually have access to the public health care system, which is normally free, although medication might not be provided free of charge, or it might be available with a reduced fee. Usually, not all treatments are offered by the public health care system, so you might still need to "go private" if the type of treatment you need is not included.

HEALTH INSURANCE THROUGH YOUR EMPLOYER

Your company might offer health insurance you can register for. In this case, typically the employer pays part of the premiums. Sometimes this type of insurance offers a health savings account (HSA) to which you can often contribute with pretax money.

PRIVATE INSURANCE

This is a type of insurance contracted for you and your family that you organize yourself. With private insurance, you're able to choose specifically which insurance company to use and what to get insured for. However, depending on where you live, this can be hugely expensive.

Characteristics of health insurance

Different insurance companies and policies include different types of treatment and health care. What should you think about when comparing health insurance options? Below are some points to look out for:

- What are the costs of high-deductible vs. low-deductible plans? If you have a low-deductible plan your health care costs will be covered completely, or you might be responsible for a very low first initial contribution when you get a medical bill. Low-deductible plans are generally substantially more expensive, though, with higher premiums than high-deductible plans. When you have a high deductible, you're responsible for paying a relatively high amount of any medical bill before your insurance kicks in and pays the rest.
- What is the minimum and maximum yearly deductible?
- How is the deductible counted? Is it one big deductible? Does it apply to the whole family or to each patient individually? Do all expenses (medication, visits to specialists) count toward it or are they counted separately?
- Is there a family plan to get cheaper rates for your partner and children?
- Is there a maximum number of doctor visits that will be covered and do you pay for any extra visits yourself?
- What types of illnesses, treatments, and surgery are included in the insurance? Think about:
  a. Basic emergency services
  b. Surgery
  c. Mental health care
  d. Dentistry
  e. Physiotherapy
  f. Emergency treatment abroad
  g. Alternative medicine
  h. Opticians costs
  i. Maternity services, both pre- and postnatal
  j. Treatments that are not medically necessary (plastic surgery, eye laser treatment)
  k. Medications: Are there any types that are not included or only partially included?
- Are you able to choose your doctor or hospital or does the insurance only have contracts with some medical care providers?

The above is just a general list of possible things to think about; of course, you might need specific services to be included depending on your family history, so make sure to add these to the above list. If you're not able to choose your insurance details or providers, use the above list to check what is covered and what isn't so you can plan or predict possible expenses you might be faced with in the future and set up a savings goal accordingly.

- -

Because health care can be extremely expensive or even unaffordable, health insurance can be equally expensive. But having decent health insurance is tremendously important to make sure that you'll be able to get the necessary treatment when needed and that you can actually afford it. Check your policy at least once a year, even if there aren't so many options to choose from. Like with anything, your situation and needs will likely change with time. A yearly check also ensures you keep up to date with any changes in the health care provisions that might have happened over the past year and that might be applicable to you.

☑ STEP 83 ACTION PLAN

Health care provision and insurance is something that widely varies depending on where you live. Below is a very generic breakdown of how to ensure you have the right type of health insurance. Note that with this topic, more than any other, it's impossible to give a one-size-fits-all solution.

☐ Find out your country's or state's current health care provision offered by the government. What are your options, how much do you contribute, what's covered, and what are some excluded conditions? In some countries, you might not be able to choose much, but rather than ignoring it, it's better to know exactly what is and isn't available. At least this allows you to plan accordingly and possibly adjust your savings.

☐ If your employer offers any health care insurance or HSA, check out how to enroll and what the conditions are. If you already participate, find out the exact details of your health savings or insurance.

☐ If you have private health insurance, find your current policy with a list of all the services that are included, the monthly or yearly premiums you're paying, and the cancelation policy.

☐ Shop around and find or request quotes for different private insurance policies from different companies if this is affordable. Even if you already have health insurance, it's worth checking not only whether it's still up to date for your needs, but also whether you could get the same coverage somewhere cheaper or with better service.

☐ Find out what other options might be available to you depending on where you live.

☐ Go through the checklist above, marking the points that are absolutely essential for you to have. Check the various quotes for whether these services are included and what the fine print is or how much extra it would cost on top of the yearly premium to include a specific treatment or coverage in the policy.

☐ Check customer satisfaction ratings via the website or on specific customer feedback websites. You want to be with a company that deals with claims and questions quickly and efficiently.

☐ Make a plan based on the information you find, whether that's to change your insurance or to set up a savings plan for costs you cannot insure against. Don't leave this one pending; the risks to your health and finances are just too high.

☐ Add a reminder to your calendar to check your insurance again in a year to ensure it's still up to date.

Disability Insurance

> *Financial security and independence are like a three-legged stool resting on savings, insurance and investments.*
>
> —BRIAN TRACY

DIFFICULTY LEVEL: Medium

OBJECTIVE: Protect yourself financially from lost future earning in case you become unable to work

REVIEW TIMES: Yearly

Disability insurance provides you with financial compensation in the event of a disability that prevents you from working. It covers your future earnings by paying a certain percentage of your wage, often around 60–70%, either until you're able to go back to work or for as long as the policy states that you're entitled to compensation.

There could be several reasons why you might become unable to work, including a sudden illness, a medical condition, or an accident. The difference between disability insurance and health insurance is that the latter purely covers your medical bills, not the potential loss of your income to support you financially. In some cases and countries, social security offers disability coverage, but conditions vary greatly and it might not kick in until after a certain time, sometimes not until after a year.

Do you need disability insurance?

The chances of becoming disabled before retirement age can be two to three times higher than the odds of dying before retirement age. Due to this relatively high chance and the possible continued payout over prolonged periods, disability insurance tends to be fairly expensive. There are several situations in which you might not need disability insurance, however, including:

- If you have enough savings to tide you over for a while (but remember that a disability could last for several years).
- If you don't currently have an income and therefore don't need to insure that income.
- If you don't rely on your income or if you could live off just your partner's income or other income streams for a while.
- If social security in your country/state has a disability payment (but check the conditions, including when it would be paid out and how long it would last).
- If your wage is relatively low and unemployment benefits would cover you instead.
- If you're already retired.

Types of disability insurance

There are different types of insurance and different factors to look at. Here are the two main points to consider when looking at this type of insurance:

DURATION OF THE COVERAGE

Disability coverage can be short term or long term,

with short-term coverage only paying between a few months up to a few years, whereas long-term insurance would cover you for many years or even all the way to your retirement age.

DEFINITION OF DISABILITY

Disability can be defined in different ways, so it's very important you are aware of the coverage you buy. Disability insurance can grant payment using one of these criteria:

- **Own occupation coverage:** Disability is defined as being unable to continue in your current profession. This means your insurance would pay out even if you were still employable in other industries or jobs.
- **Any occupation coverage:** Disability happens if you are unable to do a similar job in a similar setting/industry, taking into consideration your education level and training.
- **Some policies define disability as being unable to work altogether:** In this case, you only receive disability benefits if you're unable to take on any job, not even ones unrelated to your previous training and work experience.

The more specific the coverage—in particular the own occupation coverage—the more expensive the policy generally.

How to get disability insurance

As with other types of insurance, disability insurance varies greatly among various countries or states.

However, you can generally get insurance in the following four ways:

- **Social security disability payment:** This is disability insurance provided by the state. Some countries or states do not offer this at all whereas others might offer enough coverage to eliminate the need for any other.
- **Through your employer:** You may have disability insurance via your employer. Sometimes this will be automatic, but sometimes you need to opt in to start contributing to this.
- **Professional associations:** Depending on your profession, occupational associations and organizations might offer disability insurance specifically for your industry.
- **Private insurance:** If you don't have any of the above, buying a policy through a private insurer might be the way to go.

It's generally easier and cheaper to take out disability insurance when you're young and healthy, so even if you think you'll never need it, taking it out earlier in life might save you considerably.

- -

Disability insurance is not an excessive investment if you think about how much you would miss in future earnings if you ever had an accident that prevented you from going back to work.

☑ STEP 84 ACTION PLAN

☐ Go through the list above under "Do you need disability insurance?" and check whether you should get this type of insurance.

☐ Find out what disability insurance you might be entitled to through social security, your employer, any professional organizations, or any private insurance. Find policies, conditions, and payment details. Check for the following:

- Annual premium.
- When the insurance would start.
- Conditions of what classifies as unemployment and whether it covers your profession. Some industries might not be covered, especially in the case of high-risk professions such as certain sports instructors and construction workers.
- The upper limit of your current wage protection.
- What circumstances are excluded from the insurance (disability due to specific adventure sports or preexisting medical conditions, for example).
- Check how much you'd need to pay to get extra coverage if needed.
- Does the payout adjust to cost of living/inflation?

☐ Think about how much coverage you'd need if you were to become unable to work. You might be able to cut costs if you were without a job and got rid of some expenses (such as travel) completely—and if you're comfortable with lower monthly payouts, your premium will be lower. Bear in mind, however, that if you became disabled and could no longer work, your contributions to your savings, retirement, and investments might also end, meaning you'd stop building up these areas of financial security. When deciding on the coverage you need, consider whether you might want to take out a slightly higher coverage so you can continue to contribute to at least some of your savings goals.

☐ If you can't protect all of your desired income, you might still want to consider insuring for at least a small part of your income, even if only to cover the rent or mortgage.

☐ If you have no idea how to go about deciding how much to insure, consider getting professional advice from a certified independent financial advisor.

☐ Once you have decided to buy disability insurance or change your current plan, schedule a time to fill in all the necessary paperwork this very same week.

☐ Schedule a review of this insurance once a year to make sure it's still up to date and that any wage increases or decreases have been taken into consideration.

Homeowner and Renter's Insurance

The best way to predict your future is to create it.

—ABRAHAM LINCOLN

DIFFICULTY LEVEL: Medium

OBJECTIVE: Cover your property, possessions, and liability for accidents with the right insurance

REVIEW TIMES: Yearly

If you own a home, you really cannot do without a homeowner insurance policy. Apart from the financial protection of probably your greatest asset, it's often a requirement for getting a mortgage. If you're a renter, renter's insurance is highly recommended as it includes liability protection as well as insurance of your own belongings, the same as homeowner insurance. In the case of renting, insuring the property itself would be the responsibility of the homeowner, however, not the renter.

Why homeowner or renter's insurance?

Homeowner and renter's insurance covers you against such things as theft or damage, so that if anything happened, you would get financial compensation in order to replace or repair the loss.

What's included?

What is and is not included in your homeowner or renter's insurance obviously depends on your specific policy, but three main things are usually present:

- **Damage to your house:** (not applicable to renter's insurance), such as the structure of your house as well as the functioning of or damage to parts of your house or equipment.
- **Theft of your belongings:** both from your property, including your house, patio, shed, or car, as well as when you're away from your house, such as on vacation. Off-site loss of or damage to your belongings commonly means a substantially lower payment by the company, however, compared to when something happens on your property.
- **Liability:** Many policies include liability insurance, which is coverage for any damage you or other family members might inflict on others or on their belongings, both at your own house and when you're at their house.

What's not included?

Typically, the following items or situations are excluded from coverage in owner's or renter's insurance, although some can be added to your insurance as extra coverage resulting in a higher premium:

- Damage to your house or belongings due to poor or deferred home maintenance, i.e., if you've put off scheduling regular service or repairing a malfunction.
- Certain natural disasters such as earthquakes and flooding are often not included, though policies can include hurricanes and storms.
- The liability part of the insurance generally includes all members of your household, and this means that in some cases even your pets might be insured, although certain breeds considered dangerous might not be.
- Some of your valuables such as jewelry, silverware, and electronics likely have a limit on their coverage, meaning the insurance would only pay out up to a fixed amount if any of it was stolen or damaged.

Types of coverage

To finish off, there are different types of coverage you can choose from with homeowner or renter's insurance:

- **Cash value coverage:** This is the cheapest option and stipulates that you will be covered for the *current* value of your property or your belongings, instead of what you originally paid. This takes into consideration that most of your belongings experience a certain degree of depreciation, i.e., value loss with time, and it likely has a limit on how much appreciation, i.e., value increase with time, will be considered for a payout, if at all, which could be relevant for your house itself.

- **Replacement cost coverage:** More expensive than the cash value coverage option, this coverage pays what it would cost you to replace or repair your belongings or property with items of the same or similar quality. Similar to the cash value coverage, there is often a limit on how much you get for any appreciation of your property.
- **Guaranteed or extended replacement cost coverage:** The most expensive option of the three, this coverage gives you protection against inflation as well as an increase in the value of your property—for example, so you can replace your belongings or rebuild your home even if it goes above the original price you paid. There is often a policy limit at around 25% above the value that you insured yourself for.

As with any insurance, one hopes never to need to use their home insurance. Sustaining damage to your dwelling is not only expensive, it's also a major hassle, not to mention the psychological trauma of losing valuable items. Not having homeowner insurance for your house and belongings might mean that all your financial planning is irrelevant if you can't pay to replace or rebuild your home or replace your belongings. So be sensible: sort out your homeowner or renter's insurance as soon as possible!

☑ STEP 85 ACTION PLAN

☐ If you have homeowner or renter's insurance, take out your insurance policy and its details, including payments, inclusions, exclusions, and cancelation conditions.

☐ Regardless of whether you have homeowner or renter's insurance, request different quotes and policies from various insurance companies to compare.

☐ Compare the various quotes you received as well as your current insurance on the following:

- Annual premium.
- Inclusion and coverage of belongings, both in your house and outside of the premises.
- Whether there's a deductible (i.e., the amount you need to pay before your insurance kicks in) and how high it is. Note this might be different for different belongings.
- The limit of coverage for belongings (check the various categories) as well as for your house.
- What circumstances are excluded from your insurance (earthquakes, sewage problems, etc.).
- Whether your dog, cat, or any other pets are covered.
- How much you would need to pay to get extra coverage for items or situations you deem essential.

☐ Check customer satisfaction with the insurance company and the specific policy on websites.

☐ Once you have decided on the insurance to take out or change to, do so as soon as possible.

☐ Make an inventory of your possessions, keep receipts of valuable purchases, and consider taking photos or a video with your camera or phone of all your home's rooms so you have an overview of your possessions. This will be required for a claim, so doing this at the same time as contracting, changing, or simply checking your insurance guarantees your inventory is always up to date.

☐ Schedule an appointment in your calendar one year from now to reevaluate your homeowner or renter's insurance and take new photos or videos.

Car Insurance

We aim above the mark to hit the mark.
—RALPH WALDO EMERSON

DIFFICULTY LEVEL: Medium

OBJECTIVE: Get the right type of car insurance to cover the financial consequences of a car accident

REVIEW TIMES: Yearly

Car insurance, also known as motor or auto insurance, is often obligatory in order to use the public roads. Most countries distinguish between insuring a driver and insuring a vehicle, so in some you insure a car regardless of its drivers (as long as the driver has the car owner's permission to drive it), whereas in other countries you might insure the driver regardless of which car they drive. Make sure to check what legislation is applicable in your state or country.

Characteristics of car insurance

Car insurance generally has different parts to it. Although the terms used for coverage can vary from one country to the next, most insurance policies use a similar classification system:

MEDICAL COVERAGE

Covers any medical costs that result from an accident. This coverage usually has two parts:

- **Bodily injury liability:** Covers any injuries you may have caused to others in an accident.

- **Medical payments or personal injury protection:** Pays for any injury to yourself and any passengers of your car. In a more expensive policy, this could also include funeral costs as well as lost wages due to injuries.

PROPERTY COVERAGE

Pays for any damage to any property, including cars, mailboxes, fences, lampposts, or even buildings that were damaged as the result of an accident. Property coverage can also have two parts:

- **Property damage liability:** For any damage to people's property.
- **Collision:** For any damage to your own car as a result of a collision.

COMPREHENSIVE COVERAGE

This can be taken out as an extra part of your car insurance policy to protect yourself financially against any damage that wasn't the result of an accident. Think about damage to or loss of your car due to theft, fire, vandalism, or natural weather occurrences such as hail or storms.

- **Uninsured motorist coverage:** Covers you in the event of a traffic accident with somebody who is not or insufficiently insured and therefore cannot cover (some of) the costs of the accident. This extra policy usually also covers you if you're the victim of a hit-and-run.

When buying a car insurance policy, you're usually not obligated to contract all parts, although depending on the legislation of your country or state it might be compulsory to take out at least bodily injury liability, property damage liability, and medical coverage up to a certain limit. To determine the amount of the liability you should insure yourself for, it's usually wise to cover yourself up to the value of your assets, so that you don't run the risk of losing these if you were sued.

Extra parts of car insurance

The degree to which any of the coverage options mentioned above are included in your insurance depends on your specific policy. Apart from upping the limit on these, you can often add other parts to your insurance, such as a replacement car in case your car is in the garage, towing costs after an accident, windshield/window replacement if the glass breaks, audio equipment and sat nav coverage, and lost or stolen keys.

Most car insurance offers a deductible (or "excess") that can be higher or lower depending on the premium you pay. As with other types of insurance, if you're happy to accept a higher deductible, your monthly premium will be significantly lower than if you have no deductible at all.

- -

We've looked at the five most common types of insurance that most people will need to consider. Of course, there are many other types of insurance you might need, depending on what's best for you and your family. If you travel a lot, for example, you should consider taking out travel insurance, especially if your medical insurance doesn't cover you in foreign countries. However, there are also many types of insurance policies that you probably never need. Having a decent amount of emergency money will generally cover you in most other cases. Carefully evaluate your specific situation to decide whether you need any other type of insurance apart from the five mentioned here.

☑ STEP 86 ACTION PLAN

After going through the other insurance steps, you can probably more or less guess what the car insurance steps involve!

☐ Dig out your current car insurance policy to find out what's covered, how much you pay, what extra coverage you have, and what it would cost to add any you might want to have. If you don't have this information, request it from your insurance company. Check the cancelation policy as well.

☐ Decide how much coverage you actually need. Bear in mind that the more assets or income you have, the more you might lose if you were ever found liable for an accident.

☐ What's the value of your current car? If it's a relatively old car that's not worth much, consider taking out a policy with a high deductible on the collision coverage part, which pays for damage to your car. In the case of a collision with a lot of damage to your car, it might not be worth getting repaired if the cost is more than the value of the car. There's no point paying a higher premium to have a low deductible if you might not get it fixed anyway.

☐ How much savings do you have and what could you potentially pay for? If you have some savings or a decent emergency fund, taking out insurance with a high deductible on all parts can save considerably on monthly premiums.

☐ Contact other insurance companies for some quotes and compare them on the following:

- Yearly premium
- The coverage included
- What's excluded with each policy
- How much it would cost to add extra coverage
- How a higher or lower deductible will change the monthly premium
- Customer satisfaction
- Cancelation policy

☐ Based on the information above, decide whether to stick with your current insurance as is, make some modifications, or go with a new provider or policy altogether.

☐ Commit to following through with any changes this week and set a day and time in your calendar to complete all the necessary paperwork.

☐ Set an appointment in a year's time to reevaluate your insurance. Remember also to make any changes if you change vehicles.

Warranties and Service Contracts

Success consists of going from failure to failure without loss of enthusiasm.
—WINSTON CHURCHILL

DIFFICULTY LEVEL: Medium

OBJECTIVE: Learn more about warranties and save money on repairs and replacements

REVIEW TIMES: Yearly

When you make a big purchase such as a new car or appliance, you often get a warranty on the product. The warranty is a guarantee for a set period of time during which the manufacturer promises the correct functioning of the product and to replace or repair the product if it's faulty, providing you use and maintain the product as stipulated.

Warranties are very important to understand as they can save you a lot of money and worries if you ever need them. Here we will look at warranties and extra warranties in detail, so you can assess any current warranties you have and compare and evaluate (extra) warranties on any future purchases.

What a warranty typically includes

Normally a warranty will specify and/or include the following:

- **How long it's valid for:** For some products, this might be no more than six months,

whereas other products might be covered for several years.
- **What circumstances might void the warranty:** The manufacturer often includes several reasons why a warranty might cease to be valid, such as not having regular maintenance checkups, outsourcing the servicing, or using the product incorrectly.
- **Services included:** A warranty should specify what happens if the product is faulty. Will it be replaced or repaired, or will your money be refunded?
- **Services excluded:** This might or might not be stated in the warranty, but make sure you find out what isn't part of the warranty if your product fails. Think of costs to do with transporting the product to the shop or factory and labor charges.
- **Costs as a consequence of the product being faulty:** This would be important for situations where a faulty appliance leads to other damage, such as a broken washing machine flooding your house.

Extra warranties or service contracts

Although most products will normally automatically come with a warranty included in the price, the store where you buy the product or indeed the manufacturer itself might recommend you take out an extra warranty or so-called service contract on the product. This can be seen as buying insurance on the product. Although these extra warranties often sound tempting, it's worth checking what would and wouldn't be included before you commit to buying an extra warranty.

When you're about to make a big purchase, you're often conscious about the amount of money you're about to pay and are therefore more concerned about your new purchase breaking. Extra warranties often feed off this fear as the company knows that you're probably happy to pay a little more in exchange for extra security.

Instead of taking out extra warranties, consider saving that amount and putting it in a savings account or indeed in a special home maintenance or emergency fund. You're unlikely to need all those extra warranties, and since in most cases the extra warranty doesn't cover you for big amounts of money, it's often safe to not take it out. This allows you to build up extra savings for those specific times that a product needs servicing or replacing, in which case you have your money right there to use.

That said, there are some situations in which getting a service contract might be totally worth it, especially for very expensive items or items that are likely to break. Make sure to also consult your homeowner insurance policy because some damage might be covered there.

- -

For this step you'll probably find that having an organized filing system greatly helps you keep track of warranties, which means you're much more likely to use them when needed.

☑ STEP 87 ACTION PLAN

A problem many people have is that they lose their warranty statements or don't know whether a product still has a warranty on it, so they end up paying for a replacement or repair themselves, even if the warranty is still valid. Set yourself up to avoid this in the future:

- ☐ Find a designated place to keep all your warranties such as in your home office.
- ☐ Decide how to keep your warranties: in a big A–Z folder, shoebox, or filing cabinet.
- ☐ Go through any warranties and user manuals you have.
- ☐ Bear in mind you often need to have the receipt of the purchase kept with it to prove when you bought the product as many warranties are only valid for a limited time. Staple or tape the receipt to the warranty and file it away by date, supplier, or type of product.
- ☐ Throw out any warranties and manuals of products you no longer own.
- ☐ From now on, always check the warranty of any new product you're about to buy so you know what is and isn't included.
- ☐ If you are offered a service contract, make sure you understand the extra coverage and whether it's worth the extra payment.
- ☐ File new warranties along with the receipt and manual in your warranty filing area as soon as possible. Don't leave them lying around to get lost.
- ☐ If you decide not to take out the service contract, consider putting the money you saved in a special savings account or toward your emergency fund so you can use it in case you need it for the repair or replacement of any of your products.

Estate Planning

Tomorrow belongs to the people who prepare for it today.
—AFRICAN PROVERB

DIFFICULTY LEVEL: Difficult

OBJECTIVE: Arrange inheritance, health care, and guardianship matters for when you can no longer make these decisions yourself

REVIEW TIMES: Yearly

This may not be the most cheerful of the 100 steps to busy yourself with, but estate planning should be high up on your priority list of financial planning. Not only will you feel more at peace knowing you've made the necessary arrangements for when the time comes, but think about how you're shielding your family from having to worry about legalities and finances while also dealing with the emotional side of your demise.

Estate planning

Estate planning is about establishing what will happen to your assets when you pass away as well as making arrangements for who will make key decisions in case you no longer can. We'll look at the key parts you should arrange as part of your estate planning, including:

- A will or trust
- A health care proxy/health care power of attorney
- A power of attorney

- Beneficiary designations
- Guardianship designations
- Letter of intent

A will or trust

A will is a legal document that details what should happen to each of your assets upon your death, provided this is in compliance with national or federal legislation. Setting up a trust fund can furthermore have tax advantages for when your assets are inherited by your heirs, as tax is often lower in those cases.

A health care proxy

In a health care proxy or health care power of attorney, you assign somebody to make important health care decisions about you should you no longer be able to do so mentally or physically. You want to choose somebody you trust and who you know shares your views regarding certain important life and death issues. When you draft up this document, you need to discuss any specific wishes with that person so they can act in your interest if this were ever needed. Make sure to assign a second person in case the first person selected is unable to act at the time.

A power of attorney

By setting up a power of attorney (POA), you assign somebody the role of making financial and legal decisions, including about your estate should you not be able to do so. If you do not have a POA assigned, matters might be taken to court in order to decide what should happen to your assets, and the court's decision might not be in agreement with what you had envisioned for yourself.

Beneficiary designations

Beneficiaries are people who are named on some of your assets, such as a retirement account or certain insurance policies. Your beneficiaries will inherit their corresponding assets when you pass away. Depending on your country's or state's laws, the succession of some assets does not need to be stipulated in a will; they automatically pass on to your named beneficiary even if you haven't included them in your will. Therefore, you want to be careful that if you do take these accounts up in your will, you name the same person as the one you named in the account itself. If there's conflicting information, a court might need to decide.

Guardianship designations

One of the most difficult yet also most important parts of estate planning is thinking about any underage children, whether you currently have them or are thinking of having them in the future. It's recommended to appoint a guardian, whether that's an individual or two people, as well as a contingency guardian, in case your first choice is unable to look after your children should that need ever arise. Of course, you want to make sure that the guardian(s) are capable and willing to raise your children, have the financial means, and share some of the views and beliefs that are important to you. If no guardian is assigned, a court could get involved and decide that your children will live with a family member you might not have approved of, or they might be put in foster care or under custody. This is not an easy decision to make so be sure to discuss this thoroughly with all parties involved.

A letter of intent

In a letter of intent, you can express your views on what should happen with your assets and other financial or legal matters when you pass away or are no longer able to make any decisions. It can furthermore include arrangements for your funeral or other specific wishes you might have (for example, regarding cremation). Although a letter of intent is not a legal document, it can help a court understand your wishes should any of the previous documents be ruled invalid for whatever reason, though it would not guarantee that all of your wishes were acted upon. A letter of intent is not a binding document and can therefore never be a replacement for any of the previous documents. It is only an expression of your beliefs and ideas that can be consulted in case there is any doubt.

- -

Although this is not the most lighthearted part of our route to financial independence, it might be one of the most important pieces of planning you ever do. Regardless of how young and healthy you are, you should set up an estate plan now before it's too late. Once it's set up, it will be a lot easier to update every year and it will give you peace of mind that your heirs will be provided for.

☑ STEP 88 ACTION PLAN

☐ Discuss your wishes with your partner, children, and other important family members so that everybody can express their opinions and views related to your and your partner's estate planning.

☐ Take out your list of assets that you compiled in Step 11 and make sure it's still up to date.

☐ Decide how you would like to divide your inheritance among family, friends, other parties, and charity.

☐ Check whether you've named any beneficiaries on any of these assets and whether this is still according to your wishes. If not, get these changed.

☐ Speak to your first choice of people you would like to ask for the role of health care proxy, power of attorney, and guardianship, and let them think about your request. These are huge responsibilities, so do not pressure them! Speak to your second choices as a backup.

☐ Make an appointment with a notary, estate attorney, or whoever else is authorized in your state or country to draft the legal documents described above and discuss the arrangements you want to make in order to get the necessary documents drawn up, signed, and legalized.

☐ Set a reminder to update any of these documents if needed on a regular basis. Getting into the habit of quickly checking all is still in order yearly is definitely highly recommended. Whether it's your own situation that's changed or those of others, such as the appointed guardians for your children or your POA who might no longer wish to assume this role, your arrangements will need to be updated.

STEP 89

Protect Your Money Online

It takes as much energy to wish as it does to plan.
—ELEANOR ROOSEVELT

DIFFICULTY LEVEL: Medium

OBJECTIVE: Take measures against online scams and others gaining access to your accounts and money

REVIEW TIMES: Every three months

Having money is one thing. Making sure you don't lose it through dodgy scams or people getting access to your accounts is another thing entirely. Now that you can access your accounts via the Internet pretty much twenty-four hours a day from any of your devices and just about anywhere in the world, it has also become significantly easier for those with bad intentions to gain access to your money if they want to. This step looks at various ways to protect your money online and minimize the risk of others getting their hands on it.

Keep money in accounts with verified or associated accounts access only

Many savings and investment accounts offer the option of access via verified accounts only, which means that you cannot access your savings or investments directly but instead must transfer money into a regular checking account before being able to get to your money. That regular account needs to be validated when you set up your savings or investment account, which means that even if others gain access

to your savings or investments, they can't just divert the money into their own nonassociated accounts. It would go to your personal checking account only.

Choose difficult passwords and change them often

Most people have very weak passwords, often including their pet's or children's names that are relatively easy to work out. In addition, they don't change their passwords very often and they tend to use the same passwords for several accounts, which makes them easy targets for con artists wanting to hack these accounts. Choose difficult passwords and change them often. Two great ways to do this are:

- Using a password manager that lets you store complicated passwords so there's no need to remember each one. Examples of password managers include LastPass, KeePass, and oneSafe. When using these password managers, you only need to remember one (preferably difficult!) master password to get access to all your other ones.
- Setting very difficult passwords by keeping a long string of random characters, of which only *you* know which chunks represent your real password. You can make this as complicated as you want with a page of 1,000 characters in any random order, and only you know to look for the 100th, 200th, and 300th character. Or the eight that are in the middle of the twelfth line

in backward order—or whatever formula you decide. You can combine these two options by setting your master password with this technique for your password manager described above.

Use two-step verification

With two-step verification, you can only get access to an account if you know both the password to the account *and* have a unique security code generated at random that is sent to your phone. This means that people with bad intentions need not only know your login details, but also must have access to your phone in order to enter your accounts.

Be aware of warnings from your accounts and banks

Pay special attention to warnings sent out by your bank to inform you of phishing emails (people trying to get your login details by tempting you to click on certain links or downloading a program). Banks and account managers often alert their customers of new methods used by Internet criminals, and it's worth making sure you keep up with the latest warnings and be aware of new tricks used by online criminals. Remember that banks and account managers never ask you for your login details and passwords, so if you ever receive an email requesting these, never send along on any personal data in response.

Enable email notification for specific actions

Choose to always receive a notification to your phone or email whenever somebody logs into your account or accesses your account from a new device or when your password is changed. If all is going well, these notifications will only be about actions you've taken, but if you have the alerts set up, you'll immediately know if somebody else is gaining access to your account.

Check your accounts regularly

Checking your accounts regularly was already mentioned in Step 29. Apart from making you more

aware of where your money is going, it can also alert you to any suspicious or incorrect movements in your account. If others have indeed gained access to your money, the sooner you act, the more damage can be avoided.

Do not use public WiFi accounts or computers to access your accounts

Public WiFi accounts are not protected and scammers can get access to your accounts easily even if passwords are just temporarily saved by the website you are accessing. Avoid logging into money accounts on anything that's not a protected or safe WiFi account. Definitely never use public or shared computers to log in to your accounts, as you don't know whether any programs might have been installed on those systems that copy passwords. If you really need to access your money accounts, use your data connection on your device instead of your WiFi. Data networks are much harder—though not impossible—to hack.

Use a different email address to log in

By using a different email address from your regular email account to log into bank and financial services sites, you avoid others from discovering the email address associated with your online finance accounts. You would never use this separate one to send emails from and since it would be the one to which lost password retrieval links would be sent, making it far more difficult for criminals to work out your email and therefore gain access illegally as they likely won't be able to associate this account with your public profile.

- -

The Internet as well as data protection laws evolve continuously and new security features are released regularly to stay ahead of the game. Unfortunately, it's only a matter of time before scammers circumnavigate those new features. Take all necessary precautions to avoid being a victim of online scammers and hackers.

☑ STEP 89 ACTION PLAN

☐ Look into a password manager. There are several free and paid options available, so compare them and find which one might suit your needs best.

☐ List every online account you have and, one by one, go through the following steps:

- Enable two-step verification.
- Consider changing your contact email to a new one nobody knows about. (You might have to contact your bank for this.)
- Change the password, especially if you have not done so for a while. If you're using a password manager, get a random complicated password generated.
- Check notifications are sent every time you log in or log in from a different device or when money is moved out of the account.

☐ Never ignore warnings and notifications sent out by your bank. Read them carefully and take any necessary action if applicable.

☐ Check your accounts regularly (ideally daily).

☐ Do not use public WiFi or public computers to log into your banking accounts.

☐ Never download suspicious files, do not install programs you don't trust, and avoid clicking on links that look dodgy.

☐ Change passwords or your master password once every three to six months and set reminders in your calendar to do this.

An Introduction to Taxes

> *In this world nothing can be said to be certain, except death and taxes.*
> —BENJAMIN FRANKLIN

DIFFICULTY LEVEL: Medium

OBJECTIVE: Find out what taxes you are liable for and your tax rates for each

REVIEW TIMES: Yearly

You might have thought retirement accounts and insurance seemed boring . . . in which case, taxes probably sound even less exciting to you. Yet in order to manage your money well and plan for a secure financial future, you need to have at least a basic understanding of taxes and know where some of your money is going. And by *basic,* I mean more than just, "I know the government takes part of whatever I earn."

In this step, we'll look at a quick overview of the various taxes you're most likely to pay. Every country is different in terms of which taxes apply, their rates, whether they have a flat rate or a scale, and what the exclusion terms are. This step is therefore only meant to provide an overview of possible taxes; you will have to find out the details for your own country or state.

The purpose of taxes

Taxes are meant to fund the main expenditures of the government, such as national security (police and army), infrastructure (roads and sewage), the

legal system, health care, and the education system, among others, as well as the wages of anybody working for the state. Taxes can be raised in various ways. Let's look at the most common ones.

Income tax

Income tax is charged on the income of individuals and companies. Many countries use a scaled tax system in which the more you earn, the higher the percentage you pay. Income tax can be divided into the following categories:

- **Income tax:** Tax charged on regular income.
- **Profit tax:** Tax charged on any income classified as profit.
- **Capital gains tax:** Tax charged on sales of assets that result in a capital gain. An example of this would be the sale of your house or your stocks at a profit. Capital gains tax is usually lower than tax on regular income.
- **Dividend tax:** Tax charged on dividends.
- **Gift tax:** Tax charged on gifts received, such as from parents or grandparents.

Payroll tax

Payroll taxes are paid by both employees and employers on employees' salaries and generally include contributions to unemployment benefits and other social security charges, such as for health care and retirement accounts.

Property tax

Property tax is charged on people's assets and can include the following:

- **Property tax or council tax:** Tax on physical property such as buildings and land based on an estimation of the value of the real estate.
- **Wealth tax:** Taxes on a taxpayer's assets such as savings and investment portfolios. A wealth tax is usually charged on the person's net worth and not just their assets, meaning that the amount of any debt lowers the taxable amount.
- **Inheritance tax:** Tax paid if you inherit money, property, or other assets. In some countries, there's a distinction between estate tax (tax paid on the deceased's assets based on the total value of property owned by the deceased, before the assets are divided) and inheritance tax (tax paid by the person receiving the inheritance after assets have been distributed).

Excises and VAT

- VAT are taxes charged on goods based on a value-added tax system (VAT). This means that if somebody buys raw material, such as steel or oil, they pay VAT on the purchasing price. They then manufacture the raw material into something else and sell it to a wholesale dealer for a higher price than the purchasing price. The manufacturer charges the full VAT on top of their own price but only needs to pay taxes on the price difference between what he paid for the raw materials and what he sold the goods for (i.e., the added value to the original raw product). In essence they get a tax return of the VAT already paid on the initial purchasing price of the raw material. The wholesale dealer then sells the product at a higher price with full VAT and again only pays VAT on the difference in price. The customer is the one who ultimately cannot get a VAT refund as they are the last in line to pay and therefore need to pay the full amount. This very last charge of VAT that stops at the consumer is often referred to as sales tax instead of VAT.
- Excises are often levied on tobacco, alcohol, gas, soda, and luxury goods, excises are charged on the production and sale of these products. They are considered indirect taxes as although the manufacturer is hit with these charges, they often aim to regain them by increasing the price of the product, thereby getting the customer to pay them. Excises are usually heavier than VAT or sales taxes and can vary more from one year to the next.

Corporate tax

Any company making a profit is likely charged corporate tax on those proceeds.

- -

Understanding your taxes 100% might be a little too much to ask for, but you should know roughly what taxes you're paying. It might help you decide on a specific course of action when it comes to estate planning, saving versus investing, property management, which income stream to develop further, and more.

☑ STEP 90 ACTION PLAN

Taxes unfortunately are rather complicated, but it's a good idea to determine which of the above taxes you're liable for and how much they are.

☐ Get your notebook or digital file out and use the Internet to find out the below information about your country or state, or check with your accountant or financial advisor.

☐ Compile a list of the following taxes and note down how much each tax rate is:

- Income tax: How much do you pay in taxes on your income and what are the various percentages for different amounts? Most legislation has a scaled income tax with different tax brackets—for example, 10% on the first $10,000 you earn, 15% on the next $25,000, and so on. Find out your percentage and check it against your pay stubs.
- Capital gains tax: What is the percentage, and is there a system with increased rates for higher gains?
- Dividend tax: find out the percentage and scales.
- Gift tax. Even if you don't expect to give or receive any gifts, it doesn't hurt to know!
- Payroll tax.
- Property tax.
- Wealth tax: How much is it, and is there a minimum you don't pay anything on?
- Inheritance tax. Again, it's always best to know and be prepared.
- VAT and excises.

☐ Lastly, do a search for your country to find a list of taxes you might be responsible for that are specific for your country or state but haven't been mentioned here.

Tax Planning

The only thing that hurts more than paying an income tax is not having to pay an income tax.

—THOMAS DEWAR

DIFFICULTY LEVEL: Difficult

OBJECTIVE: Discover ways to legally reduce your taxes

REVIEW TIMES: Yearly

I know, "tax planning" might sound even more dull than our previous "introduction to taxes" step. But what's the point of knowing about taxes if you don't use any of that information to your advantage? And if you think tax planning is only for the rich, let me tell you that most tax legislation is designed to give the ordinary man and woman some tax relief in specific areas. Not utilizing this is a wasted opportunity to save some money.

Rule number one of tax planning

Before moving on, I want to start with the single most important requirement for any tax planning: never, ever, not in a million years try to mislead the tax authorities or avoid paying your taxes. Don't even think about it. The authorities are smarter than you are and you will likely end up in jail or at least paying a hefty fine, apart from being a bad example to anybody looking up to you. None of that is worth the extra money you *might* get. Besides that, it's morally wrong. Just don't do it. It's as simple as that.

Tax planning principles

Now that's been established, let's have a look at some basic tax planning principles you might be able to apply to your own life that might help you save some bucks. Be sure to keep an eye on that fine line between tax planning and tax evasion, though. If you get too carried away, you might end up on the wrong side of that line.

Please be warned that not everything mentioned below might be possible or even legal in every country or state. You must make sure to check whether these tips are actually allowed and will even give you a tax advantage in your own country. If you have any doubt or are only just starting out with your taxes, I recommend checking with your tax specialist.

Here are the basic planning principles for taxes:

- If you have a partner, you might be able to choose between filing your taxes together or separately, which can make a difference in the total tax paid. In some cases it can work out better if you file them together, but this is not automatically always the case.
- Taxes are generally charged per person and most legislation has a tax-free threshold below which there is no taxation. After an initial amount, there is usually a staged tax system divided into different brackets, with tax percentages increasing as income increases. Look at the different types of income in your household to work out whether any of it can be pushed toward

a lower tax bracket or even become tax-free by reviewing who is receiving the income.

- Imagine you're in a 25% tax bracket based on your overall annual income. Your partner has a lower income and is therefore in the different tax bracket of 15%. Instead of contributing more to your own investment account, consider having your partner contribute more to their investments instead, so that income from dividends and interest will then be taxed at a lower rate.

- As we've seen before, there are some tax-efficient savings accounts to which you can contribute pretax money, such as health savings or retirement accounts. Some might allow you to reduce your overall tax rate at the same time, if these types of contributions are seen as a reduction of your income.

- Contributions to charities can in some cases offer tax advantages in the same two ways:
  - You might not need to pay tax on the money you contribute, i.e., you might be able to give pretax money, meaning the charity gets more money than if it were after-tax money.
  - Charity contributions might also be marked as a way to reduce your overall pretax income and qualify you for a tax reduction.

- Investigate whether making gifts to others such as your children or even your spouse might lower your taxable income.

- Many countries offer tax deductions for expenses such as a mortgage, health care costs, work-related personal costs (including travel-for-work costs), losses on assets, education costs, and energy-saving investments (such as installing solar panels). Check your country's legislation regarding these options and see if you can apply for a tax relief in any of these areas.

- If you're liable for a wealth tax, find out whether there's a set time when your assets are measured—for example, January first. Some big purchases such as a car might not be classified as an asset on which to charge wealth tax, so if you plan to make such a purchase, consider making it before the tax measure date. This avoids paying wealth tax on money you'll be spending very soon anyway.

- If you can defer part of your income—for example, income from capital gains—calculate whether waiting to make that sale so that the gains enter in a new tax year might prevent you from climbing into a higher tax bracket.

- Look at the option to offset a capital gain against a loss you expect to experience in the next year—for example, if you know you need to sell some of your investments or property below the purchasing price.

- As a long-term tax planning strategy, remember that different types of income likely have different tax rates, as you discovered in the previous step when you investigated the different taxes. Assume you have an income of $40,000 per year: the tax you pay on that income depends on what type of income it is. If it's earned income from a job, you might be paying around 25% (depending on where you live). But if that money is coming from dividends or capital gains, that percentage is likely to be considerably lower. This is why it's a common observation that "the rich pay less tax": since many of "the rich" receive an income from assets such as property or dividends, they might indeed be paying less taxes than people whose income comes mainly from a job. Use this information to your advantage and start building up other income streams that have a lower tax rate.

If you want to get serious about tax planning and make sure your taxes are structured in the most effective way, you might want to consider getting the help of a certified financial planner or tax advisor (see also Step 93). Bear in mind that these people are expensive, though, so (part of) the money you save on taxes might be spent on their wage. Of course, if they do their job well, they should be able to save you more than they charge you.

☑ STEP 91 ACTION PLAN

An action plan for this step is difficult. Unfortunately, I can't spell it all out because what you can and can't do is completely different from one country or state to the next. However, below are some ideas on where to look to use your new tax knowledge to your advantage:

☐ Go through the list from above and find out whether any of these tips are applicable to you.

☐ Pay special attention to the legalities of all this. You definitely don't want to do any "tax planning" that is considered illegal where you live.

☐ Review this step once a year, to check for any changes in legislation and to adjust for any possible changes in your tax circumstances.

Digitize Your Documents

Sow a thought, reap an action; sow an action, reap a habit; sow a habit, reap a character; sow a character, reap a destiny.

—STEPHEN COVEY

DIFFICULTY LEVEL: Easy

OBJECTIVE: Set up a digital filing system for your paperwork

REVIEW TIMES: Yearly

At the beginning of our journey in Step 7, we looked at how to organize your paperwork and file important documents to make sure you never have any financial document misplaced and unavailable when you need it. Of course, in this day and age, having a physical filing system might not be your thing. Perhaps you prefer to have all your papers stored digitally. If so, this step will look at how to set up a digital filing system quickly and efficiently.

A digital system

There are a few advantages of digital filing over paper filing:

- It takes up less space in your house.
- A lot of your documents might already be digital (for example, your utility bills or bank statements might already be sent to you by email).
- Digital documents can be searched easily with tags or keywords.
- Digital files don't run the risk of fading or being accidentally damaged.

- A digital filing system can be accessed from different places or transported to another location easily.

How to digitize

The easiest ways to get all of your papers in digital format are:

- Get as much as possible sent to you digitally, such as utility bills, bank statements, and insurance policies. You could also check whether your utility companies and banks have an option to download statements from an online portal.
- Scan other documents such as receipts and pay slips that you can't download or aren't sent to you by email. You'll have to buy a scanner so you can send the documents to your computer.
- Instead of scanning, you can take a photo of the document with your mobile phone (make sure it's of a high enough quality) and send it to your computer or to filing apps such as Evernote. Alternatively, look into phone or tablet apps that function as a camera and filing system in one.

How to store your documents

Digitizing your documents is only step one. Without a digital filing system in place to store your documents, your documents will end up scattered all over the place on your computer or in your email, which would be no different from having shoe boxes with all your papers around the house. Here are some ways to set up a proper digital filing system and save those documents in a logical fashion:

- **Use your email:** Some bills might already be sent to your email account and if you use a scanner or the camera of your mobile phone, it's easy to forward these straight into your email. You can set up various folders and subfolders in your email account similar to the paper filing system we discussed in Step 7.
- **Use your hard drive:** Create a folder on your computer's hard drive for your documents and create subfolders into which you download and save the documents.
- **Use an external hard drive:** In addition to using your local hard drive on your computer, always make backups on another external hard drive. If you don't do this and your computer crashes, you'll be left with no documents. You can set up backups to run automatically, for example, once a month.

- **Use CDs, DVDs, or a flash drive as long-term backups in addition to the hard drive:** You can decide to save your entire filing system easily in a few minutes. It's a good idea to keep a copy elsewhere, away from your house, in case anything ever happened. This could be in a secure place at work, in a safe-deposit box, or at a friend's house, for example.
- **Use the cloud:** If you feel comfortable having your documents stored online instead of on your computer or on physical storage devices, Google Drive or other online storage systems work well to keep your information safe and accessible from anywhere. The advantage of this is that you can access your documents regardless of your location, as long as you have a computer and Internet connection. Make sure your online documents are well protected, though, with strong passwords, and by choosing a service with state-of-the-art file encryption.
- **Use apps such as Evernote:** These often let you clip, store, and attach photos to notes and documents. You can even set up a similar folder structure with substructures depending on your needs and preferences. Like Google Drive, an advantage of a program like this is again that you can access it from anywhere.

The action plan below tells you exactly how to create a digital filing system to get your paperwork under control. Happy scanning!

☑ STEP 92 ACTION PLAN

To start with, decide whether "going digital" is really your thing. If not, simply stick with the physical filing system. You have to use what works for you, not what you think you should be using. If you go with a system that you do not feel invested in, you are likely to abandon it in a few weeks. If you do decide that you definitely want to move onto a digital filing system, start with some preparation work:

- [ ] You will probably need a scanner of some sorts. There are great mini portable scanners available or alternatively you might want to go for a standard desktop scanner. If you would rather take photos than scan every document, check whether your phone or tablet camera suffices or whether you should install an app for better quality.

- [ ] Choose where your filing system will be stored: email, hard drive, Evernote, Google docs or any other alternative. If you are already familiar with any of these programs, it might be easier to also use them for your filing, but look around a little bit to make sure you find a system that works for you.

- [ ] Before you start scanning or taking photos of your entire collection of papers, go through everything you have and throw away anything you no longer need. No point scanning those papers if they are redundant anyway.

- [ ] Start little by little, commit to doing a section each weekend or to process 10 documents a day.

- [ ] As soon as you have scanned, make sure to file. Do not just leave stuff on your computer or in your email unprocessed, as it will all pile up and become an unmanageable chaos.

- [ ] Depending on the system you use you might be able to tag each file with keywords to make it easier to find them again at a later stage. This would be especially useful for receipts for example. Tag documents at the same time as you store the file so that you do not need to come back again later in order to find out what the document is.

- [ ] Make it a habit to scan new documents once a month and to process them immediately. Consider using the same 5 basket system as mentioned in Step 7 on organising your paperwork in which you sort your papers as soon as you come back home every day. The only difference is that your "file" basket would be a "scan" basket.

- [ ] Remember to also save any statements you have received by email over the last month and any documents available for download in your customer area.

- [ ] Clear out and update your files yearly to get rid of any unfiled documents and of any folders that you no longer need.

Checklist Part 9

Use the following checklist to make sure you've done everything in Part 9 and are ready to continue with the final part:

☐ You have taken measures to financially protect your family if you were to pass away by taking out or updating life insurance that covers your loved ones.

☐ You have bought suitable health insurance and know you can afford minimally basic and emergency medical treatment, or you're working toward saving for possible medical expenses if your insurance doesn't fully cover you.

☐ You have disability insurance that best suits your potential needs in case you're unable to work at some point in the future due to a disability.

☐ You have taken out enough coverage on your property and possessions with homeowner or renter's insurance.

☐ You have adequate car insurance that would cover your financial needs in case you were in a car accident.

☐ You know the value of warranties and service contracts and what they generally do and don't. You are aware that in certain cases setting aside the money you save by not buying an additional warranty might be a good alternative to build up funds in case your appliance breaks down.

☐ You have arranged your main inheritance, health care, and guardianship matters and feel assured your affairs and the people you love will be well looked after when you no longer can.

☐ You have taken measures to protect your online financial accounts against scams or illegitimate access.

☐ You know the taxes you're responsible for and what tax bracket you're in, and you know how you might reduce some of the taxes you pay legally in your country or state. You also know you should never avoid paying them, but to use the legislation that exists to legally reduce your annual payments.

☐ You have digitized your filing system if you prefer to work with a digital collection of your documents and you know how to access all your important documents and statements quickly if needed.

💬 PERSONAL STORY: SOPHIE

I've been wanting to give my financial life an upgrade for years. I had papers, documents, and files lying around everywhere, sometimes in unopened envelopes, sometimes hidden away behind other things on shelves and in baskets or in boxes that had accumulated layers of dust over the years.

I didn't know which types of insurance I had, I could never find any document when I needed it, and I always felt uneasy and agitated when I thought about my home office, as it made me feel like I had no control over my financial life.

I've recently started setting up a filing system. I am currently dedicating one hour a week to this. It's a slow and long process but little by little I am starting to see a light at the end of the tunnel. I already feel more organized and in control of my financial life. I am also able to evaluate the different types of insurance I have as well as finally getting a will, something I have been meaning to do for years, but always put off.

The biggest gain I got from this is a sense of peace. I am less worried now knowing that I have made the necessary arrangements to protect myself financially and although I am not completely there yet, it is absolutely worth the time and effort put in to feel more confident about my finances.

—Sophie Jennings, UK

PART 10

How to Excel at Financial Independence

The last of these 100 steps asks you to consider a few important strategies regarding financial independence now that you're nearing the end of this journey. These steps guarantee you'll take your efforts to the next level and put the final details in place that will make you not just somebody who completes the 100 steps, but somebody who will continue to excel at becoming financially independent and will keep this as a priority in their day-to-day life, while also using this knowledge to help others.

In Part 10 you'll discover whether you could benefit from the help of a coach or financial planner, develop your future earning potential by investing in your personal capital and find out about ways to share some of your knowledge and/or money.

Consider Hiring a Professional

> *To improve is to change, to be perfect is to change often.*
>
> —WINSTON CHURCHILL

DIFFICULTY LEVEL: Medium

OBJECTIVE: Determine whether hiring a financial planner could speed up your journey to financial independence

REVIEW TIMES: Every six months

Despite all the information you've read, your experiences, and maybe the relatively straightforward financial situation you feel you're in, there might be times when it's worth getting the help of a professional when it comes to your personal finances.

Advantages of hiring a professional

Finding the right person to help you with your finances can benefit you in several ways:

- They can save you money
- They can save you time and energy
- They can recommend better solutions for your situation

The first advantage—saving you money—is complicated because apart from saving you money, hiring a professional will also cost you money. Try to get a rough sense of how much an advisor would charge before signing up to this option to ensure they're worth it.

Apart from saving you money, a professional financial advisor can often also save you time and mental energy. If your financial situation is relatively complex or if you need specific help, such as with tax planning, certain investments, or insurance decisions, hiring the help of a financial planner can save you considerable amounts of time and energy, meaning you can spend that on something far more enjoyable!

A third advantage of getting a professional to look at your situation is that they might be able to recommend a better distribution of assets and help you put together a more solid financial plan thanks to their extended knowledge of the financial world, retirement account options, and legal details. Everybody has a unique situation when it comes to finances and meandering your way around the gazillion different options can be very complex to do yourself. Getting financial advice from an independent financial planner can help you greatly in ensuring you have thought about and covered all the various options. Apart from saving you money, there is considerable peace of mind in knowing you've got your finances under control, are well protected against risk, and are complying with the law.

Do you need a financial advisor?

Of course I would not have written *100 Steps to Financial Independence* if I didn't think you could manage your finances yourself. Frankly, I believe the majority of people don't need a financial advisor for the majority of their financial lives and that it's doable and desirable to manage your finances yourself. However, each person's situation is unique. If you feel you don't have the time, knowledge, skills, or patience to get your finances in shape or keep them that way, then of course getting an independent planner can greatly help you. Regardless of whether you ultimately need one, getting professional help will nearly always be better than doing nothing toward getting your finances in order.

How to get the help of a professional

Should you decide to get professional help, bear the following in mind:

- Not all financial advisors are equal. Some have your best interests at heart, while others might have their company's interest at heart and will try to sell you their products more than sorting out your finances in a way that will be most beneficial to you. Some advisors receive a commission from brokers or companies. Again, anybody working on commission will most likely put themselves, not you, at the top of their priority list.
- You should pay an advisor a flat fee based on the amount of assets they look after. Make sure you're not paying any fees for selling and buying stocks, mutual funds, or other financial products, as that will only encourage them to sell and buy more, which ultimately will cost you more but might not make you any better off.
- Check whether your financial advisor adheres to a fiduciary standard: an ethical rule stating that they put their clients' interests first and avoid any conflict of interest. Request a written confirmation or for a copy of their fiduciary oath. In addition, ask them whether they receive a commission on products on top of what you're paying them and if they are "dual-registered"

as both an advisor and a broker-dealer. Both of these can be indicators of an advisor not acting in your best interest or simply cause transparency issues.
- Find out whether the advisor is restricted in their offer of financial products. If they have no restrictions, they're more likely to recommend financial products that are truly in your interest. If there are certain restrictions they need to comply with, then most likely they are constrained by their employer to only offer products that the company sells or gets a commission on.
- Don't give your planner direct access to your accounts, or if you do, limit it to view-only.
- Remember that financial planners cannot predict the future, so you have no guarantee that what they offer you will ultimately be better protection than what you would have planned yourself.
- Last and most important: make sure you know what your planner is talking about and always stay involved in the process. Only you know what your long-term plans are, how much risk you want to take, and what alternatives you have if things go wrong. Do not become a victim of your own trust in others. Establish regular meetings with your planner to always discuss all options and alternatives before agreeing to anything.

- -

If you decide to hire a professional, always stay on top of what's happening with your finances and push to understand what they recommend. Even though they might save you time, money, and mental energy, that's not a good reason to hand over all power and knowledge over your financial situation!

☑ STEP 93 ACTION PLAN

☐ Write a list of areas you would consider getting help for from a professional. What specific parts of your financial life do you not fully understand or control? Think about specifics such as:

- Retirement account options and current retirement regulations
- Investing options
- Taxes and tax advantages
- Changes in your work situation, such as the financial consequences of becoming unemployed or setting up your own business
- Insurance needs for your specific situation
- Inheritance and estate planning

☐ Once you've identified the area(s) you need help with, jot down your questions. What exactly do you not understand or need advice on?

☐ Look at your list and determine whether to get a professional financial planner. Are there alternatives you could look at? Think about finding a book on taxes for your country, doing an online course, searching the Internet, listening to podcasts, etc.

☐ If you think it's either important enough or that there's a significant amount of money at stake, find an independent and certified financial planner. Ask others if they can recommend anybody. When you hire somebody to help with your finances you want to be sure they are competent and trustworthy.

☐ Refer back to the bullet points above and note down which questions to ask any possible candidates. Ask for written statements or documents to confirm their independence from investment or insurance companies.

☐ Determine beforehand which areas they need to help you with and which you do not need help with. Don't let them talk you into taking over more of your finances than needed, as that will just cost you more.

☐ Set meetings at regular intervals with your planner and determine what you'd like to discuss beforehand so that you keep control over the situation.

☐ Regularly evaluate what your financial planner is giving you and whether it's still working in your favor. Determine whether any changes need to be made depending on changed circumstances.

Find a Coach

*I'm a success today because I had a friend who believed in
me and I didn't have the heart to let him down.*

—ABRAHAM LINCOLN

DIFFICULTY LEVEL: Difficult

OBJECTIVE: Find a coach to help you
achieve your dreams

REVIEW TIMES: Every three to six months

Once you get further along on your journey to
financial independence, finding yourself a talented,
trustworthy, and inspirational coach or mentor
can be absolutely key to your overall success long
term. Especially if your aspirations go beyond "getting more control over my finances" and you have
indeed set yourself the target to get somewhere
between stages 4 and 8 of the eight stages of financial independence, you may find that a coach can
make an incredible difference to your progress.

Note that a coach is very different from a financial advisor. The latter is a person who will give you
practical advice, whereas a coach's role is generally
to inspire and to motivate—somebody who keeps
you committed to your goal even when the going
gets rough.

The advantages of having a coach

A coach can help you in myriad ways, including
some of the following:

- **Accountability:** A coach can encourage you to
  stick to your goals and make sure you continue
  working toward achieving them. They can
  motivate you and ask for regular self-reflection.
  Most important, they will not allow you to
  simply forget about your targets or go back to
  accepting the status quo. Being held accountable
  for something makes you much more likely to
  achieve your goals.
- **Experience:** Usually coaches bring a wealth
  of experience to the table. They have often
  overcome similar struggles as the ones you're
  facing, have discovered the ins and outs of
  various strategies, and know firsthand what
  works and what doesn't.
- **Goal setting:** Setting realistic yet challenging
  goals can be difficult, and a coach can guide you
  to achieve what's important to you, which goals
  to pursue, and how to practically implement
  them. You don't want your goals to be too
  easy to achieve, but then they shouldn't be
  completely unattainable, either. A coach can
  help you find the middle ground.
- **Honesty:** Sometimes it can be easy to either
  get too optimistic or too pessimistic about your
  financial situation or lifestyle. You may feel you
  are too far behind, that you're not making any
  progress, or that you started looking after your
  finances too late and it's not worth it anymore.
  Or you might be telling yourself all the excuses

about why you can't do more, why you've missed your own deadlines or a plan has fallen through. Conversely, you may feel that things are going well, that you're really powering through and saving and investing every penny you can find. A coach will be able to put things into perspective and tell you what you're doing right. They can see when you've maybe taken things a little too far or could afford to kick it up a notch.

- **Feedback on your plan:** Your plan might be missing a solid basis or it might be overly simplistic or complex. You might be planning too much at one time, taking on too many projects or running up more debt in favor of some investments. A coach can have a critical look at your plan, help you readjust it, and increase your chances of success.

- **Inspiration:** Your coach likely knows a lot more about personal finance than you, so they can be a great source of inspiration, new ideas, and an increased understanding of finances. They can help you learn new things, master new skills, and implement new habits. Coaches can serve as a great inspiration and set a powerful example.

- - - - - - - - - - - -

Finding a coach might be difficult at first, but stick with it. Whoever you choose has the potential to give you great advice and provide guidance for years to come. Commit to this special relationship and honor the feedback they offer to make you better.

☑ STEP 94 ACTION PLAN

If you like the idea of getting yourself a coach, here are some tips to help you find one:

☐ Write down why you'd like a coach. What do you struggle with most? Have a look at the list above outlining what a coach can offer and determine which of these apply to you. Is there anything else you need help with or would especially benefit from?

☐ Avoid asking a friend or family member to be your coach. Even though this might sound like a good (and cheap) idea, a friend or family member probably won't be critical enough and they might not necessarily have the experience you're looking for. You're also likely to become much more defensive about any type of critical questions and you might not be willing to share some of your financial aspirations with them openly. Find somebody who's not so emotionally close to you.

☐ While paying somebody will be more costly than finding somebody who might do it for free, you can get a great return on investment if you make an effort to find a professional coach who can really help you move forward.

☐ To find a coach, ask friends, colleagues, or acquaintances whether any of them have a coach they can recommend, use social platforms like LinkedIn, or reach out during conferences or workshops. You can use different criteria to find somebody—you can make your selection based on your location, profession, or their experience—but make sure to find somebody you admire and respect and whose charges are within your budget.

☐ Don't rule out working with somebody who's either quite a bit older than you or significantly younger. An older coach can provide you with more experience, whereas somebody younger might have a better understanding of new opportunities.

☐ Don't ask somebody to be your coach as soon as you meet them. Ask for a meeting or arrange for a mutual acquaintance to introduce you. Prepare yourself with some questions you'd like to ask them so you can get to know them.

☐ After the initial meeting, analyze whether you still feel this person would be a good coach to you. Did they give you any food for thought? Did they make you feel more inspired and motivated? Did they not shy away from giving you their opinion?

☐ If not, thank them for their time, then rinse and repeat until you find the right person.

☐ If they did, send them a quick message to thank them for their time and then indicate you're very interested in them being your coach, explaining some of the things you'd like to get out of the coaching sessions.

☐ Once you have found a coach, remember that you *want* them to be critical, to play the devil's advocate and call you out at times. Don't take the easy road and give up when this happens. It's what you wanted them for, to make you better, improve your plan, and get you to your financial freedom targets faster. This is usually only achieved if somebody reshapes your plan now and again, with the intention of making you more likely to succeed.

Set Aside Money for Your Children

> *Twenty years from now you will be more disappointed by the things you didn't do than by the ones you did do.*
>
> —MARK TWAIN

DIFFICULTY LEVEL: Easy

OBJECTIVE: Start setting aside money for your (grand)children and build up a fund for them

REVIEW TIMES: Yearly

I'm sure you know that children cost money. Even their day-to-day expenses seem endless—clothes, food, extra activities, and birthday parties, to name just a few. But I take it for granted that if you have children, grandchildren, nieces and nephews, or "adopted" nieces and nephews that are your friends' children, these expenses are now covered in your budget, either in your regular categories or under something like "presents." (If not, now might be a good moment to add this in!) If you don't have children now but are planning to at some point in the future, I hope you're by now financially savvy enough to have set up a savings account for your kids' "start-up costs": baby room decorations, stroller, car seat, clothes, and many other accessories. (Again, if that's still pending, do this now!)

How you can help out

With this all being covered, let's talk about "later." This might sound like a long time away still, but those children will at some point reach their eighteenth birthdays and will want to discover the world. Whether it's at college, traveling, or trying their hand at a first "real" job, there will come a time when they no longer depend on you (at least not officially—they will likely still come back home from time to time for some love, help, or even a financial contribution from time to time).

Wouldn't it be nice to be able to give them more than $50 to get them set up? Or maybe you'd like to give them something when they get married, buy their first house, or have their first child? Being able to contribute financially at an important new stage of their life is not just about the money but also shows you care through having planned and set aside something for them for years, if not decades. There are always ways you can do something now to help them later. The earlier you start, the more time that good friend of ours called compounding interest can help you out to create a small fortune for your children or grandchildren.

What and how to save

To illustrate various options of what you can do now, below are some scenarios to give you an idea of how to get started. For all of them, I'm assuming you're starting the contributions to these saving plans in the same year the child is born. Depending on the number of (grand)children you have and would like to set up a gift fund for, as well as your budget, you might be able to set more or less money aside.

SCENARIO 1

Open a savings account and set aside $10 a month. Assume an interest rate of 5%, an inflation rate of 2% and that you keep contributing $10 a month until you give the child the full amount. Your (grand)child would in this scenario and as shown in Table 18 receive the following amounts:

Table 18:
Performance of $10/month savings accounts after different periods

Years	Total paid in	Nominal value at end	Adjusted for inflation
18	$2,160	$3,467	$2,410
21	$2,520	$4,402	$2,880
25	$3,000	$5,881	$3,549

Note: Amounts rounded to nearest dollar. Exact amounts vary depending on specific calculation method used.

Imagine being able give your (grand)child $3,500 when they turn eighteen or even almost $6,000 when they're twenty-five by just saving $10 consistently every month! Once again, consistent small steps can lead to big results over time.

An important note on inflation here: even though you might be slightly put off by the difference between the nominal value of your fund and the amount after taking into account inflation, you can partially counterbalance this by adjusting your monthly contributions with the inflation rate (so $10.20 per month in the second year, $10.40 per month the second year, $10.61 the year after, etc.). The inflation-adjusted value of your savings will then be moderately closer to the nominal value stated in the table.

SCENARIO 2

What about instead of opening a savings account (which is unlikely to give you anywhere close to 5% at the time of writing), you put that money in an investment account, assuming a 7% return and 2% inflation rate? That case works out as follows:

Table 19:
Performance of $10/month investing accounts after different periods

Years	Total paid in	Nominal value at end	Adjusted for inflation
18	$2,160	$4,233	$2,943
21	$2,520	$5,586	$3,655
25	$3,000	$7,875	$4,752

As you can see in Table 19, in this case and even if you held it only until they were 18, you would be able to give them more than $4,200!

SCENARIO 3

You might be able to set aside more than $10 a month. Let's assume you're lucky enough to live in a country with a child benefit plan in which you get some financial support from the government to help with the expenses of raising children. What if you invested all that money for your child? Child benefits vary greatly by country, but let's take an average of about $75 per month. Like before, let's assume again an average of 7% return and 2% inflation rate. This is how much you would have if you continued investing that child support:

Table 20:
Performance of $75/month investment accounts after different periods

Years	Total paid in	Nominal value at end	Adjusted for inflation
18	$16,200	$31,747	$22,068
21	$18,900	$41,894	$27,409
25	$22,500	$59,060	$35,641

As shown in Table 20, by their eighteenth birthday, you'd be able to give your child almost $32,000! That's a small fortune to most eighteen-year-olds. They might be able to pay a big part of college with that money!

Or maybe you want to wait until they're a little older. Of course, most child support ends when children turn eighteen, but if you continue to pay in $75 a month for another few years until they are twenty-one or twenty-five, the fund will grow to even more impressive amounts.

Again, child support is generally likely to adjust for inflation, meaning that if you get $75 this year, it will likely adjust to $76.50 next year, and $78 the year after. As long as you keep adjusting your investments with the inflation, or really just with what you're receiving in support, the portfolio's inflation-adjusted-value should be slightly closer to the nominal value.

Of course, the above are just some examples of how careful financial planning might give your (grand)child a nice head start when they turn eighteen, twenty-one, twenty-five, or whatever age you decide. Maybe you cannot survive without the child benefit and therefore can't invest all of that money. But what about half of it? Or even just $25 a month? $10? Go back to the budgeting steps in Part 3 to see if you can free up any money anywhere for this goal. Being the child of financially savvy parents should come with some advantages, right?

- -

Saving/investing and seeing your money grow can be really rewarding, but there is an extra sense of satisfaction from setting money aside for somebody else, and seeing their fortune grow even before they're aware of it. Being part of their anticipation of how to use that money only increases the fun. Of course, you (or they) might be unlucky and the market might just hit a bad year when they turn eighteen (or twenty-one or twenty-five), but who's to stop you from waiting another few years until the market has recovered again before you hand over their investment account?

☑ STEP 95 ACTION PLAN

☐ Start with how many children, grandchildren, nieces and nephews, or other children you have in your life you (or might have in the future) and would like to help financially when they come of age.

☐ Investigate and decide how much you can invest either monthly or yearly. Remember that if you have (or might have) several children or grandchildren, you probably want to set it up equally so that you don't invest $100 per month for child one and only $20 for child two. Plan ahead to avoid arguments later on!

☐ Find out whether you can open any specific accounts that offers tax advantages, such as a 529 fund in the US to save for college.

☐ Open an investment or savings account for each child but carefully check how to do the legal side. For example, make sure you can open it in their name (in some cases only parents can do this). If you're a grandparent and can't open it in your grandchild's name, consider opening it in your name, but stipulate the child as the beneficiary and make sure to include conditions in your will that the money is to go to the child when they turn eighteen and not spread out among your heirs.

☐ Set up automatic payments into this account.

☐ Remember that the earlier you start, the more time the interest has to compound.

☐ Decide when you want to give the money or the full account to the child. Instead of giving them the money, bear in mind that your child could just continue to grow the money. Inform your child beforehand so they can start planning on what to do with the money, as otherwise they might be tempted to take it all out and spend it in one go. (See also Step 96).

☐ Remember to open a new account for any additional children who come along.

Teach Your Children about Finances

> *Many kids come out of college with a credit card and a diploma. They don't know how to buy a house or a car or health insurance or life insurance. They don't know basic microeconomics.*
>
> —JESSE JACKSON

DIFFICULTY LEVEL: Medium

OBJECTIVE: Use different strategies and activities to teach your (grand)children how to handle money

REVIEW TIMES: Weekly

In the previous step, we looked at how setting aside even small amounts of money can give your (grand) child(ren) a respectable minifortune by the time they turn eighteen or older. But what if they spend all of the money—the money you set aside diligently for many years, making the most of that compounding interest—in one weekend, on one vacation, or on a (in your view) foolish purchase?

Their money is their money

Even though you might be skimping and saving to get this fund together for them, once you give it to your child, it's their money. Whether they splurge on a luxury vacation, use it to fund their college, give it all away, or use it as a down payment for their first house, it is ultimately their choice.

That said, as a parent or grandparent, you also have a responsibility in educating your children

about finances. Funnily enough, we're totally fine with having to teach our children social skills, help them with math or French homework, and teach them about basic personal care and hygiene—but financial education is often neglected. Whether this is because people don't want to bother innocent children with grown-up matters, think school will teach them this stuff, or they just generally feel uncomfortable discussing money with their children, many parents ignore this topic, even though teaching children about money is vitally important. And if you do your job well in this respect, apart from hopefully avoiding them making big money mistakes later on in life, your child will also be less likely to spend all of that money you gift them in one go on something seemingly frivolous.

Teaching about money

Below are some practical and fun ideas about how to teach children the real value of money from an early age on. They can be adapted to your children's age and your budget, values, and ideas about what you can and want to teach them:

- Give children a small amount of pocket money early on to get them to plan how they want to spend it and how to save up for bigger purchases.

This teaches them the value of saving, planning, and prioritizing.

- Consider some type of "savings match" or interest you give children for every dollar they save if they have not (yet) got a savings account. Perhaps you could do this monthly: they show you how much they've saved, you count it up together, and then you give them a certain amount of interest or match their monthly contribution.

- Get children involved in sharing their wealth through donating to charities or fund-raising for charities so they learn to appreciate that there are many others who are far less lucky than they are and that they can make a difference in the world by giving some of their money away or by getting involved in deciding which charity you should donate to as a family.

- Give each child three jars: one for spending money that they can always use, one for savings to which they assign a specific savings objective, and one for donations to a charity of their choice.

- When they get a little older, open a savings account and have your child deposit money into it, even if it's just small amounts. Explain interest and compound interest to them and show them how their money grows if they leave it in the account.

- On a day out, weekend away, or when on vacation, give children a minibudget for themselves, or tell them that as a family you have a total budget of, say, $60 on a particular day that you need to decide how to spend. They get to vote (or decide) whether to have a simple sandwich and some money for an ice cream and a small souvenir or whether to go for that slightly fancier meal but not have any extra money for an ice cream or memento. This helps them develop skills in budgeting, planning, and understanding there's a limit to the amount of money you can spend. It can be made more fun by getting them to investigate prices and

present their plans and ideas and then all vote as a family for the best idea.

- Make sure to use cash instead of credit or debit cards for challenges such as the above so that children see there really is a limit to the amount of money.

- Make children aware of how we're constantly tempted to spend money by ads and peer pressure. Teach them how these ads work and get them to evaluate whether that new gadget or toy will really add value to their life.

- Raise children's understanding of bills that need to be paid, such as utilities, and get them to play their part in turning off lights, closing doors, and not letting the tap run when brushing their teeth.

- Turn grocery shopping into a competition by finding discounts, clipping coupons, spotting buy-one-get-one deals, and so on.

- Have a chores list with things they can do around to house to earn some extra money. You can have a maximum amount per week or month they can earn if you want to limit how much to pay them. In this way they learn that you can earn money by working for it.

- Teach children about debt and how this is expensive in the long run. The best way for them to learn this is by giving them a small loan for a purchase they'd like to make and charging interest on it. Even if they end up paying $5 on a loan of $10, those $5 will teach them a lifelong lesson on how interest and compounding interest on a loan will ultimately be a killer to their personal finances.

- Go through credit card statements together with your kids or spend your weekly money moment together with your "personal assistant" to teach them the importance of checking financial statements regularly for errors and staying up to date on the health of your finances.

- When your child is a little older, explain the concept of the stock market and investing. Show them to sit tight when the market falls and the importance of patience in the long run.

- Tell them about the savings or investment account you've opened for them, how much is in it (if you want), and how you've managed to save it. You can decide not to tell them it's theirs (yet) and just say you're saving it for "a special occasion." Ask them what they would do with that amount of money. Point out how the money grows over time.

If done well, these financial lessons can help your children hit the ground running when they come of age and become responsible for their own finances, as it gives them so many skills that others might take years to discover by themselves. Just make sure the lessons are appropriate to your child's age and maturity and remember that every child learns differently and has different interests. Some might be more open to this topic than others; just see that as part of the challenge. Happy teaching!

☑ STEP 96 ACTION PLAN

- ☐ Discuss with your partner the importance of teaching your children the value of money and agree on a basic approach to this. It's important to be aware of each other's involvement and ideas so that you don't clash over this.

- ☐ Consider a set time each week, maybe on the weekend, that's dedicated to discussing finances with your children. This could be between five and fifteen minutes, depending on their age. Use this time to discuss something new, develop a new savings target for the week, count up savings, or update financial statements.

- ☐ Decide which ideas from above to implement depending on your child's age and interest and what you feel comfortable with.

- ☐ Find a balance between teaching your children the value of money and concepts such as saving and investing without taking away from the fun. Make sure not to turn *all* of your family days into budgeting days. Kids should also be able to enjoy these days without constantly thinking about money. Rather than overload your children with information, treat it as a step-by-step progression that takes time, skills, and awareness to develop (a bit like compounding interest, come to think of it!).

Invest in Your Individual Capital

An investment in knowledge pays the best interest.

—BENJAMIN FRANKLIN

DIFFICULTY LEVEL: Medium

OBJECTIVE: Invest in your personal and professional development and increase your future earning potential

REVIEW TIMES: Every three to six months

Hopefully by now, you are at a point—or will soon be getting to the point—where:

- You have a good, solid budget you're happy with and able to stick to.
- Your emergency reserve and three-months-expenses funds are well funded.
- You're paying off debt.
- You have short-term savings goals set up, such as a vacation or a new laptop, and you contribute to them monthly.
- You have your long-term savings on track through retirement accounts, paying off your mortgage, and/or investing in the stock market.

On your way to financial independence, it's tempting to be completely caught up in the popular personal finance motto: "Earn more, reduce your spending, invest the difference."

And although there's nothing wrong with the above guideline on paper, it's easy to get a little too distracted by this, to focus on cutting expenses too

much and forget what else is important. In Step 50, we looked at how spending a little on yourself every now and again, with a reward or treat, helps you remember the importance of YOU in this process.

But what about your intellectual or professional development? When you get too carried away by the notion of financial independence, be careful not to overlook the importance of investing in your individual capital, too.

Individual capital

Your individual capital is made up of the unique skills, talents, creativity, wisdom, and experience that you possess. You use your individual capital to create, perform, produce, guide others, or otherwise contribute to the world.

There are three main reasons to invest in your individual capital:

1. It can be fun, entertaining, absorbing, and challenging.
2. It increases your earning potential.
3. It contributes to the compounded learning effect.

The first reason is fairly self-explanatory: learning something new can be fun and motivating and give you a new challenge or goal to work toward. Let's look at the other two reasons in more detail.

Increase your earning potential

Contrast the following two scenarios:

1. An employee with a stable job, earning $24,000 a year, manages to live off $18,000 a year and save and invest the remaining $6,000. His superiors are happy with his performance and he gets a 3% pay raise every year. He puts half of every pay raise directly in his savings and adds the other half to his regular expenses—to combat the effects of inflation and allow for some extra splurges. Ten years down the line, his earnings will be $32,254 a year, and his annual savings will have increased to $10,127, as you can see in Tables 21 and 22.

2. An employee with the same job also earns $24,000 but lives off $19,000 a year ($1,000 extra), therefore saving and investing only $5,000. Why the extra $1,000? This employee spends roughly $1,000 per year investing in herself—courses, seminars, books, and workshops. The first two years nothing notable happens (she gets the same 3% pay raise every year as the first employee), but then her superiors quickly notice she has a lot of talent and potential as she continuously develops herself, so they give her a promotion after the second year with a 15% pay raise. Like the first employee, she adds half of this pay raise to her savings and allows herself to spend the other half. All along, she continues investing $1,000 a year in herself, and every other year she gets a 15% pay raise. This cycle continues until ten years later her yearly earnings are $55,961, of which she now saves $20,981 annually.

It makes a big difference to invest in yourself, right? Of course, the second person started with saving "only" $5,000 a year instead of the $6,000 the first person saved. But after ten years, she quickly caught up and overtook the first person. The difference will only continue to increase with every year to come.

Even though this example is a little extreme, remember you can easily invest in yourself without spending even half of that $1,000 per year from the second scenario. By investing in yourself, you get an edge over others or even your past self which, with time, will likely increase your earnings and earning potential.

The compounding effects of learning

Investing in yourself abides by the same laws of compounding as money and interest: with every new thing you learn, you build up your knowledge, skills, motivation, and dedication. The more you learn and adjust your course to supersede the average, the bigger the difference over time. Like with compounding interest, you might start with a 1% difference, but that 1% soon becomes 2%, then 3%, until you've moved so far away from the starting point that you can't even see it anymore. You can use this to your advantage by continuously pushing yourself to learn, improve, and set new goals—perhaps to become the expert in your professional area, the top performer in your company, or whatever else you aspire to.

Strive to continue to develop your skills and knowledge and it will build more confidence and experience, which in turn will help you implement all you've learned. The more you practice or apply your knowledge, the more you'll perfect your skills, and the better you'll become. The better you become, the more you'll be asked to put your skills into practice, leading to a perpetual cycle of improvement and development.

Examples of how to invest in yourself

You can invest in your individual capital in many different ways. A common way is by taking courses. They don't have to be graduate-level courses, especially not if you consider how expensive these often are. Consider courses that cost far less and might take up a lot less time, yet provide you with valuable new skills and information for your career, such as a writing class, a course on computer skills or public speaking, brushing up on another language, a management class, a training on how to improve customer experience or taking an e-course on online marketing.

Table 21: Spending and savings patterns of two different employees

	Net pay	Regular spending	Investments in personal capital	Saving
Employee 1	$24,000	$18,000	$0	$6,000
Employee 2	$24,000	$18,000	$1,000	$5,000

Table 22: Pay increases, net pay, and annual savings of two different employees

	Raise	Yearly extra saving	Net pay after 10 years	Annual savings after 10 years
Employee 1	3% every year	50% of his raise	$32,254	$10,127
Employee 2	3% every year, 15% every other year	50% of her raise	$55,961	$20,981

The advantage of taking courses is that you often get some type of diploma or certificate to confirm that you've completed the course. That said, this doesn't mean you can only invest in your individual capital through courses. There are other ways to develop your skills. Think about the following options:

- Reading books
- Reading professional magazines and articles
- Listening to podcasts
- Subscribing to blogs
- Listening to webinars
- Attending seminars and workshops
- Attending conferences

I'm sure there are many different areas in which you might want to develop more and that might help you increase your future earning potential, be that in your current career, one you're considering switching to, or even for your side hustle. The key is finding an area you feel motivated about and that you think will help increase your earnings over time.

☑ STEP 97 ACTION PLAN

☐ Think about courses and training that might teach you new skills or improve skills you already possess. Use the ideas from above to help you decide what you might be interested in and what would also be beneficial.

☐ Investing in yourself doesn't have to be related to just your job. If you're setting up a side hustle to generate income, maybe you can take a course, read a book, or attend a conference on establishing a blog, selling online, or designing websites. Write down some areas you'd like to become better at or learn more about.

☐ Estimate how much money you think you need or would like to designate to learn or develop your skills.

☐ Set aside a yearly amount to invest in yourself. Find that money in your budget and determine a yearly plan to use that money in the best way possible.

☐ If you get worked up about the amount of money it will cost you, think of it like this: Imagine you invest $1,000 in a course that, with time, might lead to a promotion with an accompanying $10,000 annual increase in your wages. If you still have twenty-five working years ahead of you by the time you get to the $10,000 yearly increase, that promotion alone will amount to an extra $250,000!

☐ Think about a schedule or time frame regarding these investments in your personal capital. If you decide to enroll in a course, how long will you need to complete it? If you're going to read books on a new topic, when would you like to have read these books by?

Give to Charity

We make a living by what we get, but we make a life by what we give.
—WINSTON CHURCHILL

DIFFICULTY LEVEL: Easy

OBJECTIVE: Pick a charity you identify with and start making contributions

REVIEW TIMES: Yearly

Enough about *your* finances for a moment. Now that we're nearing the end of this book, I think it's right to talk about others who are less fortunate than you and who could do with even just a tiny fraction of your wealth. I appreciate that you probably have many new plans and targets from all the previous steps on how to create and save more money. And I'm sure you might already be planning to start giving to charity sometime soon.

But let me just remind you of Step 21, Beware Lifestyle Inflation. There we saw how you will never have enough money—not now, not tomorrow, not next year. If you don't remember or if you're convinced you do not have money for charity, please return to Step 21 now and see if you still feel the same after rereading it. If you still do, then please read on anyway, as you will learn that you can also give to charity without giving money.

If, on the other hand, you're aware that part of the path to financial independence lies in prioritizing and appreciating what you already have and knowing that no matter your debt, struggles, and hardships, you have so much more than others less fortunate

than you, then the good news is that giving to charity doesn't have to mean donating hundreds of dollars a year. It's just like saving money: start with it early, even if you can only contribute $1 a month, or $10 a year. Not only is that still $10 a year, it also gets you into the habit of giving, so that every time you have a little more money, it's easy to increase that contribution—even by a small amount—and remember there are many for whom your (however small) contribution can make a considerable difference.

Types of charities

There's no point giving to charity if you don't feel particularly connected to their cause, so before you donate, spend some time finding a charity you can identify with. Of course, you don't have to limit yourself to just one charity; you can choose to have two or three different charities to give your money to.

To get started, below are some common themes along with specific examples that you might feel particularly connected to.

- **Health and health care:** Cancer research, new medicines, patient and family support charities, mental health care
- **Animals:** Endangered species and wildlife conservation, local animal shelters, animal welfare organizations
- **Human and civil rights:** Human Rights Watch, Amnesty International, War Child, American Civil Liberties Union

- **Children:** Poverty, education, orphans, children who have a parent in jail, the Scouts
- **Environment:** Greenpeace, the Sierra Club, renewable energy initiatives
- **Arts and culture:** performing arts, music education, museums and historical societies
- **Social and community:** the homeless, the elderly, social services, local neighborhood groups

There are many more charities, but these give you a rough idea in order to start looking at the type of charity you might want to donate to.

Types of contributions

Although the most common way to give to charity is by giving money, there are other ways to contribute, too. Normally you can give to charity in the following ways:

- **Monthly or yearly contributions:** You can make regular financial contributions often presented as a membership in exchange for which you might get a (bi)annual magazine, special discounted products, or regular events you can attend.

- **Inheritance:** Leaving some of your inheritance to a charity by stipulating this in your will is a common way to give money when you ultimately no longer need it.
- **Your time:** Become a volunteer—help out with yearly events, at a local shelter, or by promoting a charity's mission.
- **Fund-raise:** Participate in a bake or yard sale, put a collecting box at work, or add a link to a charity on your personal blog or social media to bring the work of your charity to the attention of others and encourage them to give, too.

It's easy to get distracted by your own finances and focus entirely on your own path to financial independence. But remember that you're not alone in this world and there are many good causes that can do with some of your money, time, or attention to make this world a better place.

☑ STEP 98 ACTION PLAN

☐ Find a moment to sit down and decide what you care about. If needed, brainstorm about your core values or what news items make you sad, angry, or inspired.

☐ Imagine you were given $1 million dollar on the condition that you had to give it all away. How would you spend it?

☐ Look at the list of types of charities above and see what resonates with you most. Is it children in poor countries, the street animals in your neighborhood, or the closing of the local art gallery?

☐ Research some charities and check that their ideas are in line with yours. Read their mission statement, their membership information, promotional materials, and financial accounts declarations.

☐ Look at your budget or calendar and determine what you can and want to contribute, whether it's a yearly amount of money or a free Saturday three times a year. Or could you organize a yard sale with your neighbors sometime soon and give the proceeds to charity?

☐ If you decide to donate money, check that the charity of your choice complies with the requirements needed in order to qualify for a tax break. Not all charities do, so if this is important to you, make sure to confirm it first.

☐ Make a final decision on one (or two or three) charities and start giving now. Add a new category to your budget, change your will, schedule in your time, or mark your calendar with a fund-raising event.

☐ Review your charity contributions once a year and adjust where needed.

Play the "What If" Game

> *Before you speak, listen. Before you write, think. Before you spend, earn.*
> *Before you invest, investigate. Before you criticize, wait. Before you pray,*
> *forgive. Before you quit, try. Before you retire, save. Before you die, give.*
>
> —WILLIAM A. WARD

DIFFICULTY LEVEL: Difficult

OBJECTIVE: Prepare for adverse financial situations by analyzing the possible consequences of certain scenarios

REVIEW TIMES: Yearly

Being prepared for adverse financial situations is an important step on your way to financial freedom. Just like we touched on some common doubts regarding this journey to financial independence in the introduction of this book with different "what if" scenarios, the current step takes a similar approach with a "what if" game to prepare yourself for future concerns that might arise. Without wanting to be demotivating, the "what if" exercise forces you to think of possible situations that might set you back on your journey to financial freedom, or in some cases would have far bigger consequences than just the financial ones.

How emergency funds are not always enough

We've already established the importance of an emergency fund for unexpected one-off expenses. You should also by now be well on your way to getting together a three-months-expenses (or even six-months-expenses) fund in case you or your partner

lose your main source of income and need to make ends meet until you find another job.

Whereas the emergency and living funds prepare you to financially deal with the consequences of a financial setback quickly and efficiently, the "what if" game prepares you psychologically for any changes you might need to make to adjust to smaller or bigger changes that may require you to adapt on more long term.

So let's get playing. . . .

What if your income went down by $100?

Imagine for a moment that for whatever reason from this month onward, your monthly income decreased by $100—maybe your salary goes down, your taxes go up, you lose a bonus, or your union makes a deal to cut wages in order to keep jobs. The question is, what would you do if you lost $100 in monthly income? Where would you cut in your expenses? How would you adjust your budget? What stays and what goes? Would your savings take a direct hit? Could you cut out those monthly salon appointments? Would you mow your own lawn instead of paying somebody else to do it?

What if your income decreased by 50%?

Let's take it one step further and say that from next month onward, your monthly income decreases by

50%. The reason could be various: your hours are cut or your contract is not extended and your new job is only 50% of your old salary. Where could you cut now? Should you get rid of your second car? Would there be no more eating out? Cancel that vacation you were planning?

What if you lost your job?

Of course, we all hope this won't happen, but you never know how stable your job situation truly is (speaking of which, how's that three-months-expenses fund coming along?). Or you might have your own company and it could go bust. Or your clients might all decide to take their business elsewhere. Then what would you do? Could you still pay your mortgage? Could you make your minimum payments on your debts and still pay for food and shelter for your family? Would you need to start an immediate side hustle? Would you end up eating into your long-term savings?

What if you lost all your savings?

What if you have all of your savings in the stock market, and just before your retirement date or the time you're going to take a short break from work, the market plummets and you see your portfolio lose 50% of its value in the span of just a few months? Or the bank that has all your savings goes bankrupt and your money goes down the drain? Would you have any other retirement account or savings you could rely on? Would you have another income stream to fall back on? Sadly, these things have happened, and they will likely happen again. Nothing is certain, so be careful not to put all your eggs in one basket.

Play "what if" before any big purchase

That new $30,000 car you were looking to buy at $600 a month seems like a good idea now, but what if (insert your own scenario) happened? Would you

still be able to make those payments? Just because you can afford it today doesn't mean you'll be able to afford it next year, or the year after, or in three years' time. Before you commit to any big purchase, think things through and decide how well you're protected in the case of potential harmful events.

Of course, you never know if any of the above will happen, and if so, when they'll happen. But even though you can't predict any of these factors, you can certainly try to be prepared for them if they do. Keep asking yourself these questions and add questions that are applicable to your situation. Make sure you review your insurance, asset allocation, and income plans regularly to further build your safety net.

There's no need to become pessimistic about the economy or your finances, but some realism is absolutely needed to ensure you don't fall victim to unrealistic optimism that might make you think you have it all under control. The truth is, you can't predict what will happen in the future. The rest of the world does what it does, regardless of how you've organized your finances.

- -

Although the "what if" game isn't very uplifting, it's an important one to play now and again. I hope you can appreciate even more that having the right insurance and legal documents and more than one income stream will be huge if you ever find yourself in any of these situations. This exercise isn't meant to discourage you from taking risks by making new investments, buying a rental property, or setting up your own company. It's simply meant to help you prepare for some less-than-ideal situations in life.

☑ STEP 99 ACTION PLAN

I'm sure that by now you're probably aware I'm a big believer in writing things down to make them more real and make it easier to put together an actual plan. Here goes:

- ☐ Get out your notebook.

- ☐ Write down at the top of a new page: What if I lost $100 of my monthly income?

- ☐ Go ahead and answer the question. Make sure to find $100 in your budget and write down each item you'd scrap and the corresponding amount until they add up to $100. Of course, you could also just take $100 out of your savings contributions. But if you decide to do this, calculate how this will affect your savings over time.

- ☐ When ready, write down the next question: What if I lost 50% of my monthly income?

- ☐ Write down the answer until you've adjusted your budget completely.

- ☐ Remember you can use your savings funds if you have to, but you want to avoid building up any more debt when at all possible! (I presume you're pretty clear on this by now.)

- ☐ Write down the next question: What if I lost all of my monthly income? Try and answer this one as best as you can. If you have a full three-months-expenses fund, you might need to rely on it here. But how long will that last? A good follow-up question would be, What if I lost all of my monthly income and my living fund ran out?

- ☐ You can keep playing this with anything, so continue with other questions that seem appropriate:
    - What if it took me two years to find a tenant for my rental property?
    - What if I lost 50% of my savings?
    - What if I became chronically ill and couldn't work anymore?
    - What if my partner couldn't work anymore?

- ☐ Review your answers and see how well you're doing in all these areas. What adjustments do you need to make to your current expenses and savings in order to better prepare yourself for any of these scenarios? What can you do today that should not wait until tomorrow?

- ☐ Review your answers once a year to remind yourself of the possible solutions and to make any adjustments to monthly savings deposits, retirement plan contributions, or debt repayments if you realize you're not prepared well enough for some of the scenarios.

Life is never without risk, so go ahead and start new projects or take on new challenges. Just be prepared for all possible outcomes. Being prepared doesn't mean having the perfect solution for all of the above scenarios. But knowing how you would adjust—and even just thinking about the possibility of these things happening—gives you a head start, to say the least.

STEP 100

Stick to Your Journey

To learn and not to do is really not to learn. To know and not to do is really not to know.
—STEPHEN COVEY

DIFFICULTY LEVEL: Easy

OBJECTIVE: Continue to implement the 100 steps to financial independence to take your journey to the next level and achieve your dreams

REVIEW TIMES: Yearly

Congratulations! You have come to the end of the 100 steps! Along the way, you have set important new goals, maybe already completing a few; you've implemented new habits; you've acquired a wealth of information on finances; and, most important, you've started your journey to financial independence, getting closer with each step you've taken and are still taking.

How each end is also a beginning

The first most important moment on this journey was when you decided to change your situation and embark on this project. You have now come to the second most important moment: your determination to continue on your path, stick to your habits, keep learning, implement new plans, and progress toward financial independence.

Remember the examples of people who quit smoking or start a new diet and how often they fail and give up their resolutions altogether? With all that you've learned and everything you've started, now is

the time to make a new commitment to keep financial independence as one of your top priorities for tomorrow, next week, next month, next year, the next five years, and, indeed, the rest of your life. Don't let all that you've learned go to waste. Keep tracking your monthly spending, making new budgets, noting down your net worth, reviewing your investment strategy, and monitoring your progress toward your various financial goals whenever you can.

Create your definitive master plan

The very last step of this mission connects all previous ones and turns them into a perpetual cycle of a continuous journey. Step 100 is essentially Step 1 again, though your starting point is no longer the same. With all that you've learned, you are now continuing your efforts on a higher level. With your regular finance reviews, you can link your objectives and actions even more, so that every single step you take will fully align with your final goals. And the further you travel along the path to financial independence, the more you might start to push those goals to loftier levels.

To help you stick to your journey and to make it easier to know what to do and how often, there is a checklist at the end of this book in Appendix A with an overview of all the 100 steps along with a guideline of how often I recommend you review each step. You can easily refer to this list on a regular basis, see how you're doing, and stay true to your plan of reaching financial independence.

☑ STEP 100 ACTION PLAN

☐ Schedule time in your calendar to go through the list in Appendix A.

☐ Make sure you know what each step entails or, if not, refer back to the various steps.

☐ Each step has a recommended time frame for review:

- Daily: continue to execute these steps as part of your daily routine, for example, in the morning or in the evening.
- Weekly: these are the steps to complete during your weekly money moment.
- Monthly: complete these at the start or toward end of the month as part of your monthly finance review.
- Every three to six months: these steps usually require an update on goals or targets and are therefore at less regular intervals.
- Yearly: analyze or review specific steps to ensure that you're continuing to stick to a plan that still works for you, or make adjustments where needed. Some of the steps with yearly reviews might simply be reminders of specifics you have learned during this journey.

☐ Make sure you've scheduled in time for these steps so you know exactly when you will do the daily, weekly, monthly, every three months/biannually, and yearly tasks. Put them in your calendar, carry the list with you to be checked weekly, use Post-its, photocopy the list and hang it up, or set up your own reminder system.

☐ Whenever you review a step, be aware that your circumstances might have changed and that your financial plan might need to change with them. Stubbornly holding on to a plan just because that was the one you once set up will not help you achieve your goals. Always evaluate and readjust as you go.

And that really is it!

I'm sure there have been some easy as well as some far more difficult steps you've gone through, but if you've made it this far, I'm confident you can see your hard work paying off in many financial areas by now.

Good luck and I hope you feel inspired to keep progressing on your path toward financial independence and that you will continue to work toward realizing your financial dreams!

Checklist Part 10

Use the following checklist to make sure you've done everything in Part 10:

☐ You have decided whether you could benefit from hiring a financial planner, and, if so, you have taken steps to find a good planner worth your money and time.

☐ You have carefully analyzed whether a coach might be able to further help you on your way to financial independence and, if so, have designed a plan to get one.

☐ You have started setting aside money for your (grand)child(ren) in a savings or investment account in order to build up a small fund for them.

☐ You are passing down your knowledge about finances to your (grand)children to give them a head start in their financial lives.

☐ You have set up a plan for investing in your individual capital to stay at the top of your game and increase your earning potential with time.

☐ You have identified one or two charities you identify with and have determined how you can contribute to their cause.

☐ You are prepared for possible negative financial situations that might happen to you so that you can deal with these in the most effective way and plan for them ahead of time.

☐ You understand the importance of continuing your journey and keeping the *100 Steps to Financial Independence* at the forefront of your planning. You have reviewed Appendix A and know what you need to do daily, weekly, monthly, biannually, and yearly.

💬 **PERSONAL STORY: PATRICK**

I've never been great at managing my money. I used to always survive from paycheck to paycheck, becoming increasingly worried as the month went on. I've had overdrafts, credit card debt, and loans hanging over me that I shouldn't have had. It's never been massive but I never seemed to get out of it as there was always something new that needed money (birthdays, holidays, fixing my car, etc.).

I've recently started to take control of my money. It's been six months and I've just made my last payment to pay off all the debt I had, I've been continuously saving toward the down payment on a house, I've been inspired to start a small business on the side, and most importantly am feeling happier than ever!

I wouldn't say I'm financially independent, but I believe that it's possible now and am committed to achieving it.

—Patrick Alvarez, Ireland
www.alvarezpatrick.com

Acknowledgments

When I set out on this journey, I had no idea it was going to take me almost three years to write this book. I'd like to thank everybody who has helped and contributed in some way to this project.

There are a few people I'd like to thank in particular:

Patrick Alvarez, Ilse van Driel, Jenny Galligan, Liz Grabo, Esther van den Heuvel, Sophie Jennings, Carolina Rodriguez, Esteban Sanchez, Sue Thomas and Kylie Watson for sharing their personal stories with me. You have all, more than you probably know, inspired me throughout my journey, and I hope you will inspire others, too!

My editor, Susannah Noel, who has provided me with her invaluable advice, experience, and improvements. I can't believe how much this book has progressed since the first draft!

My proofreader, Heidi Dorr, for checking even the smallest details.

My designer, Domini Dragoone, for the amazing work she's done with both the cover and interior design and layout!

The team at EbookPbook, for their fabulous work creating the ebook version.

Jillian Maxwell, for her help, great ideas and contagious enthusiasm.

My parents, May and Els, for always believing in me and supporting me, even though I've made some unexpected decisions in life. I am forever grateful for everything you have done for me. Dad, thank you also for going through the many calculations in this book!

My sister, Martine, for always being enthusiastic whenever I come up with a new plan. I admire your determination to follow your own path regardless of what others believe you should do and your success as an entrepreneur made me want to keep up with you. You know where I'll be writing my next book!

My pet-loving friends in our Mission Impawsible group for their encouragement and support when I needed it. My friends Patrick Alvarez and Kike Bodega deserve a special mention for our many conversations and discussions regarding this project and for their helpful contributions when this book was first completed. This book is not what most people would regard as holiday reading. . . .

My cat Monkey has been my most loyal supporter throughout and I'd like to show my appreciation for the hours of company and her supervision, which were often characterized by her sitting next to my computer for long times on end, or, more frequently, her attempts to play with and mess up my papers or lie on the keyboard to stop me from typing. It was a much less solitary experience with her by my side!

Lastly, I'd like to express my eternal gratitude to my husband, Douglas Haines, for always being there for me and believing in my dreams. Your endless support and encouragement made me trust that I was actually able to do it. You've been amazing all along and I'm so incredibly lucky to have you by my side!

Appendix A:
The 100 Steps in Action

Daily
- Read your goals (Step 0) and your FI vision (Step 1).
- Look at your vision board (Step 3).
- Remind yourself of your financial objectives (Step 4).
- Register your expenses (Step 9).
- Check your bank accounts (Step 29).

Weekly
- Track your progress on your various targets (Step 5).
- Check your budget is still accurate for the rest of the month (Step 22).
- Schedule in a money moment to update your expenses, file receipts, and quickly check your budget (Step 24).
- Review how much you have saved by limiting one expense (Step 26).
- Make your weekly (or daily) contribution to your piggy bank or coins jar and appreciate what you have saved (Step 46).
- Do an activity or play a game to teach your children about the value of money (Step 96).

Monthly
- Review your progress toward your targets and celebrate your victories if you reach a milestone (Step 6).
- Update the amounts of your outstanding debts (Step 10) and your assets (Step 11).
- Update your net worth (Step 12) and review your net worth target (Step 13).
- Update how much you spent last month on your various expense categories and on fixed, variable, discretionary, and savings expenses (Steps 15–18) and how much that amounts to in time costs (Step 25).
- Calculate last month's cash flow (Step 19).
- Organize a finance check-in with your partner (Step 23).
- Close last month's budget and set a new budget for next month. Remember to pay yourself first, using your version of the 50/20/30 rule and your financial objectives and checking your yearly budget (Steps 4, 22, 30, 31, and 34).
- Check your progress toward building your emergency fund and keeping it fully funded (Step 28).
- Check your progress toward getting one month ahead (Step 32).
- Automate any payments that have not yet been automated (Step 33).
- Conduct a monthly finance review (Step 35).
- Check your progress toward becoming debt-free (Step 43).
- Check your progress toward building a three-months-expenses fund (Step 45).
- Calculate last month's savings rate (Step 48).
- Track any crowdfunding payouts (Step 79).

Every three to six months
- Remind yourself of the eight stages of FI and update your financial goals to ensure they align with your targets (Steps 2 and 4).
- Update your financial objectives (Step 4).
- Set a new net worth goal (Step 13).
- Update your money map (Step 20).
- Calculate the amount of interest paid on all of your debts over the past three to six months (Step 37) and analyze whether you can make bigger contributions to paying down your debts in the next few months and the effects of those extra payments (Steps 40 and 41).
- Review your progress toward paying off your mortgage (Step 44).
- Track how much you have contributed to your savings goals and adjust or set new goals (Step 49).

- Spend some money on just yourself (Step 50).
- Update your income overview with the various amounts you make per month per income stream (Step 51).
- Change passwords to online accounts (Step 89).
- Analyze your need for a professional financial planner (Step 93) or a coach (Step 94).
- Review your budget and strategy to invest in your individual capital (Step 97).

Yearly

- Update your financial goals (Step 0).
- Review your money allocation strategy (Step 8).
- Check that your expenses are still categorized in the most logical way (Step 14).
- Remind yourself of the temptation to give in to lifestyle inflation (Step 21) and confirm you've been setting aside 50% of any extra money you receive, such as a bonus or pay raise (Step 42).
- Recalculate how your hourly costs translate into your time costs (Step 25).
- Check that your bank and bank accounts are still meeting your standards (Step 27).
- Review your emergency fund and plan on how to add more to it if needed (Step 28), taking into consideration the effects of inflation (Step 47).
- Set your yearly budget (Step 34).
- Remind yourself of the effects of compound interest (Step 36).
- Review your credit score (Step 39).
- When reviewing your targets for savings and extra funds, adjust for inflation and new interest rates (Step 47).
- Review and update your targets and plans for your income from the seven income streams (Steps 52–59).
- Review your retirement accounts to update projected income and make any adjustments to your plans to ensure you reach your target (Steps 61–65).
- Review your investment strategy for stocks and bonds (Steps 66–72).
- Rebalance your portfolio back to its ideal allocation (Step 75) or to your lifestyle investment plan (Step 76).
- Review your investment strategy regarding gold, commodities, real estate, and crowdfunding options (Steps 77–79).
- Review your long-term investment targets using the 4% rule (Step 80) and by analyzing the likelihood of sequence of return (Step 81).
- Check that your various insurance policies are still up to date, including your life, health, disability, homeowner or renter's, and car insurance, and make changes where needed (Steps 82–86).
- Go through your warranties and service contracts and throw out what you no longer need or what has expired (Step 87).
- Review your estate plan and make any necessary changes (Step 88).
- Review any changes to national, federal or local tax laws and how they affect you and make any changes to your tax planning strategies (Steps 90–91).
- Clean up your paperwork and dispose of any outdated documents (Steps 7 and 92).
- Review your donations to charity (Step 98).
- Analyze your contributions to your children's savings or investment funds (Step 95).
- Play the "what if" game and update the scenarios (Step 99).
- Review the 100 steps in action (Step 100).

Appendix B:
Discussion Points
with Your Partner

Below are the main topics covered in this book along with some suggestions and discussion points to cover in your meetings with your partner as described in Step 23.

TAKING CONTROL OF YOUR FINANCES

This is probably the most important area to discuss. So many people do not take control of their finances and live paycheck to paycheck without making any plans for the future. Maybe you were the same until you picked up this book? But taking control of your finances also takes sacrifices, time, and patience. Now that you've identified your vision and targets, share them with your partner so they can see the advantage and bigger picture of your mission.

DIVISION OF MONEY

How do you currently share your money? Do you have individual accounts, a joint account, or a combination of individual and joint accounts? What about savings and investment accounts? Are you still happy with the way this is set up, or should you adjust how these accounts are shared and the monthly contributions you make to the shared accounts?

NET WORTH

What is your joint net worth? What assets and debts make up your current value? What are your short-term and long-term targets? How can you both work toward increasing your net worth?

EXPENSES

What do your joint monthly expenses look like? What does your monthly and yearly budget entail? How much money have you allocated to each category? Is your partner in agreement with these allocations, or

do they feel that some categories need more or less assigned? How are decisions being made when making a purchase from a joint account? Can you come to an agreement in terms of your spending goals, or do you need to consider giving each of you free "spending money" to use in whichever way you want?

DEBT

How much debt do you both have, individually and together? Do you want to pay off debt faster? Do you or your partner need to stop accumulating debt? Can you set a goal together on when to have paid off all loans? How will you achieve this? Is your partner on board with this, or is it worth discussing how compounding interest affects your balance each year?

SAVINGS

How much do you currently have in savings? What are some of your short-term, midterm, and long-term goals when it comes to building up savings? How can you hit those targets faster? Do you have any big expenses you need to save for—a new house, a wedding, children? How will you get ready for this?

INCOME

What is your joint annual income at the moment? Do you both feel content with this? Is your income likely to change anytime soon? Would you like to increase your income in some way, either in your current job or in other ways? Discuss whether either of you might want to pursue any additional ways of generating some extra money.

RETIREMENT ACCOUNTS

What retirement accounts are you both building up at the moment? Do you have retirement plans in place? Should you or your partner make more or less contributions to a workplace or private retirement account? Are you concerned you might not have enough built up for your (early) retirement? What can you both do about this?

INVESTING

Do you or your partner want to invest and do both of you feel comfortable with this? Can you discuss options, risks, possible returns? Can you read more books together about this topic? Could you agree on a (small) initial amount to start investing with if you're both new to investing?

FINANCIAL SECURITY

Review your insurance policies and estate planning together. Do you both feel secure with them, or do you need to make changes and discuss further arrangements?

Feel free to add in any other topics to the list above as you go through these points together.

Appendix C: Glossary

Active income – Income earned through active work, often a job, in which you trade your time for money.

Amortize – To pay off a loan or mortgage.

Annuity – An investment that pays out a monthly income or lump sum by the time you retire.

Asset – Something you own that has value and that you can sell in order to get money, for example, real estate or an investment portfolio.

Asset allocation – The distribution of different assets in an investor's portfolio.

Bear market – A time when stocks and bonds go down in value.

Bonds – Loans given to a company or government traded on the stock market. Investors receive interest on bonds they own.

Budget – A plan detailing how to spend your money, often elaborated per month, taking into consideration your projected income and expenses with the aim to not spend more than what comes in and to work toward long-term financial goals.

Bull market – A time when stocks and bonds go up in value.

Capital gains – Income received from selling an asset at a much higher price than what you paid for it.

Cash flow – The net monthly difference between your income and your expenses.

Commodities – Unprocessed natural resources and primary agricultural products such as oil, gold, and cotton that can be traded on the stock market.

Compounding interest – The addition of interest, increasing exponentially, to a principal sum of a loan or deposit. In other words, the interest that accumulates on interest payments.

Crowdfunding – The raising of capital to fund a new project or start-up by collecting many small sums of money from a large number of people.

Deductible – An initial amount of money that your insurance doesn't reimburse you for. The higher your deductible, the lower your insurance premium.

Default – Not being able to repay a loan.

Defensive investing – An investment strategy aimed to reduce risk and maintain wealth. Defensive investment portfolios often have safe bonds and stocks of large, well-established big companies.

Deflation – An increase in the value of money, leading to being able to buy more with the same amount of money.

Discretionary expenses – Expenses that are not essential for daily living but add fun or comfort to your life.

Diversification – The act of taking up a lot of different assets (stocks, bonds, real estate, commodities, etc.) from different markets (US, Europe, upcoming markets, etc.) and industries (technology, manufacturing, services) in order to spread investment risks. In this way if some markets or industries experience a downfall, other investments are able to hold up the portfolio.

Dividends – Parts of a company's profit paid out to its shareholders.

Dollar cost averaging – An investment strategy in which you invest a regular amount every week or month to buy new investments, thereby averaging out the high costs of investments during peaks and using the opportunity to buy cheaper investments during a bear market.

Emergency fund – Savings set aside to cover an emergency expense, thereby ensuring you don't need to take on debt in case of an unexpected expense. I recommend having $1,000 in your emergency fund.

Financial independence – A stage at which you can pay for all of your regular expenses through a passive income without needing to work.

Fixed expenses – Expenses that are essential for daily living, have a regular payment interval (such as monthly or quarterly), and are always the same amount.

Index – A specific group of stocks and bonds that trade on the market.

Index investing – A way of investing that aims to replicate the market results by copying a particular index.

Inflation – The devaluation of money leading to money being worth less and not having the same buying power. The effect of inflation is that you can buy less for the same amount of money.

Insurance premium – The amount of money paid for an insurance policy.

Interest – The fee paid on loans to a loan provider. As a consumer, you can either pay interest on your outstanding loans or you can receive interest on money in a savings account or bonds.

Liabilities – Something that costs you money, such as a debt.

Lifestyle inflation – The perceived devaluation of one's lifestyle resulting in an increase in expenses every time your income increases in order to live more comfortably.

Lifestyle investment strategy – An investment strategy in which an investor's portfolio slowly moves from a more risky asset allocation to a safer distribution of assets. This is often done by reducing the number of stocks and increasing the relative number of bonds in an investment portfolio.

Liquidate – To sell an asset and convert it into cash. If you liquidate your investments, you sell them in exchange for money.

Money allocation strategy – A long-term plan describing how to use your money on your way to financial independence using different methods to "make money with your money," such as through investing, saving, and income development.

Money moment – Weekly time dedicated to analyzing and updating one's financial situation as well as goal setting for the week ahead. Usually approximately thirty minutes.

Mutual funds – Investment funds in which money from various investors is pooled together and invested by a fund manager who makes all the decisions regarding when and what to buy or sell.

Net worth – The amount of money you would have if you sold all of your possessions and paid off all your debts. Your net worth can be positive or negative.

Offensive investing – An investment strategy aimed at building wealth, often through taking more risk and investing in stocks that might generate a higher return but could also result into more losses.

Passive income – Income from sources that require little or no time to maintain after you have done the initial work to build the income stream.

Pension or **social security (US)** – Provision for retirees often in the form of a monthly income. Pensions are often paid into by an employee and/or employer.

Portfolio – An investor's collection of investments.

Principal – The initial amount of a loan, not including any interest payments.

Progress tracker – A visual representation of your progress toward a goal that shows how much you have completed as well as how much you still have to go.

Rebalancing – The selling of a particular asset in an investor's portfolio in order to return to the investor's ideal asset allocation.

Safe withdrawal rate – The safe withdrawal rate is the percentage of a portfolio an investor should safely be able to sell (or "withdraw") on a yearly basis without the portfolio going down in value. This is also referred to as the 4% rule as that is commonly seen as a safe amount.

Savings expenses – Expenses that aim to improve your financial situation such as payments toward savings, investments, or outstanding debts.

Savings rate – The percentage somebody saves from their monthly income for long-term savings targets.

Sequence of return risk – The risk of your portfolio decreasing in value due to negative returns over a certain number of years after you start withdrawing from it.

Shares – Stocks of a particular company.

Stocks – Small parts of a company investors can own that are traded on the stock market. Stocks provide investors with dividends.

Three-months-expenses fund – A savings fund that covers three months of your living expenses in case you are without an income for a while. I recommend building up this fund to six months as soon as you can.

Variable expenses – Household expenses that are essential for day-to-day living that vary a little from month to month depending on your use of an item, service, or product.

Appendix D:
Recommended Reading List

Books

Adams Miller, Caroline, and Michael B Frisch. *Creating Your Best Life: The Ultimate Life List Guide.* New York: Sterling Publishing, 2009.

Clason, George. *The Richest Man in Babylon.* New York: New American Library, 2002.

Covey, Stephen R. *The 7 Habits of Highly Effective People: Powerful Lessons in Personal Change.* New York: Simon & Schuster, 2013.

DeMacro, M. J. *The Millionaire Fast Lane: Crack the Code to Wealth and Live Rich for a Lifetime.* Phoenix, AZ: Viperion Publishing, 2011.

Duhigg, Charles. *The Power of Habit: Why We Do What We Do in Life and Business.* New York: Random House Trade Paperbacks, 2012.

Hallam, Andrew. *Millionaire Teacher: The Nine Rules of Wealth You Should Have Learned in School.* 2nd ed. Hoboken, NJ: John Wiley & Sons, 2017.

Hill, Napoleon. *Think and Grow Rich.* Anderson, SC: Mindpower Press, 2015.

Keller, Gary, and Jay Papasan. *The One Thing: The Surprisingly Simple Truth Behind Extraordinary Results.* Austin, TX: Bard Press, 2013.

Khalfani-Cox, Lynnette. *Zero Debt: The Ultimate Guide to Financial Freedom.* 3rd ed. Mountainside, NJ: Advantage World Press, 2016.

Kiyosaki, Robert. *Rich Dad Poor Dad: What the Rich Teach Their Kids About Money That the Poor and Middle Class Do Not!* Scottsdale, AZ: Plata Publishing, 2011.

Lowry, Erin. *Broke Millennial: Stop Scraping by and Get Your Financial Life Together.* New York: Penguin Random House, 2017.

Malkiel, Burton G. *A Random Walk Down Wall Street: The Time-Tested Strategy for Successful Investing.* 11th ed. New York: W. W. Norton, 2015.

Olson, Jeff. *The Slight Edge: Turning Simple Disciplines into Simple Success.* Austin, TX: Greenleaf Book Group, 2013.

Ramsey, Dave. *The Total Money Makeover: A Proven Plan for Financial Fitness.* Nashville, TN: Nelson Books, 2013.

Robbins, Tony. *Money Master the Game: 7 Simple Steps to Financial Freedom.* New York: Simon & Schuster, 2016.

Robin, Vicki. *Your Money or Your Life: 9 Steps to Transforming Your Relationship with Money and Achieving Financial Independence.* New York: Penguin Group, 2008.

Rubin, Gretchen. *Better than Before: What I Learned About Making and Breaking Habits—to Sleep More, Quit Sugar, Procrastinate Less and Generally Build a Happier Life.* New York: Broadway Books, 2015.

Sethi, Ramit. *I Will Teach You to be Rich.* 1st ed. New York: Workman Publishing, 2009.

Stanley, Thomas J., and William D. Danko. *The Millionaire Next Door: The Surprising Secrets of America's Wealthy.* Lanham, Maryland: Taylor Trade Publishing, 2010.

Templar, Richard. *The Rules of Wealth.* Harlow, UK: Pearson Education, 2015.

Waring, Mary. *The Wealthy Woman. A Man Is Not a Financial Plan.* Surrey, UK: Wealth For Women Publishing, 2014.

Blogs and websites

The Balance (blog). https://www.thebalance.com

Hol, Inge Natalie (blog). *100 Steps to Financial Independence.* 100stepsmission.com

Lowry, Erin (blog). *Broke Millennial.* brokemillennial.com

Pant, Paula (blog). *Afford Anything.* affordanything.com

Podcasts

Hol, Inge Natalie. *The Financial Harmoney Podcast.* https://ingenataliehol.com/financialharmoneypodcast

Pant, Paula. Afford Anything podcast. http://podcast.affordanything.com/listen/

Choose FI podcast. https://www.choosefi.com

Mad Fientist. Financial Independence Podcast. https://www.madfientist.com/podcast

Endnotes

1. Seventeen Facts About Women's Retirement Outlook, from 17th Annual Transamerica Retirement Survey – Transamerica Survey: https://www.transamericacenter.org/docs/default-source/women-and-retirement/tcrs2017_sr_women_and_retirement_17_facts.pdf

2. 17th Annual Transamerica Retirement Survey: https://www.transamericacenter.org/docs/default-source/retirement-survey-of-workers/tcrs2016_sr_retirement_survey_of_workers_compendium.pdf

3. One in Three Americans Prepare a Detailed Household Budget: https://news.gallup.com/poll/162872/one-three-americans-prepare-detailed-household-budget.aspx

4. Changes in U.S. Family Finances from 2013 to 2016: Evidence from the Survey of Consumer Finances: https://www.federalreserve.gov/publications/files/scf17.pdf

5. 17th Annual Transamerica Retirement Survey: https://www.transamericacenter.org/docs/default-source/retirement-survey-of-workers/tcrs2016_sr_retirement_survey_of_workers_gender.pdf

6. I classify insurance as a fixed cost, hence "substantial financial risk."

7. Consumer Expenditures (Annual) News Release: https://www.bls.gov/news.release/archives/cesan_08292017.htm

8. Jeffrey Dew. Bank on It: Thrifty Couples Are the Happiest: http://www.stateofourunions.org/2009/bank_on_it.php

9. Report on the Economic Well-Being of U.S. Households in 2017: https://www.federalreserve.gov/publications/2018-economic-well-being-of-us-households-in-2017-preface.htm

10. Most Americans Have Inadequate Savings, but They Aren't Sweating It: https://www.bankrate.com/banking/savings/financial-security-june-2018/

11. Changes in U.S. Family Finances from 2013 to 2016: https://www.federalreserve.gov/publications/files/scf17.pdf

12. Changes in U.S. Family Finances from 2013 to 2016: https://www.federalreserve.gov/publications/2017-September-changes-in-us-family-finances-from-2013-to-2016.htm

13. 17th Annual Transamerica Retirement Survey: https://www.transamericacenter.org/docs/default-source/retirement-survey-of-workers/tcrs2016_sr_retirement_survey_of_workers_gender.pdf

14. Usual Weekly Earnings of Wage and Salary Workers Second Quarter 2018: https://www.bls.gov/news.release/pdf/wkyeng.pdf

15. 17th Annual Transamerica Retirement Survey: https://www.transamericacenter.org/docs/default-source/retirement-survey-of-workers/tcrs2016_sr_retirement_survey_of_workers_gender.pdf

16. In the U.S. the term "Social Security" commonly refers to retirement benefits from the federal government, whereas in other countries, the term "national" or "state pension" is more common, as "social security" in those countries covers a wider range of welfare care offered by the government, such as health care or unemployment benefits.

17. Social Security Fact Sheet: https://www.ssa.gov/news/press/factsheets/basicfact-alt.pdf

18. World Pension Ages on the Rise: When Will You Retire? https://www.schroders.com/en/insights/economics/world-pension-ages-on-the-rise-when-will-you-retire/

19. 17th Annual Transamerica Retirement Survey: https://www.transamericacenter.org/docs/default-source/retirement-survey-of-workers/tcrs2016_sr_retirement_survey_of_workers_gender.pdf

20. The S&P 500 is short for the Standard & Poor's 500, an American stock index of the 500 biggest publicly traded U.S. companies.

21. Portfolio Success Rates: Where to Draw the Line https://www.onefpa.org/journal/Pages/Portfolio%20Success%20Rates%20Where%20to%20Draw%20the%20Line.aspx

Next Steps

I hope you enjoyed *The 100 Steps* and that you've started to make some important progress toward financial independence in order to gain control of your financial life! Here's what you can do to continue your journey:

Free materials

Get your free copy of the blueprint *Kickstart your Dream in 10 Steps* and start pursuing your true dream, to live a more purposeful and financially secure life on https://resources.ingenataliehol.com/dreamlife

Podcast

I have a weekly podcast, *The Financial Harmoney Podcast*, in which I dive deep into creating your dream life step-by-step by streamlining your financial habits, goals and mindset, without compromising today's happiness or time. You can find it on all the major podcast platforms, or on my website https://ingenataliehol.com

Social media

You can connect with me via:

- **Twitter:** https://twitter.com/ingenataliehol
- **Website:** https://ingenataliehol.com
- **Facebook:** https://www.facebook.com/ingenataliehol
- **Instagram:** https://www.instagram.com/ingenataliehol

Review

If you enjoyed this book and have a spare moment, I would really appreciate a short review on Amazon, Goodreads or the website you ordered your book from! Reviews really help in getting the word out and I would be very grateful if you could leave me one!

Your story

I would love to hear about your journey and how *The 100 Steps* has changed your (financial) life. Please contact me at inge@100StepsToFI.com and share your story with me!

Here's to your Financial Independence and to achieving your financial dreams!

—Inge Natalie Hol